PURITAN RULE
UNDER
CROMWELL

JANE HAYTER-HAMES

AMBERLEY

First published 2024

Amberley Publishing
The Hill, Stroud
Gloucestershire, GL5 4EP

www.amberley-books.com

British Library Cataloguing in Publication Data.
A catalogue record for this book is available from the British Library.

ISBN 978 1 3981 1353 4 (hardback)
ISBN 978 1 3981 1354 1 (ebook)

1 2 3 4 5 6 7 8 9 10

Typesetting by SJmagic DESIGN SERVICES, India.
Printed in the UK.

PURITAN RULE
UNDER
CROMWELL

Contents

List of Maps

List of Illustrations

Between pages 192 and 193

Introduction

My original aim was to explain the events in England, Scotland and Ireland from the beginning of Charles I's reign to the restoration of Charles II. Initially, I had hoped to cover the whole revolutionary period of the three kingdoms in one volume. That proved impossible and in 2022, *The Fall of Charles I* was published, which begins with the accession of James I and ends with the execution of his son.

This volume takes up the story after the king's death. In key places, as the revolutionary government takes control, I have reminded readers about people or events from before 1649 about which I wrote in the previous book. I hope that *Puritan Rule under Cromwell* can stand alone and be read as a single volume but it will be of more use and interest to the reader if they have already read *The Fall of Charles I* and are familiar with the arguments and events which led to the king's death.

The civil wars were a terrible period for all three kingdoms. Charles I lost the war and several of the victors subsequently attempted to negotiate with him, but none found a satisfactory compromise. To the more radical of his enemies, ending the king's life seemed the only solution. Actually, it was the beginning of a struggle over government for England, Scotland and Ireland which proved beyond the abilities of those concerned. This book attempts to explain why. Although details of constitutional arrangements can be tedious, they are the core and essence of the story as they define how power is managed. The efforts to make various systems work during the 1650s were an experiment which eventually failed. Yet the modern forms of government under which we now live were forged in this period; the experiment proved invaluable. It showed both what was essential in the monarchical system as it had evolved, and what would have to be altered to make it sufficiently flexible and representative amid a societal transformation that was only picking up speed as the century progressed. Nor was it a dry experiment but a matter of religious urgency and personal advantage for many.

I have tried to depict the main characters in all their complexity and to discuss their ideas, aspirations and fears as they struggled to reform the mass of the people and the way in which the three nations were ruled. Although there were several changes of government, there were only two written blueprints, which I have given in abridged form in the appendices.

As the period from 1625 to 1649 was defined by the character of Charles I, so the period from 1649 to 1658 was dominated by Oliver Cromwell. After his death, various men of influence tried to take control of the revolution. The events which led to the restoration of the king's son have a bittersweet character, as the hopes and fears of so many were overtaken by an unstoppable tide. The reader can draw their own conclusions about that.

After the Puritans lost power in 1660, the struggles over the constitution and for commercial advantage continued in different ways. I hope to cover the remainder of the century in a subsequent volume. The later Stuarts lived and ruled in a very changed society, with new ideas to draw on. More colourful but no less challenging, they found novel solutions to many of these problems.

Jane Hayter-Hames
January 2023

1

The King's Burial and the New Regime

King Charles I was executed in Whitehall on 30 January 1649. His death was the culmination of a decade of conflict in which neither warfare nor negotiations over forms of government for the three kingdoms had brought settlement. Charles had been a captive since May 1646, held by a succession of his enemies all of whom tried to reach an agreement with him. The army had possession of the king in late 1648, and it was army officers who purged the parliament, leaving only a compliant 'Rump'. Under their remit the trial of the king was carried out. A High Court of Justice was set up, which charged Charles I with ruling outside the law and with making war on parliament and the people which it represented. The king was found guilty and condemned to death. Fifty-nine men signed his death warrant; some were MPs, some were officers of the victorious army, but the majority were both. The judge also signed.

Although his trial and execution were carried out under the auspices of parliament, it was the army officers who made the decision, purged the parliament and saw the execution carried through. Fairfax, the commander of the army, who had inherited his father's title and was now Lord Fairfax of Cameron, had removed himself as the trial commenced and was said to have urged his officers to spare the king's life. Lieutenant General Oliver Cromwell, second-in-command of the army, preferred conciliation and had been slow to make up his mind, but his son-in-law Henry Ireton had determined to bring the king to justice and led the officers who demanded his trial. Cromwell took several weeks to come round to their view, but once his mind was made up he emerged as their leader and was energetic in seeing the process to completion. The execution was a revolutionary act; the radicals felt the enormity of it. Cromwell and the other regicides wanted as many signatories as possible to give the deed a wider legitimacy and to cover themselves; it was Cromwell who rounded up his fellow MPs and officers, hurrying them into the Painted Chamber where the death warrant lay ready for signing.

Charles I was an anointed king and the embodiment of the nation; his death shocked his English subjects profoundly and left them alarmed, not knowing how they would be governed in future. For Scotland and Ireland, the execution of the king increased the threats against them. Some Englishmen were jubilant – intellectuals like John Milton, radical members of the army and some republican MPs exulted – but generally, English people feared what might follow. After the execution a soldier supposedly asked Cromwell what form of government they were going to have. The answer: 'The same that now was.'

In fact, power had already been transferred. On 4 January 1649, the House of Commons had passed a resolution stating that authority lay with them:

> That the people are, under God, the original of all just power; that the Commons of England, in Parliament assembled, being chosen by and representing the people, have the supreme power in this nation.

They stated clearly that law no longer required the consent of king or peers.[1]

The House of Commons now ruled. The leaders of the Levellers had pressed for a very different form of government, and the previous winter Ireton had several meetings with them as they created the latest version of the Agreement of the People. This document was a design for the constitution which aimed for a balance of power between institutions, but the execution of the king had been hurried forward and now there were few other bodies to check the power of parliament. Moreover, the House of Commons in January 1649 was only a fraction of the original Long Parliament which had more than five hundred members at its first sitting. To make parliament compliant, the army had excluded about one hundred MPs during Pride's Purge the previous December. After that, other members stayed away, so in January 1649 only seventy or so sat in parliament, men who were at the core of the revolution. Some were army officers and some were friends of the army but many were determined to oppose military influence. Gradually, more MPs returned but the Rump parliament which remained after the Purge never got over 211 members. So rule by the Commons was deeply flawed. However, a statement of popular sovereignty was important. How would parliament follow it up?

With the death of the king, the system of government which he headed came to an end. Throughout the years of war, the Commons had run an administration but it was partial. Now it must create a new executive and replace the ministries and courts by which the king had ruled. First and foremost, the new rulers had to safeguard their own survival. Killing the recognised monarch of three kingdoms would provoke opposition and the new rulers knew they would be challenged.

The body of King Charles and his severed head were gathered from the scaffold and taken to be embalmed. They were then put in an open coffin at St James's Palace, where soldiers charged the public to see the body. The soldiers were delighted with the amounts they earned. One was heard to say, 'I would we could have two or more such Majesties to behead, if we could make such use of them.'[2]

Oliver Cromwell seems to have made his own visit to regard the dead king. There are various versions of the story but the clearest, and perhaps the most likely, supposedly originated with the Earl of Southampton, who was keeping vigil over the king's body in the Banqueting House the night after his execution, sitting 'very melancholy' with some fellow royalists. Around two in the morning, someone could be heard treading slowly on the stairs. A man entered, muffled in a cloak which obscured his face. He came over to the body of the dead king, gazed at it for some time and murmured, 'Cruel necessity.' Then he turned and left. Southampton could not see his face but recognised, by the voice and the way the figure moved, that it was Oliver Cromwell. In a different version of the story, Cromwell says that 'if he had not been king he might have lived longer' – which is clearly accurate as an observation but less likely than the terse 'cruel necessity', which rings true for General Cromwell. The Southampton story did not appear in print until the next century, although the second quotation was printed in 1663.[3] Since the people of London paid money to see the dead king, it seems probable that the chief regicide would also wish to visit the corpse and dwell on the reality of what had been done.

Parliament would not permit the king to be buried in Henry VII's chapel in Westminster Abbey so he was taken to Windsor for burial in St George's chapel. Parliament provided the funds, and the king's attendants and courtiers accompanied the body as the only mourners, although there was hardly a service. The coffin left St James's by night on 7 February in a coach with six horses, hung with black velvet, the way lit by torches, until the cavalcade arrived at Windsor Castle where the body was taken to the king's chamber.

It was difficult to decide where to bury him. The Tomb-House was a possibility but it was outside the chapel and was named for the magnificent but unbuilt monument which Henry VIII had planned for himself. Charles's attendants felt that a grave beside Edward IV in the choir would be more suitable. They began excavating but several noblemen arrived with Bishop Juxon and found a vault beneath the centre of the choir, where Henry VIII had been buried beside Jane Seymour pending the completion of his unfinished monument. There was space for another burial, and it was decided this should be used for King Charles. Both courtiers and soldiers moved the body to St George's Hall in preparation for burial in the chapel.

When the coffin was carried out of the hall on 9 February, snowy weather ensured the velvet pall shrouding the coffin had gone from black to white by the time they entered the chapel. There had also been disagreement about the form of service as the military governor of the castle forbade the *Book of Common Prayer*, but Juxon was there to give the king a last blessing. Charles I had been monarch for twenty-three years and, despite his end, was buried as a king among kings. A lead band on his coffin bore the legend 'King Charles 1648'. His remains lie at the chapel still.[4]

Parliament was in session, although the numbers attending were low, with fewer than ten peers in the Lords and seventy members in the Commons. On 1 February, when the Lords had suggested a joint meeting to discuss the future form of government, the Commons reacted aggressively, questioning the need for an upper chamber. Cromwell and the lawyer Bulstrode Whitelocke wanted to retain the Lords but Henry Marten was energetically opposed. On 6 February, the Commons voted to abolish the House of Lords, and on the day the king's coffin left London parliament voted to abolish the office of king; they said experience had shown that having all the power in a single person was 'unnecessary, burdensome, and dangerous to the Liberty, Safety, and publick Interest of the People of this Nation'.[5] An Act would follow to confirm these decisions and the Commons hurried on, first to dissolve the committees which had managed business during the war and then to create a new executive body which would take over the functions of the king.

There was to be a Council of State. A small committee was formed to decide who should be councillors and what the functions of the body should be; they reported the following week. The Council was to have full powers to manage home and foreign affairs but would be chosen by the Commons and act for one year only. Clearly, power would remain in parliament: the Council was subordinate to the Commons and, unlike the king, could not dissolve parliament. The Agreement of the People had aimed to balance one against the other.[6]

The Council of State would have forty-one members; those chosen for the first iteration were mainly MPs but three judges, five peers and three army officers – Fairfax, Cromwell and Skippon – were included. Ireton and Harrison were nominated but rejected by the Commons; both were radicals, the former politically and the latter theologically. Ireton, so influential in the king's trial and execution, wanted backing for those decisions and insisted that councillors take an oath approving the revolutionary changes, but some held back.[7] Council attendance was low – sometimes there was barely a quorum to vote through decisions.

The Rump was still composed of radicals. Pride's Purge had removed the peace party who hoped for agreement with the king, but more MPs subsequently left of their own accord. The seventy who remained began to worry that the Commons was far too small and unrepresentative. Who should be allowed to return? Those who had rejected further talks with the king the previous December were now considered acceptable and were allowed to re-join the Commons. The war party had triumphed but now it was essential that parliament fulfil its normal functions as representing the nation, so moderates were encouraged to return. Some came of their own volition while others had to be cajoled – Cromwell was keen to reinstate as many as possible. As they took their seats, the House lost much of its radical character and a wider spectrum of opinion emerged; the country gentlemen and burgesses attended not to cause revolution but to promote local issues, as they always had.

For such a famous and closely studied body, the Long Parliament has proved hard to analyse. The right to vote in elections depended on property and the members came from the property-owning classes: merchants, lawyers and country gentlemen. The real revolutionaries, men who rejected monarchy and planned significant social change, were a small group. Cromwell, for example, signed the king's death warrant and was concerned for the poor but generally hoped to maintain the status quo, in which he was a minor gentleman and landowner. In religion there was a range of opinion. Most were Puritans, their views based on Calvin, but there was divergence.

The Independents wanted freedom of worship while the Presbyterians wanted a national church and had agreed a form of service with the Scots. Pride's Purge had excluded most of the Presbyterians who made up the peace party, but even without them there was a spread of belief.

What kind of government would the men now sitting at Westminster create? There had been a revolution but how much would change? Some hoped for reform, others dreaded upheaval. Henry Marten, one of the most radical MPs, was agitating on behalf of imprisoned debtors – but in the febrile condition of the country, some members feared anarchy and tried to silence the more extreme ideas. Many MPs had stood against Charles I to maintain the rights of parliament, not to revolutionise the system. Essentially conservative, they wanted a return to normality. For many MPs the main concern was trade and national wealth, which had been so disrupted by a decade of war.

Membership of the Commons had altered enormously since 1640. Royalists had left or been excluded; some had died. By-elections had brought in new men, many of them army officers, generally with propertied backgrounds but holding radical views. When the army had mutinied in 1647, many MPs had fled before Pride's Purge excluded still more. From the Purge to the king's execution was the crisis period, but now that it was over experience and competence mattered, so less radical men were welcomed back. The established traditions of parliament gave it stability as it set about its work.

Sir Henry Vane had withdrawn from the Commons in mid-December but was at his office in the Admiralty on the day of the execution and joined several parliamentary committees. His father had been a diplomat and the younger Vane, although a religious idealist, was himself a capable public servant. Sir Arthur Haselrig returned to the Commons in February; he had been governor of Newcastle since 1647, which had kept him out of London during the crisis. Previously considered radical, he opposed the Leveller programme and helped to stabilise the new government. Haselrig and Vane, both able administrators with a power base in the north, became leading figures in the parliament which gradually reassembled at Westminster. Of the army officers who had won by-elections in 1645 and 1646, the most prominent were Ireton, Hutchinson, Harrison, Ludlow and Fleetwood. Their support network in the army gave them influence but their aims would clash with those of Vane and Haselrig.

Since the army had won supreme power for parliament, the soldiers expected reform to follow. Their officers did too, but they were more cautious. Ireton had already shown his hand by his role in the regicide and his work with the Levellers, but the Agreement of the People which he had negotiated had not been taken up in parliament. The Levellers were disillusioned – John Lilburne said he would prefer rule by a king than rule by the sword – but the army was standing back as MPs trickled in and committees got to work. Hopes of change were still high.

The republican government was creating new structures and institutions, but also symbols and artefacts. Before the execution, a new Great Seal had been created with the House of Commons on one side and a map showing England and Ireland on the other. Henry Marten wrote the motto: 'In the first year of freedom, by God's blessing restored.' The new regime also needed new flags and coins, liveries for watermen and cloths on barges all needed redesigning, and later the royal arms on public buildings were ordered taken down. The symbols of monarchy were visible right across the nation and had to be replaced.

It was not clear what role the army would play. There were officers in the Commons and three in the Council, but would the army obey parliament? What line would the army leaders take? Fairfax had been against the execution of the king but was appointed to the Council of State. In public opinion, Oliver Cromwell played a different role. Even before the king's execution, newsbooks had accused him of a hunger for power and at the king's trial Lady Fairfax had called him a scoundrel, but among his men Cromwell was highly regarded. He had made them into a magnificent fighting force and led them to victory. He had navigated the Putney Debates skilfully and delayed in the north while parliament was purged, but during the trial and execution of the king he had acted decisively. He was skilful at managing his restive forces, with their religious fervour and political demands. With Leveller influence in the ranks but property-owning officers holding republican ideals, there was an unresolved tension in the army. Cromwell sought to both lead and tame; this was the army which had made his career, and it now held the nation's fate in its hands.

The Commons might have supreme power in England but it faced pressing problems. Trade had been disrupted and the finances of the country needed immediate attention. Most urgent of all, however, was the security of the nation and of its new governors.

The people of England, many of whom had never understood why the king and his parliament were at war, were in uncertain temper. Even those who criticised Charles I for his illegal taxation and for taking up arms had no quarrel with his son. The army spoke of freedom and rights but when swordsmen displayed their political power, people feared the consequences. Those with strong Puritan beliefs were in a minority; the English people had become accustomed to the forms of the Elizabethan church, with the monarch at its head, and showed no signs of wanting to change that. War had greatly increased taxation and was collected more widely. Landowners had been fined and property confiscated, but often it was the military men who benefitted, so already there was suspicion. On the other hand, those who longed for greater religious liberty or social change were hopeful. Everyone waited to see how the new government would develop.

People already knew what to expect regarding social behaviour. The Puritans were passionate about a reformation of manners, attempting to bring the whole nation into a state of godliness. Fast days had sometimes been called by the king but in the army, days of fasting and prayer were highly charged events, frequently called before great decisions were taken. The men had been drilled to avoid swearing and lewd behaviour, but far more was envisaged by the new government.

Atheism had been outlawed: the Blasphemy Ordinance of 1648 stated that 'all such persons as shall maintain that there is no God', or deny his attributes, would be punished by death. Charles I had condoned Sunday recreation once church services were over but the Puritans were determined on the strict observance of the Sabbath, which was sacred, while considering other feast days offensive because of their Catholic origins or their rituals of pleasure. Parliament had already abolished Christmas, Easter and holy days while weddings, baptism and burials had been stripped back to a bare form of words. A new secular holiday was created, held once a month, which had none of the trappings of the traditional feast days. Around the country, the Puritan way of life was resisted – parishioners played noisy games outside houses where the devout were praying and in Kent excrement was daubed on stiles which Puritans had to climb to get to church. Some particularly severe ministers had been beaten.

The Puritans were inspired by the Bible and Calvinist doctrine as well as humanism with its values of diligence, sobriety, civility and good order; but those ideals appealed to educated people, mainly those in towns with business interests and social aspirations. In rural England, where most of the population lived, traditional feasts and pastimes marking the agricultural year were a deeply ingrained way of life.

Nor was Puritanism attractive to all city dwellers. The theatres had been closed in 1642 and in 1648 the law became permanent and draconian; actors flouting it were to be whipped. The last four theatres still open in London were raided in January 1649, after which only private performance continued, or recitations in pubs. Perhaps more serious for intellectuals was a new Licensing Act passed in the same month. The same parliament which had freed from captivity 'Laud's martyrs' – Prynne, Bastwick and Burton, and then John Lilburne – now found unbridled publishing dangerous and set out to control it. The courts which Archbishop Laud had used for censorship – Star Chamber and High Commission – had been closed by parliament early in the war. During the conflict, offensive books had been burned. Now a parliamentary committee on printing was established which, although it was far less draconian than Laud's, required printers to be certified in order to publish. The Act ran until September 1651, when it was not renewed.

Throughout the war, parliament had tried to destroy idolatrous images by ordinance and through a committee of demolition, but this was limited to paintings and windows. When the sects started demanding that churches be demolished, parliament took fright; a 1648 ordinance ordered their repair and maintenance. 'Reformation' of cathedrals allowed soldiers to seize plate and valuables. Some of the buildings were used as stables, barracks or prisons but the damage to churches was at its height during the war. Now, the Puritan government concentrated on creating a godly nation. Swearing, drunkenness, lewd behaviour, animal baiting, pub music and licentious dancing were to be crushed. The people were to learn less carnal and more modest forms of enjoyment.

The revolution had sown dread among many but hope among others. Some had wild expectations. Time would show who would be rewarded, who would be disappointed and who would be destroyed. But first the new government had to establish itself and ward off its enemies.

2

The Claimant to the Thrones

The new regime in London had many enemies but the threat to its survival centred on the heir to the three kingdoms, who was a young man of eighteen living in exile on the continent. Prince Charles had escaped from Cornwall early in 1646 as his father's armies were overwhelmed. He had stayed in the Scilly Isles and in Jersey, where he spent the spring sailing a specially made pinnace, before joining his mother in France, where he was received at court and stayed for two years. In 1648, he had briefly commanded a small fleet during the Second Civil War but they had been blocked by a parliamentarian force and the prince had returned to the Netherlands, where he was made welcome by his sister Mary and her husband William II of Orange.

Charles was still in the Hague when news of his father's execution reached him. His nervous chaplain entered and addressed him as 'Your Majesty', at which the young man realised that his father was dead, which left him – shocked and grieving – with the appalling mesh of claims and responsibilities which he had watched his parents grapple with. He burst into tears.

He was proclaimed king in Ireland by Ormond, and in Scotland by Argyll, with conditions; but in England, only cavaliers and clergy dared to make minor gestures towards his claim.

The royal Stuarts were now prisoners or in exile; only Mary, Princess of Orange had a position and a court of her own. Charles I's eldest daughter, Mary had come to the Netherlands as a child-bride and grown up as a princess on the Orange estates. As stadholders – governors and military leaders – the princes of Orange held a commanding role, but the United Provinces of the Netherlands was a republic where the

States-General, not the princes, held sovereign power. Princess Mary's father-in-law had died in 1647, so when Charles and then his brother James, Duke of York arrived in The Hague, her husband William had only recently become head of the House of Orange. Charles and James had last seen their sister when she left England aged nine. Now Charles was nineteen and Mary two years younger. Prince William made the two teenage princes welcome and offered them every assistance; the Orange family had already been generous to their father.

Mary had some of her parents' hauteur and hardly spoke Dutch, but the other Stuart exiles in the Hague were quite different. Elizabeth, Queen of Bohemia had been there since she and her husband Frederick had fled from the emperor's armies in 1620. When Charles arrived his aunt Elizabeth had been a widow for fifteen years, but she had much of her father James I's boisterous personality and, despite limited funds, kept court and entertained. Extrovert and convivial, Elizabeth had been left two old houses by her deceased husband and here she kept up as much royal style as she could. She had borne thirteen children, of whom nine were still living. Princes Rupert and Maurice

Elizabeth of Bohemia.

had fought for Charles I and were close to him; his death had been a cruel blow for them too. Now in The Hague with their cousins Charles and James, the young princes of the Palatinate were restless.

Only two of Charles I's children were still in England. Princess Elizabeth and Henry, Duke of Gloucester had been put in the care of the Sidneys, Earl and Countess of Leicester, at Penshurst Place in Kent; they would stay until 1650.

The widowed queen was in France. In crisis, Henrietta-Maria had naturally turned to her own family, who had taken her in and provided for her. Her brother had died in 1643 and her nephew was now king; Louis XIV was eleven when Charles I was executed. His mother was regent and ran the French government with Cardinal Mazarin as her chief minister. France had its own problems – a war with Spain and internal unrest – so the upheaval in Britain and a revolutionary government there created a complex foreign policy issue for France. Henrietta-Maria, who as a young woman had been headstrong and impulsive, was still learning the slow and painful lessons in statecraft by which she had attempted to succour her husband and with which she tried to aid her son. If she could enlist the help of Mazarin or other potential allies, if she could co-ordinate the nobles who came to her from Britain and Ireland, surely a workable strategy could be devised.

The French royal family had given Henrietta-Maria apartments in the Louvre and then the use of St Germain-en-Laye, a palace outside Paris, with a monthly pension of 30,000 livres. When Prince Charles joined her from Jersey in 1647 this was increased by 25 per cent but the money was paid irregularly. Charles had gone to the Netherlands by the time his father was executed; the only one of her children who was with her was Henriette, who had been born in Exeter as the queen fled the war and had been brought out of England by her guardian. When the grieving widow met her eldest son again, he was king and she the queen mother, a small and no longer pretty creature who tried to rouse her wounded spirits to help and advise him. James was on his way to join his mother when his father died, but he had stopped for a month at a Benedictine monastery and was only told of the execution when he reached St-Germain.

In exile, the Stuarts had returned to their religious roots. Elizabeth of Bohemia was in the Protestant Netherlands with her children, while Henrietta-Maria was in Catholic France. Charles, who had three chaplains and spent an hour each day with one of them, knew that it was vital that he remain a Protestant if he was to regain his thrones in Britain. In that respect, being in the Protestant Netherlands with William and Mary helped his public image.

As soon as he succeeded his father, Charles had to assume command of the royalists and devise a strategy to regain his kingdoms. His most immediate problem was money. The French income was paid to Henrietta-Maria, making Charles financially dependent on her. Around the exiled Stuarts clustered their ministers, advisers, friends and servants, most of whom looked to Charles for their living. In Jersey, he had maintained a retinue of three hundred people whose debts had not been paid when he left. Nor could the costs of his court be met by the Prince of Orange for long. Some of the exiles brought wealth with them but many were impoverished. William II had to be careful, as the States-General had not been sympathetic to Charles I's policies nor his relations with Catholic Ireland. The Netherlands was Calvinist and as a trading nation with a fleet, the country was growing in importance; they meant to hold that position and were aware of the military might of the new government in London. The States-General would not compromise their own position to aid the Stuart claimant. If Charles hoped to regain his inheritance, he would have to be an astute politician and turn the considerable sympathy for him into tangible force – but money was essential. There were rulers who in theory would support Charles's legal claim but politically might have doubts – was he really a good bet?

The European powers were unwilling to recognise the new regime in London but were also cautious about Charles. The Dutch States-General recognised him as King of Scotland but not of England. France entertained him as a king without formally recognising his presence in the country. If he could put himself at the head of a viable army, he believed that other princes were more likely to aid him. He had supporters in both Scotland and Ireland but the former country was Presbyterian, the latter mainly Catholic. Stitching them together would require skill. If there was a choice between the two kingdoms, to which should he turn?

Charles formed a council, appointing those of his father's privy councillors who were in the Netherlands: Sir Edward Hyde was his chief adviser, along with Hopton, Culpepper, Cottington, Brentford and Sir Richard Lane, to which Charles added his secretary Robert Long. Charles's training for kingship had been irregular; he had spent his teenage years with his father, fighting a civil war. They had been together at headquarters in Oxford or out on campaign, but since he was twelve they had had no access to the royal palaces, and his father controlled only part of the country and had only a patchy administration to run. But war breeds a special kind of leadership. After Prince Charles was sent to Bristol, he had his own council and in theory led the war effort in the west – but it soon collapsed. Taking on the duties of kingship is never easy but now he was starting his reign in exile. It was a massive challenge with no lands, no revenue and no tax income, meaning his first struggle was to obtain grants and loans.

Charles had natural strengths, however. Unlike his small parents, he was unusually tall and well-made, with a sensual mouth, dark eyes and thick, dark hair. Vivacious and assertive, the young man's charm was often remarked on. Both his parents had been serious about their faith but Charles seemed to take a pragmatic and political position on religion. In that, he perhaps looked to his French grandfather, Henri IV, who had become a Catholic in order to take the throne of France. Charles resembled Henri in other ways: he was tall, energetic and a great ladies' man. Charles's first love – or the first we know of – was Lucy Walter, whom he met in the Netherlands in 1648. She was calling herself Mrs Barlow and seems to have made all the running. A son James was born, probably in April 1649. The affair was carefully managed: Lucy went to France with Charles but was housed discreetly. John Evelyn, who had travelled in a coach with Lucy, described her as 'brown, beautiful, bold but insipid'.[1]

Henrietta-Maria wanted her son to join her in France, where Hyde could be side-lined and she could direct the new king, but Charles stayed on in The Hague, trying to devise a strategy. Through Scotland or Ireland, Charles hoped eventually to dislodge the Puritans from their grip on England, by far the richest and most powerful of the three kingdoms. Hyde was a devoted Anglican and demurred from this policy, believing that an alliance with the Scottish Covenanters would be disastrous and that it was only through the strength of English royalism that Charles would eventually regain his thrones. However, the exiled king had to make alliances; diplomatic missions which had already been set up were confirmed and new ones were launched. Some of the privy councillors also became ambassadors; Cottington and Hyde were appointed for Spain while Culpepper set off for Moscow, where he was received by the Russian Tsar and given a loan of 20,000 rubles paid in corn and furs. The Queen of Sweden provided Charles with some arms and the Portuguese made harbours available for royalist ships. Otherwise, support was thin.

The only fleet Charles had was a modest one under the command of Prince Rupert. To the royalists, Ireland looked the most promising of the three kingdoms as Ormond was still at the head of a considerable army there. So, Rupert sailed west with his small fleet and based himself in the harbour of Kinsale, west of Cork city. He lacked sailors but linked up with the Earl of Antrim who, although antagonistic to Ormond, had a privateering fleet that allowed Rupert to continue funding himself by seizing merchant ships as he had in the North Sea.

In the spring of 1649, Charles received news from both Ireland and Scotland. A messenger from Argyll arrived first at the exiled court, then representatives from both the Scottish parliament and the kirk appeared, but intense rivalries and bitterness persisted between the Scots. The Duke of Hamilton was imprisoned in England but his brother and heir was in The Hague, as was the Earl of Lauderdale. The latter advised reconciliation with the Covenanters, but since the defeat at Preston the kirk party had loathed and scorned these aristocratic 'Engagers'. Also to Charles's side came James Graham, Marquis of Montrose, who had proved so formidable a champion for Charles I in 1644–45 and was still brimming with confidence. Montrose was all for taking Scotland by force of arms, whereas Hamilton and the Engagers wanted Charles to sign the Covenant, which would make him a religious lodestar to the Scottish people. The parliamentary commissioners from Edinburgh wanted far more.

To Charles I, the Scottish leaders had proved severe and unreliable; they had sold him to parliament and by their intransigence over the Covenant had delayed a deal which could have saved his life. The Scots had considered the late king obstinate, obstructive and blind to their deeply held beliefs. To Charles II, they might prove useful or duplicitous; he was polite but cautious.

The commissioners, in return, liked the young man, whom they found courteous and charming. They urged him to satisfy their conditions, so that he could swiftly be restored to his rights, 'before Democracy or any new modell of government under the name of an Agreement of the people, or any other name', was set up in England.[2] Charles certainly wanted support from Scotland but Montrose advised him to look to Ireland first. If Charles took command there, he, as the king's captain general, would invade Scotland and rouse the royalists. But which Scottish party should Charles choose for his ally? Clearly, it would be best to gain his Scottish throne by agreement but the demands of the Scottish commissioners were rigid and prohibitive. Charles remembered how his father had struggled with the same party over the structure of the church and especially over bishops. He could not abandon the principles for which his father had died – or not immediately.

The commissioners thought the young man was one of the most 'gentle, innocent, well inclined princes', but they thoroughly distrusted his advisers.[3] Revolutionary changes had been made in Scotland in 1640–41 without his father's consent and Charles offered to confirm those but he refused to impose Scottish Presbyterianism on England and Ireland – at the very least their parliaments would have to be consulted. The Scots commissioners were dissatisfied with this reply; they dourly shook their heads and the negotiations came to an end.

So, Charles made plans to leave for Ireland. His companions, the young swordsmen who had followed him into exile, were unemployed, angry and poor. Their restlessness, squabbles and duelling started to cause trouble. The States-General strongly disapproved of the alliance which Ormond had made with Catholic Ireland on behalf of Charles. They offered him no help and the position was becoming tense, so William II found the travel money and Charles once more set off west, first to visit his mother in France. He arrived in June, and Hyde, who deplored the queen's emotional schemes, left for Spain on his diplomatic mission. Henrietta-Maria wanted Charles to marry the richest of the French princesses but Charles demurred, while the lady in question thought him silent, or even gauche. He seems to have known he could not marry a French Catholic at that stage in his career but to tell his mother so might remind her of the greatest flaw in her own marriage; as a French Catholic her behaviour in England had contributed to her husband's conflicts and vulnerabilities.

During those few months in 1649, Charles impressed on his mother that he was her affectionate son but that in affairs of state he would not be consulting her. As summer ended, he took James with him and sailed west. It was September when he reached Jersey, preparing for the onward journey to Ireland, but by then Oliver Cromwell's campaign in Ireland had already begun.

3

Security

The challenges facing the government at Westminster were daunting. A revolution had been pushed through before any new constitution was established. There was a viable claimant to the three kingdoms just across the English Channel with supporters in Scotland, and in Ireland the Duke of Ormond led an army on behalf of the crown. The Commons would soon turn its attention to Ireland but first it had to decide how to rule and deal with internal security.

As to the nature of the state, by May 1649 parliament had decided on the name and nature of the new polity. An Act declaring England to be a Commonwealth was passed on 19 May. By it, 'the people of England, and of all dominions and territories thereunto belonging' were to be 'a Commonwealth and Free State ... and that without any king or House of Lords'.[1] There was no mention here of the sovereignty of the people. The concept of a Commonwealth was an old one; the same term was used of the common law and had been explored in More's *Utopia*. It was used as an English translation for *res publica* and it postulated the good of all in a well-regulated state, with implicit ideas of social justice. The concept was hard to define of course; even More, with a long line of older authors behind him, had struggled to map out an ideal society.[2] Now the Commons of England had an opportunity to reshape the state; how radical would they be?

The English people had opinions of their own and the revolutionaries were concerned about those. They knew something of people's attitudes by book sales; ten days after the execution of Charles I, *Eikon Basilike* was published. A 'portrait of His sacred Majesty in his solitude and suffering', it purported to be the meditations and prayers of the king during his final captivity. The text was compiled by John Gauden, later Bishop of Winchester, who may have revised or possibly written some of the book. On 16 March, the government banned it but the gesture was futile; the book had enormous appeal and was reprinted thirty times during that year, while appearing in translation in several European languages. To rule against this tide of public opinion would take considerable intelligence – or dominating force.

Among the new men in power there was great divergence of belief and motivations, from the visionary millenarians to the pragmatic reformers, but in the early weeks of 1649, as the drama of the king's death gave way to the urgency of security and administration, the government had to set priorities. Having declared its own power and defined the Council's remit, the Commons turned swiftly to security. They needed to deploy their forces and gather information, but also set up diplomatic channels to deal with foreign states.

The new regime was not a novice – from a legislature working with a monarch, it had grown during the wars to a government which controlled increasing territory – but now it had to take on the full weight of managing England: foreign and domestic policy, the justice system, policies for the regions and counties, the funding of the state. The Commonwealth set up diplomatic missions, with Strickland and St John sent to the Netherlands where a Protestant and republican government might be an ally. John Milton was appointed Secretary for Foreign Tongues to manage all the Continental correspondence, much of it in Latin.

Meanwhile, the army had to be paid and troop numbers reduced, while the navy had to be beefed up. Sir Henry Vane proved invaluable, an efficient administrator who oversaw sailors' pay, shipbuilding and naval supplies. Inheriting his father's skills in diplomacy, Vane was adept at finding advantage for England among foreign rivalries. To gain intelligence about the fledgling state's enemies, the MP and Buckinghamshire attorney Thomas Scot set up a spy network. During the civil war, fear of retaliation had meant few executions of enemy officers; now that concern receded. The leaders of the Second Civil War were sentenced to death: Hamilton, Holland and Capel were executed in London and Huntly in Scotland. There was no sympathy between London and Edinburgh, but the death of Hamilton and Huntly suited both capitals.

For the Commonwealth, the subjugation of Ireland was urgent. It was a dependent territory, had rebelled against English rule and had a viable army. Land was owed to the Adventurers, who had funded the Irish war. The new government had to regain control. The regiments would have to be rationalised and army pay was overdue, so preparing the forces was a challenge. In March, the Council of State asked Cromwell to command the forces for Ireland, but he delayed a decision until funds and the mood of the army were clear.

England was emerging as a leading military power. After Naseby, the army chaplain Hugh Peters, preaching to the soldiers, had told them, 'The Lord hath made us warlike, awaked us thoroughly out of our effeminacie and we are become formidable to our neighbours.'[3] Already, Peter foresaw England showing leadership to the Palatinate, Germany, France and the Netherlands, for few armies in Europe had the discipline and effectiveness of the New Model Army. As an island nation, however, the navy was always uppermost in English rulers' thoughts; Vane's task was to reorganise and increase naval capacity, which meant greater funding.

While strengthening its forces against the enemy without and preparing to retake the subordinate island of Ireland, the English government was all too aware of the enemy within. Many of the leading royalists had gone into exile with the king or taken jobs overseas but

Oliver Cromwell.

the royalist presence in England was still strong. Landowners who had fought for the king had seen their property sequestered until they paid heavy fines, and some had lost their property altogether. These were men who were known and could be watched, but more dangerous were the younger sons who had no land to lose, as well as the artisans, merchants and labourers whose sympathies lay with the young king or might drift in his favour.

A more tangible danger lay in the radical groups who could cause uproar in the cities and who had infected the army with their views. Above every danger was that posed by the New Model Army itself, the army which had won the war for parliament but then rebelled against it. If radical politics infected the army, its cohesion and obedience might not hold, stability would be undermined and the new government would be in jeopardy. Leveller ideas had infiltrated the army in 1647 and led to long debates on the constitution, with demands for greater voting rights as well as social reforms. A confrontation at Ware in November that year had led to courts-martial and one soldier had been shot as an example to others. The Second Civil War had broken the momentum for political change within the army but the same ideas emerged again once the fighting stopped. The constitution which Ireton negotiated had not been taken up in the Commons.

In John Lilburne, the new government, as well as the army and Cromwell himself, had an enraged but brilliant adversary. Throughout his life, he published a blizzard of pamphlets which gave him notoriety and a large following. He believed that all men and women were born free and that all should be equal before the law; that the people could only be ruled by an agreement between the government and the governed. His swift absorption of new ideas, his lively intelligence and burning determination for equality made him a potent political activist, but his effectiveness was constantly undermined by his inchoate rage. To John Lilburne, every institution was the enemy, which made him incapable of negotiation. He was furious that the king had been executed without due process of law or before a new constitution had been built. He thought the army a threat and the parliament unrepresentative and too long-lived. He complained about the excise, customs, monopolies and forced loans, as well as the treatment of the soldiers, but he showed little understanding of how government was funded or the scale of the debts.

Imprisoned by both Charles I and the Long Parliament, he was freed in 1648 but the revolution of that winter quickly drove him into print. In February 1649, Lilburne published *England's New Chains*

John Lilburne.

Discovered, rejecting the 'military juncto', the new Council of State and the 'puppet parliament'. When he published a second part to this diatribe in March, the government jailed him again. Walwyn, Overton and Prince were also imprisoned.

The Levellers were not the only protest movement the government faced in England. Religious upheaval underlay the whole structure of society. The monarch had been head of the English church since the reign of Henry VIII, but with monarchy abolished, men of influence clamoured for an end to the national church as well. Over time, the Rump consistently blocked its abolition but the church survived among a fever of religious ideas. The agreement made in the 1640s with Scotland over church structure was not implemented; too much was in contention. Sects were springing up and revolutionary ideas, previously hidden, now burst forth. The Reformation had already aroused expectations of Christ's imminent kingdom. During the war, preachers with millenarian views lived among parliament's army as it struggled for the cause of God, and Stephen Marshall had told parliament, 'All Christendom except the Malignants in England, do now see that the Question in England is, whether *Christ*, or *Antichrist*, shall be Lord and King.'[4]

With the king dead and political revolution achieved, the new age seemed to be dawning and expectations became urgent. Theological speculation was lively and widespread, reaching from clergy in the national church across the spectrum to the radical sects. Much of it was infused with apocalyptic and millenarian views. Sects such as Baptists and Seekers found new adherents. Since 1647, the preaching of George Fox had created the Religious Society of Friends and these 'Quakers' posed a challenge to all forms of authority. But it was the Fifth Monarchists who had the most potent aim – the godly to rule in a theocracy of the 'saints'. Revolution was leading to highly charged expectations.

For Puritans who believed in predestination, this was the moment for the godly to prevail. Surely the true revolution was that foretold in the Bible, when old corrupt empires would end. Among some, an obsessive reading of the Books of Daniel and Revelation took hold, in which four monarchies are described. When the last is overthrown, it was prophesied that the Fifth Monarchy would arise when the saints – the godly or God's elect – would rule and Christ's kingdom be established. This vision was so urgent that for some, it far outweighed issues of constitution, law or land tenure; but it had great danger for the state, with its talk of the overthrow of kingdoms and rulers. The Fifth Monarchists made their presence felt loudly in London, with vehement and often ecstatic pronouncements.

The Diggers addressed what was probably the most acute issue for poor people in rural England: land rights. Feudal strip farming had become inefficient and over the previous century, by land exchange or purchase, larger holdings had been enclosed into single units. Population growth had left little waste to bring into cultivation, so enclosure produced more food but reduced land for small farmers; it caused controversy under the Tudors and was opposed by Archbishop Laud. The collapse of feudalism might be welcomed, but often the fragile rights which poorer people still held were broken too. The Levellers wanted copyholds, for example, to be translated into freeholds but those were uncommon. As established landowners were dispossessed, smaller tenants found it difficult to roll over their traditional copyhold agreements, so change often disadvantaged the small man.[5]

Rather than tackle the legal problem, the Diggers were idealists. Calling themselves True Levellers, they were as much a part of the millenarian mindset as the Fifth Monarchists, and they had also studied the books of Daniel and Revelation. Gerrard Winstanley, leader of the Diggers, believed the kingdom of the saints would occur when people gave up lordship and property. Adam's sin had driven people away from the garden of the earth; by sharing land, mankind could achieve spiritual regeneration. In February 1649, Winstanley published *The Law of Freedom in a Platform*, which he dedicated to Cromwell. In it, he described a property-less commonwealth held together by strict laws and education so that ideas could not stray.

To put these ideas into practice, a group of about thirty Diggers had chosen common land on St George's Hill near Walton-on-Thames, dug it up and sown it with vegetables. However, the right to the land belonged to the local commoners, who complained. The Council of State asked Fairfax to remove the Diggers. He sent a captain of his own regiment who had a discussion with the Diggers, during which the men refused to remove their hats, showing their lack of deference – something for which the Quakers became notorious. Captain Gladman thought the small group harmless and left them during the summer, but when a new Digger encampment appeared on Cobham Heath the Council insisted on action. This time their huts were taken down and their crops destroyed. By the summer of 1650 no more Digger settlements had sprung up. They were a small movement but a symptom of expectations.

The Commonwealth also had widely dispersed territories to subdue, claiming Ireland, the Channel Islands and the young colonies in America as dependencies. The American settlers, with charters from the crown, had remained largely neutral during the war. Trade was essential to their survival and being far from the upheaval in the British Isles they had protected their interests as best they could. Parliament claimed authority over the colonies in 1643 and appointed the Earl of Warwick to oversee their trade but little was done and the colonists traded freely during the war, finding new markets and selling to the Dutch who came into their ports.[6] After years of commercial freedom, when the Commonwealth began to assert its authority over their affairs, they resisted. But their aims varied; in colonies dedicated to religious freedom there was greater support for parliament, whereas those with commercial charters looked to the crown – in 1649, Virginia, Maryland, Antigua, Barbados and Bermuda proclaimed Charles II as king. In Puritan colonies, where internal struggles were emerging over religious conformity, attitudes were not simple: Massachusetts denounced Independents, who were forced to leave the colony.[7] The London government would have to tackle the American colonies but they were not the first priority.

The Levellers were. From March they became active again in the army, demanding a revival of the General Council which had included agitators to represent the men's views. A pamphlet attacked Cromwell and Ireton for advancing themselves and betraying the soldiers' interests. But after Lilburne and his colleagues were imprisoned, the Levellers lost supporters and influence. However, women were a strong and vocal part of the movement; thousands signed petitions for the prisoners' release and hundreds demonstrated outside parliament. In Colonel Whalley's regiment, dissatisfaction over unmet Leveller demands, pay and the forthcoming Irish expedition reached a mutinous stage. Fifteen men refused to march and were court-martialled. Cromwell wanted to pardon them but Fairfax insisted on discipline and one man, Lockyer, was shot as an example. His funeral attracted a massive demonstration, again with many women among the 4,000 who followed his coffin.

In this atmosphere, choosing regiments for Ireland was going to be contentious. When the process began on 20 April, the orders were met with discontent and disobedience. The imprisoned Levellers published a new Agreement of the People. Early in May, genuine signs of mutiny were appearing in the cavalry regiments, although not among the infantry. As the disaffected regiments were far apart, the commanders acted decisively to prevent them meeting. When several hundred malcontents tried to amalgamate, they were routed near Banbury. The centre of army unrest was in Bristol, so Fairfax and Cromwell took a force of 4,000 men to meet them. While on the march, Fairfax published a document confirming that none of the men would be sent to Ireland against their wishes, that the Agreement of the People was under consideration and that the mutineers' grievances would be heard. If they returned to orders they would be pardoned. Negotiations led to no solution and a real confrontation occurred at Burford where 340 mutineers were taken prisoner while the rest escaped. Five leaders were court-martialled, of whom three were shot.

This was the last action by the Levellers within the army. The movement drifted apart – the leaders were never of one mind but had used the army to further their aims. The strategy had failed and they had no other. Walwyn had shown himself a more persuasive political actor than Lilburne but it was the latter who attracted attention and was known to the London crowds as 'Freeborn John'. Their attempts to get power within the army were sternly met but they were persuasive political agitators and, with time, the foresight of their demands would be recognised.

With the mutiny crushed, Fairfax and Cromwell had full control of their forces once more. The commanders could turn their attention to the Irish campaign.

4

Cromwell's Expedition
to Ireland

In 1649, choosing men to serve in Ireland ignited seething resentment within the army, as it had two years previously. The soldiers viewed Ireland as very high risk and resisted being sent overseas when their political demands had not been met. Who was to command? They had always served under Fairfax and Cromwell. In February, fifteen regiments were chosen but the men were restive. In April, the selection was made again by drawing lots, a more Biblical method and not open to manipulation, but it failed to calm the men. Arrears of pay were the primary complaint but the soldiers also wanted their regiments intact and their known commanders; they thought Ireland a likely graveyard, while Leveller agitation widened their causes of unrest. Government in England was unclear: why had the Agreement of the People not been taken up? Tithes and taxes were high while Leveller pamphlets complained about the newly powerful rulers, arguing that monarchy had only been replaced by aristocratic tyranny and the nation overrun by lawyers.

There was some disquiet about the aims of the expedition.[1] 'Will you go on still to kill, slay and murther men, to make [your officers] absolute lords and masters over Ireland, as you have made them over England?'[2] one pamphlet asked. Henry Marten, the radical MP, challenged the religious motive. If the Commonwealth cherished religious toleration, why would they impose a settlement which was alien to Ireland?[3]

For the government in London, however, Ireland was a possession and a security threat; it was imperative to get the expedition underway. Cromwell took two weeks to consider the offer to command, while he studied parliament's terms and his own conscience. His views on the Irish had not altered: 'all the world knows their barbarism,' he wrote.[4] The reports of the 1641 rebellion had lodged in his mind and poisoned his attitude towards the whole nation. Besides, the Irish service was perilous; in the past, many English commanders had lost their reputations in Ireland as disease, guerrilla warfare and a lack of support weakened their armies. If Cromwell went, he meant to succeed. He already had investments there: in 1642 he had 'adventured' £600, which was to be repaid in land. At the end of March, satisfied that his powers and military supplies would be sufficient, Cromwell accepted the command.

With war debts to settle, funding the re-conquest was a challenge. The Commonwealth planned to sell confiscated property – land and goods belonging to the church and royal family – but sales would take time, so they borrowed from the City to fund the Irish expedition.[5]

Ormond had been appointed Lord Lieutenant of Ireland by Charles I and was working to bring all the royalist forces together. His own troops were Irish Protestants but he needed an alliance with Irish Catholics and Ulster Scots if he was to withstand the army of the Commonwealth. That army's role in executing the king had had a galvanising effect, and in mid-January Ormond made a treaty with all the Confederate Catholics except the veteran fighter Owen Roe O'Neill, who was still active in Ulster. The Ulster Scots were much weakened but allied their forces with Ormond. Prince Rupert's fleet arrived in Kinsale and teamed up with the Earl of Antrim's privateers. Confident that with £5,000 he could hold the island, Ormond invited Charles to Ireland. The Commonwealth's intelligence reports suggested that the Stuart claimant was on his way. For the republican government, there was no time to lose.

Ormond had brought all the royalists together but religion divided them and they lacked money and arms. His Protestant officers were unhappy with the treaty; they saw the Catholics as a threat who might demand changes in politics and land rights, undermining their position. In the north, Owen Roe harried parliament's commanders Monck and Coote, but still he resisted alliance with the crown forces. Even with Ormond's treaty, the Irish factions were not united.

Once Leveller activity in the army was crushed at Burford, discipline was no longer a problem for Cromwell but he had other concerns. He was leaving London while the new government was finding its feet and he would be unable to influence its direction while he was away. He intended to accumulate money and armaments to take with him, and not rely on promises that supplies would be sent later. Ireland's climate and water had often depleted armies and Cromwell, now almost fifty, might be tested personally. For the new government, the stakes were high; for him personally, failure in Ireland would probably mean political failure too.

The costs would be considerable. Twelve thousand men were to be shipped over with all their equipment and supplies. The lieutenant general was to be well paid. Not only military commander, Cromwell was also appointed head of government and now styled Lord Lieutenant, with a salary of £5,000 a year and an additional £8,000 while he was in Ireland, giving the handsome annual sum of £13,000. Cromwell thought the expedition could be done on £20,000 a month and determined not to leave until he had £100,000 to take in coin. He never quite got hold of that amount, despite loans from the City and his actually seizing £10,000 sent to the navy, but he was not far off it when he set sail. In fact, over a seven-year period, almost a million a year was spent on subjugating Ireland, although once the English forces took territory they imposed fines and taxes to help fund the full conquest.[6]

Cromwell would land on the east coast and knew that the province of Munster, especially the port towns, would be crucial. The disquiet of the Irish Protestants over Ormond's treaty gave Cromwell a weakness he could exploit. He sent Colonel Phayre ahead, with money and persuasive terms, to win over Protestant officers. Key men were propositioned by both sides. Ormond tried to sway Michel Jones, the commander of Dublin, but he stayed firm for parliament. Roger Boyle, Viscount Broghill, had changed sides during the war and in 1649 was in London but expected by Charles at the exiled court. Cromwell got to Broghill first and, whether by threat or persuasion, won his allegiance. The vast Boyle estates in Ireland had been taken by the Confederates and a parliamentary victory might be the best chance of restoring them. By whatever blandishments, Broghill gave Cromwell his support and since his influence in Munster was enormous, turning him proved valuable to the English.

As Cromwell was making his plans, the balance of forces in Ireland altered again. Inchiquin held the Munster ports for the crown and in April joined Ormond in Tipperary for the summer campaign. While Ormond moved up to challenge Dublin, Inchiquin and Castlehaven took key strongholds in Leinster. Irish by birth, Protestant by allegiance and daring in command, Inchiquin moved on north of Dublin to take first the port of Drogheda, then Dundalk and Newry, while the Ulster Scots took the fortress of Carrickfergus. Monck surrendered and took ship for England. The royalist position had been greatly strengthened but now Ormond miscalculated. Expecting Cromwell to land in Munster, Inchiquin returned to Cork, but in Dublin Jones received reinforcements and when he led his troops out of the capital to fight Ormond at Rathmines on 2 August, Charles's Lord Lieutenant could not withstand him. The royalists were routed, losing cash and their artillery. Ormond's forces were seriously weakened and he warned Charles not to sail for Ireland yet.

By then, Cromwell was at Milford Haven in West Wales, gathering his troops and supplies. He had left London on 12 July with solemn ritual. A fast day was ordered, three ministers blessed his expedition and Cromwell spoke at length. His lifeguard of eighty officers mustered, trumpets sounded and his coach set out, pulled by six grey mares with a white standard flying overhead. The new government was developing a style which was grand and symbolic, but Puritan. To the millenarians, conquering Catholic Ireland was both a military necessity and a crucial religious step. For them, overthrowing papist rule would fulfil the prophecies in the Book of Daniel, bringing closer the rule of the saints and the reign of King Jesus. For both strategic and religious reasons, the Puritans had to conquer Ireland.

The Irish expected Cromwell to land in Cork. Why else would he have chosen a southern Welsh port? But at Milford Haven, Cromwell heard the news of Jones's victory at Rathmines which he hailed as 'an astonishing mercy'. Throughout the wars, God had shown his favour by awarding victories – here was another. 'The Lord fills our souls with thankfulness,' Cromwell wrote.[7]

The success at Rathmines meant that Cromwell could sail directly for Dublin and on 13 August his fleet left harbour. This was the first and only time he departed the island of Britain. The sea was rough and he was violently sick; Hugh Peters the preacher said the commander was as seasick as ever he saw a man in his life.[8] The crossing took three days. Ireton followed and a third squadron brought more troops; Hugh Peters returned with the first fleet and came back with the last of the troops – about 14,000 men were shipped to Ireland along with horses, munitions and supplies. By late August, Michael Jones could welcome the Commonwealth's Lord Lieutenant to Dublin Castle, a massive fortress within the city walls. Throughout Cromwell's youth, Ireland had had a reputation for everything which he detested and he had invested a sizeable part of his fortune in its reconquest; now he could see it for himself. He spent about a week in Dublin, taking intelligence and organising his campaign. The fighting season was advanced and his funds had to be used to maximum effect. He planned carefully with the robust and practical mind which made him the exceptional soldier that he was.

Soon after his arrival, Cromwell gave instructions to his troops not to plunder or take free quarter. He also put out a statement to the local people that all provisions brought to the army would be paid for, and this helped him gain both supplies and goodwill. His aim was to take the walled towns on the east coast, of which Drogheda was to be the first. He spent a week in Dublin and then marched up the coast, but it took a further week to ship the artillery and get it into position, so the storming of Drogheda did not begin until 10 September. As a military action it was successful and swift, but Cromwell's work in that town left an indelible stain on both Irish history and the commander's reputation. In fact, Cromwell's decisions at Drogheda are just one example of how he, along with his fellow officers and officials, conquered and planted Ireland, inflicting such radical changes that Irish society could never recover – as was their aim.

Drogheda was physically defensible but the royalist army lacked strength. As Cromwell was coming ashore, Ormond was organising the defence, appointing Sir Arthur Aston as governor and assigning him four of the best infantry regiments to hold the town. The governor and his officers were almost exclusively English: Aston had fought in Europe, been governor of Oxford during the Civil War and had come to Ireland the previous year. He was a Catholic but his officers were Protestant.

Their sense of identity was playing on the loyalty of the soldiers. Some of Ormond's cavalry, unhappy at the alliance with the Catholics, rode away to join the English as they approached. Outside Drogheda, Cromwell made his dispositions. The town had stout walls with a ravine outside to the south; here Cromwell stationed his artillery on the bank of the ravine and so level with the walls. The town was bisected by the River Boyne and Cromwell judged it unwise to split his troops to attack both sections of the town. On 10 September the bombardment commenced. It took all day to breach the walls so it was late afternoon when Cromwell's infantrymen were sent through the hole; inside, the defenders were behind earthworks and fiercely repelled them. The Puritan response was a cannonade to blast the defenders away from the walls, after which Cromwell and Hewson accompanied the troops through the wall. This time they drove the defenders back, poured into the town, took St Mary's church and opened the gate for their own cavalry to enter. Some English troops raced down to take the bridge over the Boyne. Cromwell had captured the town in a simple assault – but now the slaughter began.

The royalists had been separated, one group with Aston on Mill Mount south of the Boyne and the others north of the Boyne, many of whom took refuge in St Peter's church. As the Puritans attacked Mill Mount, they offered quarter to the royalists penned in there and many surrendered, but Cromwell, whose previous war record had been of discipline and moderation, now showed a different face. Aston had defied the original summons, and under the conventions of war Cromwell's orders were not exceptional, but they contradicted the offers given by his subordinates and were carried out with brutal efficiency. Aston, his officers and men were put to the sword; Cromwell later estimated that 2,000 men were killed. North of the Boyne, around St Peter's church, Cromwell's troops piled furniture and set fire to it. The defenders were either burned or captured trying to escape and shipped to Barbados.

Cromwell wrote to Lenthall, Speaker of Parliament, 'I am persuaded that this is a righteous judgement of God upon those barbarous wretches, who have imbrued their hands in so much innocent blood; and that it will tend to prevent the effusion of blood for the future, which are the satisfactory grounds to such actions, which otherwise cannot but work remorse and regret.'[9] For Cromwell, the town and the Irish generally carried blood guilt for the 1641 rebellion. He went on to explain and justify his strategy further, but it was a poor defence. The men killed in Drogheda were not the Ulster Catholics who had risen in 1641; they were largely Protestant settlers from England. Even Ludlow, who came to Ireland in 1651 as commander of horse for the Commonwealth, was uncomfortable with the slaughter in Drogheda.

Nor was this violence only seen in the heat of battle, for records show that for three days after the town was stormed, prisoners were taken out and run through. Hugh Peters, Cromwell's chaplain, gave the final death toll as 64 parliamentary soldiers and 3,552 enemy; historians have not greatly altered these figures. Of these casualties, 2,800 were soldiers and the rest were non-combatants; every friar found was said to have been killed.

Why did Cromwell order this killing? He seems to have lost his head as he entered the town with his troops, but the continuing executions probably reflect just how high the stakes were for him. He was overseas for the first time, he believed the terrible reports about the Irish and he could not afford to fail. He reasoned that severe measures now would terrify his opponents and bring a swifter victory. At first, this seemed to work, but later Irish resolve hardened and took its toll on Cromwell's army.

Cromwell was back in Dublin by the time he wrote to Lenthall, but already the conditions on the island were weakening his men. 'We keep the field much, our tents sheltering us from the wet and cold, but yet the country-sickness overtakes many,' he reported.[10] From the time they landed, dysentery ravaged his troops and he begged for more recruits. As he took royalist garrisons, so he left his soldiers to man them, but this too depleted his forces.

However, the alliance of royalist forces was an uneasy one, and this made Cromwell's job easier. Owen Roe O'Neill now agreed to join Ormond but this alienated more Protestant officers and caused them to defect to Cromwell. Many walled towns refused Ormond's troops, demanding Catholic officers. The population of Ireland, so recently transformed by plantation, could not fight as a coherent nation. Ormond wrote to the exiled king that it was incredible how fearful the Irish had become, 'though they know themselves designed at best to the loss of all they have, and to irrecoverable slavery'. The Irish had the numbers, yet Ormond could hardly goad them into defending their country.[11]

Cromwell now sent Colonel Robert Venables north to secure Ulster while he turned south to secure the Munster ports. Venables took Lisburn and Belfast, while Coote took Coleraine; the east coast was quickly subjugated. Only the massive fortress of Carrickfergus held out against the English until winter. (*See map 4, page 101.*)

Cromwell's next target was Wexford. Here, one of the defenders opened the castle to the English forces, allowing easy access, and when panic ensued in the marketplace the Cromwellian troops mowed down the fleeing populace. As in Drogheda, killing was indiscriminate. This time it was not on Cromwell's orders – he lost control of his troops. New Ross fell to Cromwell on 19 October, having capitulated quickly. The town was not plundered but when they asked for freedom of religion, Cromwell made the position clear: 'I meddle not with any man's conscience. But if by liberty of conscience you mean a liberty to exercise the mass, I judge it best to use plain dealing, and to let you know, where the parliament of England have power, that will not be allowed of.'[12]

By then, Broghill had arrived in Ireland. He would prove exceptionally useful to Cromwell. Under Charles I, he had competed with Inchiquin for the presidency of Munster; the two men were also divided by race and religious culture. Now Broghill reminded the

Cork officers that Inchiquin was party to Ormond's treaty with the Catholics and insinuated that their Gaelic commander was reverting to type. The officers deserted Inchiquin and opened the gates of Cork city to Cromwell. Youghal, Kinsale and Dungarvan followed. Admiral Robert Blake brought his ships into Kinsale harbour, flushing out Prince Rupert who escaped with his small fleet, leaving Charles with no naval presence in Ireland. The east coast had fallen to Cromwell in just a few months. Only Waterford held out: here the rain made siege manoeuvres difficult for the English and disease weakened the troops, so Cromwell abandoned his attempt on the port and marched his men away to decent winter quarters in Cork. In November Venables took Carrickfergus, and by Christmas no major Ulster strongholds were left in Irish hands.

Ormond's difficulties were not just lack of arms and morale but preserving his treaty with the Catholic forces. His alliance with Owen Roe was short-lived as the elderly commander died in November without reaching Ormond, but his nephew Hugh O'Neill, also a veteran of the European wars, brought his officers and troops to join the royalists. Hugh Dubh (Dark Hugh) proved a formidable soldier and inflicted unusual damage on the New Model Army in the following year.

Increasingly, the Catholic Irish looked to their bishops for leadership and viewed officers who were English or Protestant with suspicion. A meeting of the Irish Catholic clergy at Clonmacnoise in December published a manifesto warning that Cromwell intended to extirpate the Catholic religion and that this meant removing the Irish people.

This document enraged Cromwell, who replied in forceful style. *For the Undeceiving of Deluded and Seduced People*[13] stated his policies for Ireland but displayed his own lack of knowledge. As a Puritan, he described the authority of the Catholic clergy over their people as 'anti-Christian'. Then he moved on to the rebellion. 'I will give you some wormwood to bite on; by which it will appear that God is not with you,' he told the priests. 'Remember, ye hypocrites, Ireland was once united to England. Englishmen had good inheritances, which many of them purchased with their money; they or their ancestors, from many of you or your ancestors.' He wrote that Englishmen lived 'peaceably among you ... you, unprovoked, put the English to the most unheard-of and most barbarous massacre'. He ignored the political tensions of the previous century and attacked the religion. 'You are a part of Antichrist,' he wrote. He questioned Irish loyalty to the king: which king? he asked, 'Is it France, or Spain, or Scotland?'

He accused them of arbitrary power, 'a thing men begin to weary of, in Kings and Churchmen'.

Then he outlined what the Irish should expect from his own regime. He had already stated there would be no mass. If Catholic priests fell into his hands, they should expect the full rigour of the law. He would not meddle in the consciences of the people, but offered to 'walk patiently and in love towards them', hoping that God would 'give them another or a better mind' – he hoped to convert the Irish. He sneered at the idea that an English army had invaded solely to take land for the Adventurers. His army had come in a righteous cause, to 'ask an account of the innocent blood that hath been shed ... to break the power of a company of lawless rebels'. Then he emphasised England's sovereignty over Ireland and offered English liberties. 'We come to hold forth and maintain the lustre and glory of English liberty in a nation where we have the undoubted right to do it; – wherein the people of Ireland ... may equally participate in all benefits, to use liberty and fortune equally with Englishmen, if they keep out of arms.'

In their own declaration, the Catholic clergy had warned the people that they would be 'massacred, banished and destroyed' by parliament's forces. Cromwell railed against this propaganda. 'Give one example,' he challenged, 'only men in arms have been so treated.' But people needed to know what to expect and Cromwell set it out. People not in arms would not lose their lives; those taken in arms might be banished. As to land confiscation, Cromwell responded to the priests' warning. The Adventurers Act had been a just response to rebellion. Those who had never rebelled would be protected by law, common soldiers still in arms should lay them down and go home, but for those who continued to fight Cromwell would 'rejoice to exercise utmost severity against them'.[14] This document was written in Youghal and published in Cork during January 1650.

By the time it came out, Cromwell's army was taking the field once more. Increasingly, the Catholic clergy were leading the resistance to the English, rather than Ormond. Ulster Scots troops had drifted towards parliament. The walled towns demanded Catholic garrisons but ended up with weak defences; yet when attacked, they were slow to surrender.

Throughout the winter, Charles remained in Jersey. Ormond had warned him not to come until the royalists took Dublin, but since the king's party reached the island in September 1649 all news from Ireland had been of royalist losses. Sir Edward Hyde and Cottington had departed as ambassadors to Madrid, leaving several councillors with the king. James was there too and the royal brothers were conspicuous on the island, dressed in mourning for their father and attending chapel, while Charles kept court but had to sell crown property in Jersey to maintain his entourage. In adversity, Charles was developing poise, secrecy and political cunning. Messages and envoys reached him: from Ormond and Montrose, from possible supporters like Sweden. While waiting for an opening in Ireland, he watched for the same in Scotland.

In Edinburgh, the kirk party was in power but there were disagreements among them. Johnston wanted to ally with the Commonwealth but the Covenanters had sworn allegiance to the king in a sacred document. Would the young Stuart conform to their religious ideals? That was the problem for the kirk. In his heart, Argyll may have leaned towards the Commonwealth too but as a politician he acted the royalist. Messages were sent to Jersey and in December a lawyer named Wynrame arrived with Colonel Titus, who was in touch with both Henrietta-Maria and the English Presbyterians, bringing a message from Argyll suggesting further negotiations.

However, Montrose had the king's commission for Scotland and was scouring northern Europe for funds and recruits. He had visited Elizabeth of Bohemia and was one of the gallants whom she welcomed to her court. This gave him standing among English Protestants, for whom Elizabeth was a shining star, but although Montrose spent the winter gathering support for a landing in Scotland, raising funds and troops proved hard. The Covenanters heartily loathed Montrose, yet Charles hoped for support from both parties. He stayed on in Jersey over Christmas and into the new year, still waiting on news from Ormond although increasingly he saw Scotland as a better option. Perched on his island, the young king received visitors and sent letters as the news from Ireland seemed less and less hopeful. In January 1650, Charles's council invited the Scots to negotiations at Breda in the Netherlands.

With so much at stake, Cromwell was back in the field early in the year. In London, the Council of State was already agitating for him to return because of the Scottish situation. Cromwell however, was on campaign in a pincer movement with his commanders. They already held the east coast; now they turned inland to the nearest river valleys with their fortresses. Cromwell was southernmost, working his way up from Cork through Tipperary to Kilkenny, the capital of the Confederate Catholics. Ireton marched out of Dungarvan and Hewson came south from Dublin. Broghill protected their western flank as the Puritan forces advanced. There were no pitched battles, as Ormond could not mount one; rather it was a laborious business of taking fortresses. Methodically, Cromwell marched to each walled town, brought up artillery and summoned it to surrender. If it did, there would be negotiations and terms; if it did not, the guns would breach the walls and troops would pour in. Cromwell's forces took Fethard, Cahir and Callan. Ormond's cousin commanded at Kilkenny and the city held out for several weeks but surrendered on 28 March. Since the initial attacks on Drogheda and Wexford, which had created shock and awe, Cromwell had reverted to his usual methods and took his conquests with less bloodshed and more mercy. If terms for surrender were agreed, legal documents were drawn up for the commanders to sign.

Ormond wrote to the Earl of Clanricarde that the whole kingdom was 'terrified beyond imagination, and no means left for me to persuade them in any settled way of resistance'.[15] His own loyalty to the king was unshakeable but the Catholic population was unsure, looking to the clergy for leadership and unsure what to expect from Cromwell: slaughter or mercy, honourable terms or dispossession? During April, more Irish Protestants deserted Ormond for Cromwell. This increased Catholic suspicions: if Ormond put a Protestant garrison into their town, it would surely open the gate and abandon them to the English.

Ormond was a careful administrator but had few military skills. He doggedly carried out his commission from the king but the cities of eastern Ireland were falling one by one. Cromwell was an unrivalled commander with a battle-hardened army and supplies, whereas the Irish were split and Charles, who might have been a figurehead, was overseas. The previous summer, Ireland had seemed the royalists' best hope but by Christmas the situation had changed. In February 1650, Charles left Jersey for France, discussed the situation with his mother and then continued to the Netherlands to meet a new Scottish delegation at Breda. He hoped to gain their support but moderate their demands. Like his father, he would discover they were as unbending as granite.

As Charles travelled to Breda, his aims were still broad. His policy was to unite all royalists and enemies of the Commonwealth under his leadership. His problem was the religious divergence among those groups. The Covenanters were uncompromising Presbyterians, antagonistic to Irish Catholics and furious about Ormond's treaty with them. Nor were the Scots tolerant about the Church of England, to which most English royalists belonged. The kirk was in sympathy with English Presbyterians, but they were a minority group. So, there was a religious chasm among royalists. As claimant, Charles had youth and tradition on his side, whereas the new English regime had yet to win support, but the divergence among his supporters weakened his cause and created impossible choices for him, as it had for his father. To the Commonwealth leaders in London, however, any alliance between Charles and the Scots would pose an immediate threat. Presbyterianism was strong in London and the Scots might find support there. The new government began to arrest leading Presbyterian ministers in the capital.

In Ireland, Cromwell took Kilkenny, and during April more Protestant forces surrendered. The Catholics still held Waterford but late in April, Cromwell turned his attention to Clonmel, on the River Suir, at the base of the Comeragh mountains. Here, Hugh Dubh O'Neill commanded the Irish and, having seen Cromwell's methods, made his own preparations. As the English artillery smashed a breach in the town walls, the Irish created an alley between rubble walls just inside the breach, leading to a ditch where they planted their guns. English infantry and cavalry poured through the wall, realising only too late they were in a trap. Fired on from above, and attacked with every available sharp weapon, the English were unable to turn back. About 1,500 of Cromwell's men were killed – one of the worst maulings ever inflicted on his army – but in the night, having run out of ammunition, Hugh Dubh led his men out of the town. Cromwell gave Clonmel generous terms for surrender, only to discover, to his fury, that his adversary had disappeared.

The Irish, after the initial shock of Drogheda and believing that an English victory would mean total loss, hardened their resistance. Clonmel was the end of Cromwell's campaign in Ireland; parliament repeatedly sent orders for his return because of the Scottish situation. He handed command in Ireland over to his son-in-law Henry Ireton, appointed him Lord Deputy and sailed from Youghal on 26 May. It had been his only overseas journey and the cost to his reputation was heavy, but he had prosecuted a successful war: the Adventurers would be paid, that much was sure. However, when Cromwell left in the spring of 1650, the conquest was unfinished and many decisions about the final settlement were yet to be made.

Ireton was slender and energetic, fiercely Puritan, a clever lawyer and constitutional theorist. He had married Bridget Cromwell and worked closely with his father-in-law but lacked the older man's military abilities. The Irish were regrouping. Cromwell had taken £100,000 with him to Ireland and the government had sent further supplies but the conquest proved tough and dragged on. While the Lord Deputy and his commanders turned their horses towards the walled towns in the west, Cromwell crossed the Irish Sea and made for London to take up a further command.

5

The Struggle for Scotland

The potency of Charles was as a figurehead, especially in Scotland where a royal Stuart was bound to attract support. Cromwell's strength was military, but Charles had some experience of warfare, so he posed a substantial threat and reports of the meeting in Breda alarmed London. The English government had no legal claim on Scotland and had suggested a treaty, but when the Scottish parliament refused to acknowledge 'the present authority', the Commons renounced all former treaties and obligations.[1] If the Scots now installed Charles Stuart as their king, there was no doubt that England would mobilise against them.

Potentially, Scotland might withstand the English. David Leslie still commanded about 4,500 men and a Stuart king would bring in more; the Highlands were likely to rise. Montrose was recruiting for the royalist cause overseas, and if all these factions coalesced they could defend Scotland and possibly threaten England. However, the kirk party controlled the Committee of Estates, directed government in Scotland and had its own aims; eventually the narrowness of the kirk position worked to England's advantage. In the spring of 1650 there was urgency on all sides. In fact, in contrast to the Irish expedition, Charles arrived in Scotland before Cromwell.

During the winter, as Cromwell laboured in Ireland, Montrose tried to fulfil his own commission by recruiting in northern Europe. Queen Christina of Sweden, the daughter of the late but mighty Gustavus Adolphus, allowed Montrose to buy military supplies in Gothenburg; other princes spoke warmly but gave nothing. Montrose had the support of Elizabeth of Bohemia; he was a favourite at her exiled court in The Hague and corresponded with her regularly to keep her abreast

Scotland in 1650.

of his plans. This friendship enhanced his profile but not his supplies. The Winter Queen was still gracious, sparkling and wild-hearted in her widowhood. She could remember her childhood in Scotland and it was to her that the Scottish exiles principally came. Among the gallants who gathered around her, Montrose was a star. His portrait had been painted by Honthurst at her request and hung in her cabinet, for among the Scottish royalists Montrose was a general of the first order whose courage reflected Elizabeth's own. The Covenanters, however, had excommunicated him, casting him 'out of the Church of God ... upon whose head lies more innocent blood than for many years hath done on the head of any one, the most bloody murtherer in our nation'.[2] Many of the men who had led the effort to raise armies and fight the wars of the previous decades had accused each other of similar outrages.

The real enemy of the Scottish royalists was London. The Commonwealth not only had the most powerful army in Europe but was building up its navy. The position of England made it formidable to all the states of northern Europe with coasts and shipping to protect. The Commonwealth's spy network was known to be active in the northern ports. So, although the rulers of Sweden and Denmark, as well as the German princes, had sympathy for Charles and listened to Montrose, they were cautious. While he tried to win more support, Montrose sent an advance party under Kinnoul who arrived in Orkney in September 1649. The islands, untouched by the passions of the Covenanting movement, offered a base for building up the expedition. From here, royalist Highland lords like Mackenzie were close while both Edinburgh and the Covenanting army under Leslie were a long march away. If the north rose for the king and held, the central Highlands would surely rise too. Bad news reached Montrose in November: Morton, his chief ally in the north, had died. Kinnoul, Morton's nephew, died soon afterwards. However, the messenger assured Montrose that Scotland was restive, chafing at the exactions and repressions of kirk rule, and that thousands would rise were he to come ashore as the king's captain general.

The enmity between Montrose and the Covenanters weakened the royalist position in Scotland. For Charles to succeed, the Scottish people would have to cleave to the king more than to the kirk. Even then, he would need additional support, from English and Irish royalists as well as European friends. Montrose hoped to rouse the Highlands and sweep up all Scotland, including the Covenanters, behind the king. He had sworn loyalty to the Stuarts long before and stayed true to his word, despite the odds shifting against him.

He believed his mission was sacred and he accepted God's will. In his declaration to the Scottish people, he wrote, 'Let the Lord do whatever seemeth Him good.'[3] Johnston, one of the purist Covenanters, had this document publicly burned in Edinburgh.

Men and arms were sent on to Orkney during the winter, the men hired in Scandinavia and the shipments ravaged by wild weather. Montrose waited on letters but in late March 1650 he left Sweden and sailed to Orkney where he gained more troops. Here two letters from Charles reached him, one public and one private. The former informed his commander of the negotiations with Edinburgh, assured him that any agreement would protect him and told him to proceed, as any military success would improve Charles's bargaining position. The private letter added assurances that Charles would protect Montrose. Events showed that both men had seriously overestimated their strength, but by the spring of 1650 Montrose recognised how perilous the strategy was and warned Charles of being outmanoeuvred in negotiations: 'Have a serious eye, now at last, upon the too open crafts [that] are used against you.'[4] Then, from 9 April, despite his modest resources, he began dispatching forces to the mainland. Charles's public letter was leaked and published in Paris, so the main points of his strategy were known in London and Scotland.

In Edinburgh, the leaders were motivated more by religious purity than national survival. They had weakened their army by purging it of the ungodly the previous year. When overtures came from London, they were rejected out of hand unless the Commonwealth repented of Charles I's execution. Yet the Scots would not restore his son to the Scottish throne unless he signed the Covenant and embraced their beliefs. To the kirkmen, both Montrose and the Commonwealth were enemies, while the Engagers were dreadful malignants. This left them with a narrow base and even among the government in Edinburgh there was divergence about their plans. In February, after a stormy meeting of the Committee of Estates, a delegation set off for Breda with a mandate to negotiate.[5]

Charles spent three weeks with his mother, who advised against signing the Covenant, as did many of his council. There was clearly a chasm between Charles and the Scots; on both sides there were those who thought it could be bridged, and others who rejected compromise. Charles himself was anxious for agreement and thought a deal signed now could be softened later, once he was in Scotland and could work his royal magic. He met the six-man delegation at Breda with courtesy, but their demands were severe: Charles was to sign the Covenants and apply them to all three kingdoms, recall Montrose, confirm all the acts of the Scottish parliament since it had sidelined his father in 1641, disown Ormond's treaty with the Catholics in Ireland and persecute that religion in all three realms.

Charles charmed them and negotiated patiently but he continued to use the *Book of Common Prayer* by day and to dine and dance at night. It was obvious he did not share their brisk Calvinism, but the Scots needed Charles. In Scotland, feeling ran high against England and its government of 'sectaries'; Charles would boost the Scottish cause. For Argyll's party, the king would cement rule by the aristocracy, although the Scottish negotiators did not envisage Charles governing the country on his own terms. For the young king, Scotland seemed his only hope of restoration. As time for negotiation ran out, the delegates suggested that details could be settled once Charles met the Scottish parliament and on 29 April, they accepted the king's concessions and invited him to Scotland. Hyde and Cottington were still in Madrid but other councillors advised against the deal; Charles, however, accepted.

Believing that problems could be overcome once he was in Scotland with loyal followers and an army, Charles sent messages to his supporters in all three kingdoms alerting them and making offers. He had received communications from his agents which seemed hopeful; the London and Cornwall royalists had schemes, while feelers had been put out to the Levellers who, furious at Lilburne's reimprisonment and the suppression of their agents at Burford, had made overtures to Charles themselves. First, he must establish himself in Scotland. The Prince of Orange had tried to assist in the negotiations but found the Scots intransigent and had abandoned the effort with disgust; nonetheless he provided three warships for the journey.[6]

Just as Charles reached agreement in Breda, tragedy struck his loyal commander. Montrose came ashore in Caithness in mid-April. His forces were few and many Highland leaders could no longer raise men, although some joined him. The Covenanting troops under Leslie reached Brechin in Angus by late April, where Strachan was sent on ahead. Montrose, as always, kept to the hills and camped at the head of the Dornoch Firth in Ross. Waiting for local clans to join, with a steep hill behind and the shore before him, he waited to move south. But Strachan crept forward and as soon as Montrose's infantry moved onto low ground near Carbisdale, the Covenanters fell on them. The small numbers of Scandinavian and Orcadian troops were overcome and Montrose's own horse shot under him. A fellow officer pulled him onto his horse and they fled into the hills.

Attempting to reach the coast without food or support, and hunted down the glens by Strachan, Montrose was taken to the castle of Ardvreck where he hoped Macleod would assist him; instead he was taken captive and sent to Edinburgh. His captors led him south on a poor pony, hoping to humiliate him, but friends greeted him and the journey showed how warm public feeling was towards Montrose. The Covenanters had determined that the 'great Graham' would not be beheaded, as was normal with noblemen and state prisoners, but would be hanged and dismembered. He was brought into Edinburgh, where the kirkmen lectured him, but he walked to the gallows with calm dignity and, despite the cruel sentence, died bravely, making a strong impression on the watching crowd. His limbs were put up outside four cities with his head in Edinburgh. His torso was buried but Lady Napier had his heart secretly removed from the common grave, embalmed in a casket and sent to his son in Europe.

Montrose died on 21 May. Charles was still in Breda and Cromwell about to leave Ireland. Commonwealth spies had been warning that agreement was imminent in Breda. If Charles Stuart reached Edinburgh, with the Scots hostile over religion and vengeful over their dead king, the north of England was endangered. Fairfax was still commander-in-chief of the army but his behaviour over recent months had been ambivalent and England would need their finest officers for Scotland: Cromwell must return. When he sailed from Youghal, he had achieved much of his purpose; the conquest of Ireland might take time but it was hardly in doubt. He arrived in Bristol late in May, but by the time he reached London Charles had embarked for Scotland.

Cromwell returned to London as a conquering hero. As a reward for his success, parliament had given him the use of a townhouse in Whitehall called the Cockpit, with command of St James's Park, and subsequently they lavished manors and lands on him.[7] Whitelocke records Cromwell's arrival in the capital:

> He was met on Hounslow Heath by many members of parliament and officers of the army, and at Hyde-park saluted with great guns, and a volley of shot from Colonel Barkstead's regiment, and lodged in Whitehall ... In great ceremonies and appearances of joy upon the coming of the lord-lieutenant of Ireland to London; most of the persons of quality, the members of parliament, and officers of the army about the town, paid their visits to him, and congratulated the safe arrival of his excellence after so many dangers both by sea and land, wherein God had preserved him, and the wonderful successes which he had given him.[8]

Andrew Marvell wrote *An Horatian Ode upon Cromwell's Return from Ireland* after his return, probably composed in pursuit of patronage. It brilliantly sums up all the issues which must have been tumbling through the minds of English people: the fear of Ireland, the dignity of the king in death, the awe in which Cromwell was viewed and the hopes that he would obey parliament.

> 'Restless Cromwell'
> 'cast the kingdoms old
> Into another mould.'
> 'How good he is, how just
> And fit for highest trust:'
> 'And now the Irish are ashamed
> To see themselves in one year tamed.'

Even Scotland must cower:

> The Pict no shelter now shall find.[9] .

England had to mobilise; there was no time to lose. It was known that the Scots were levying troops and that Charles was destined for Scotland. Fairfax initially agreed to lead an expedition to protect northern England but when the Commonwealth decided that attack was better than defence and that an invasion of Scotland was necessary, Fairfax refused the command. This was a serious development and a deputation went to visit the General in his Whitehall quarters, among them the lawyer Bulstrode Whitelocke, Cromwell himself and several officers. Cromwell suggested 'there seemed to be some hesitation in yourself as to that journey'. Fairfax reiterated his duty and affection to parliament but said an invasion of Scotland was not warranted as 'we are joined in the National League and Covenant', making it unlawful to invade.[10]

The visitors tried to persuade the General and Harrison says they stayed long into the night but Fairfax would not alter his position. It was widely believed that his wife, a forceful woman and a Presbyterian, had influenced him. Since he could not be swayed, Fairfax resigned his commission. He returned to his estates in Yorkshire, where Andrew Marvell was hired as tutor to his only daughter, Mary, and described the beauties of Appleton House in verse.[11] Naturally, Cromwell was promoted to Lord General and commander for Scotland.

Out in the Scottish countryside, in small towns and rural parishes, the kirk was raising funds and men. They had enormous power, as they controlled education and punished social behaviour but also managed tax collection for the armies. Scotland had been at war since 1638, leaving the resources of this modest northern country sorely stretched. The Scottish people were restive and grumbled, but the kirk remained obdurate in its aims.

On the day that Montrose was brought into Edinburgh tied to a cart, the Scottish parliament rejected the Treaty of Breda and insisted its full conditions be met. Charles with his courtiers and entourage had reached Terheiden on the coast of Holland when a letter reached Scotland's commissioners. They were aboard a ship when they read the missive, in which the Scottish parliament demanded Charles's full compliance. The commissioners decided to procrastinate. Among the king's entourage were Scottish noblemen such as Hamilton and Lauderdale, who had been Engagers in 1648; the kirk found them obnoxious and demanded they be left behind, but Charles ignored their demands. All might be settled when he landed and could speak to his parliament.

The commissioners weighed anchor but the wind was treacherous and the voyage delayed. While they awaited better conditions at Heligoland, extra demands arrived from the Scots. Charles was now in an awkward position – if he said no, his reception in Scotland might be thwarted; if he abandoned the journey, his political strategy would be wrecked and his prospects greatly reduced. He was trapped and very angry, but after more prevarication he agreed to sign both Covenants and to disavow Ormond's treaty. The kirk party had what it wanted but it was a hollow victory; their greatest problem, which they later recognised, was that the king had no interest in their religious programme. He had been brought up to head the Church of England, his father had died a devout Anglican and his mother was a Catholic. The commissioners had complained that Charles even denied that the scriptures settled all issues, questioning how 'people knew it was the word of God, but by the testimony of the Church'. How could this young sceptic, who danced and drank until late into the night, possibly be considered a 'covenanted king'?[12]

They sailed for Scotland, the king with his councillors and friends, the commissioners for kirk and parliament, all aboard the Dutch warships. To avoid the English fleet, they came near land far north in the Moray Firth but the king could not disembark until he made his fateful signatures. So he signed the two Covenants and, already angry and now knowing of Montrose's execution, with his full entourage around him to thwart the strict kirk leaders, set foot on Scottish soil. The kirkmen would extract more painful concessions from him later.

Nonetheless, Charles Stuart set out on a royal progress south to his palace of Falkland in Fife, warmly greeted by the people of Scotland. He arrived on 6 July, so on this expedition he had a head start over Cromwell, who left London on 28 June with a long march ahead. The Scots were levying troops and more came in swiftly. Leslie began to dig trenches to defend the approaches to Edinburgh.

Nervous about a resurgence of support for the Stuarts, the Commons moved Charles I's two younger children from the care of the Leicesters at Penshurst Place in Kent to Carisbrooke Castle on the Isle of Wight, where their father had been held in 1648. Elizabeth was a clever and gentle girl but was not robust. She said she was not well enough to travel, but she was moved anyway. On the journey the fourteen-year-old princess caught a cold which became pneumonia. She died on 8 September 1650, leaving Henry as parliament's only Stuart captive.

Cromwell had set off north with 16,000 men – eight regiments each of cavalry and infantry. The English army was disciplined and experienced but Leslie was a notable commander and by the time that Cromwell crossed the Tweed on 22 July, the Scots and English forces were matched in numbers. While the armies took shape and defined territory, the king and the Covenanters wrestled politically.

The Marquis of Argyll acted as intermediary but his task was difficult. The Scots wanted a king but the kirk party regarded the one they had as wholly unsatisfactory. With spasms of religious zeal, they attempted to remould him. They had different aims: the Scots to consolidate power and fulfil the Covenant, Charles to regain control of Scotland and then use it to retake England and avenge his father's death. For the Commonwealth, the alliance of king and kirk was indeed seen as a declaration of war. For the kirk, Charles was a goad; he refused to send away the Engagers in his entourage, told the kirkmen how to prepare for war and then joined the army in Leith, where he proved popular with the soldiers. Furious, the Committee of Estates demanded that he leave and threatened to withdraw their support, so Charles, with bad grace, withdrew to the royal palace of Dunfermline. He could live as a king but could not visit his capital nor his army.

In reaction, the kirk party continued their purges of that army and demanded a declaration from the king which would affirm his devotion to the Covenants and denigrate his parents – his father for opposing the Covenant and his mother for idolatry. The Covenanters were making him do a horrible penance. Argyll begged him to sign and Johnston threatened to withdraw support if he did not. Charles did eventually sign but the public repudiation of his parents weighed heavily on him, and although he also stated his respect for them the declaration made him miserable. The crown and sceptre were brought to Dunfermline but there was no sign of a coronation. Sad and angry, Charles withdrew to Perth and wrote to secretary Nicholas in Holland to send a ship which should wait off-shore for him, in case he needed it. Perth was an important move for Charles; the ancient capital stood on the fertile coastal plain and nearby was Scone Palace, the crowning place of kings, held by a royalist. From Perth northwards was royalist country, where Charles could more easily communicate.

Meanwhile, the armies had come close to each other. This time Cromwell was up against a formidable general. David Leslie had strengthened the defences of Edinburgh and the port of Leith, building earthworks between the two, and when Cromwell's forces probed into Edinburgh from the south they were ejected. Leslie had stripped the Borders of both people and food, so the English withdrew to Musselburgh on the coast, from which they could be supplied by sea.[13]

The Covenanters were formidable enemies, implacable in their religious aims and without mercy for their defeated foes; they were defending their homeland and their beliefs were impregnable. For Cromwell this fixity was appalling. He issued a declaration of his own, addressed to them:

> Your own guilt is too much for you to bear: bring not therefore upon yourselves the blood of innocent men ... Is it therefore infallibly agreeable to the Word of God, all that you say? I beseech you, in the bowels of Christ, think it possible you may be mistaken.[14]

The English were equally devout but their religion was enquiring and searching; they read the Gospels and both men and preachers argued about their meaning. All the same, both armies believed themselves sustained by God.

At Musselburgh, Cromwell's supply ships could not get in against the wind, but Dunbar, further along the coast, was more protected from the westerlies and became essential to the English. Throughout August, Cromwell marched north again to probe at the Scottish defences but could find no weakness and achieved nothing; Leslie had outmanoeuvred him. In addition, Cromwell's men were more exposed to field conditions which brought on dysentery. He retreated south, only to find on reaching Dunbar once more on 1 September that Leslie was already occupying the high ground on Doon Hill. Although the Scot had numerical superiority, his men were less experienced and the purges of both officers and men, undertaken to satisfy the Covenanters, had removed some of the army's strength. As Leslie had the high ground and the numbers, Cromwell would have to use all his skills; behind him lay the sea, and Leslie had blocked his line of escape to the south.

Oliver Cromwell had enormous physical stamina and a marvellously disciplined army but his successes often rested on the speed with which he seized opportunities. Whether or not it was true of his political life, there is no doubt that in battle he was a master opportunist. Nonetheless, he was in a difficult position. He wrote to Haselrig on 2 September, 'We are here upon an engagement very difficult. The enemy hath blocked up our way at the pass to Copperspath [Cockburnspath] ... He lieth so upon the hills that we know not how to come that way without great difficulty, and our lying here consumeth our men who fall sick beyond imagination.'[15] Cromwell's second-in-command was Major General John Lambert, now aged only thirty but a clever soldier who had risen swiftly through the ranks during the civil war. A Yorkshireman, he had played an important role during the Preston campaign and was now invaluable at Dunbar.

Leslie justifiably hoped that he was the man who would maul the Ironsides and, with luck, drive them out of Scotland. He expected to decimate them as they tried to escape from the small coastal promontory on which Dunbar stood – but now the Committee of Estates intervened. They had recently joined the campaign and apparently urged Leslie not to wait on the high ground, where his men were exposed to the weather and short of water. Leslie's position meant he could fall on Cromwell's army when it tried to move, but he obeyed and moved his troops down from the hill, drawing them up in battle formation on the lower ground below. He still controlled the defile through the hills which led to the Berwick road, and his troops lined the lower slopes which opened onto that track.

The English scouted and Lambert detected a possible weakness in Leslie's formation; Cromwell agreed with him. That night – 2 September – the Scots slept while the English prepared. Before daybreak, Lambert opened the fighting with a cavalry assault on the troops blocking the road south. It was a risky strategy which depended on iron discipline among his men, who would attack along the full stretch of Leslie's front line. Cromwell used diversions to distract the Scots commander from the main plan. Monck, who had rejoined the army and was well thought of by Cromwell, led the infantry in the centre while Lambert's cavalry had the job of breaking through onto the Berwick road. The element of surprise was telling: Leslie's men had to scramble into formation. The Scots still held the higher ground but those of them on the lower slopes were soon drawn onto the same level as the English.

Cromwell's gamble paid off. Both his cavalry and infantry performed their task magnificently, and by the time the sun was fully up the Scots had lost their army – 3,000 were dead and almost 10,000 taken prisoner, leaving Leslie only 4,000 men. Many of the Scottish prisoners died on the march south, and the survivors were sent to New England as penal labour.

Cromwell, who had been in a very weak position on 1 September, saw his victory at Dunbar as an especial providence of God. On the following day, he wrote to the Speaker with his report. The battle cries of each army reflected their beliefs: 'The enemy's word was, "The Covenant," which it had been for divers days,' he wrote. 'Ours was, the "Lord of Hosts",' he told Lenthall. 'The best of the enemy's horse and foot being broken through and through in less than an hour's dispute, their whole army being put into confusion, it became a total rout.' To Cromwell this was the work of God and showed his blessing on their cause. In return, he urged the Commons to press on with social reform: 'to curb the proud and insolent, ... relieve the oppressed, hear the groans of poor prisoners in England; be pleased to reform the abuses of all professions; and if there be any that makes many poor to make a few rich, that suits not a Commonwealth'.[16]

Dunbar was a decisive defeat for the Covenanters. As Cromwell wrote to Haselrig, rather more pithily, 'Surely it's probable the kirk has done its do.' But, as he also remarked, the king was still in Scotland and 'will set up upon his own score now, wherein he will find many friends'.[17] The war was not yet over.

6

Completing the Conquest

While Charles II was negotiating with the Scots and making his fateful journey to Scotland, Ireton had been pushing westwards through Ireland. Cromwell's son-in-law was an experienced soldier but his real abilities were intellectual – he was the theoretician in the army. Cromwell had left him in a strong position, controlling most of the eastern seaboard and with able subordinates. But Ireton lacked Cromwell's driving martial energy and his unerring eye for terrain. In the summer of 1650 an English victory looked inevitable, yet the full conquest took until 1652 and even after that a guerrilla war continued. Driven from their land or under sentence for their actions in war, the Irish 'tories' subsisted in the forests, bogs and moorland, appearing suddenly to goad and challenge the conquerors.[1] They harassed settlers and worried the government well into the next century, starting a resistance to conquest that never really ended, despite the ambitious plans of the Commonwealth for settlement and improved governance.

The River Shannon, deep and navigable far upstream, creates a natural boundary around Connaught, the most Gaelic province. It has a major bridging point at Athlone, and Limerick sits at its mouth. When Cromwell left Ireland, the Irish held Connaught while the English held about half the land east of the Shannon. Ireton had to take the other half and wrest Waterford from the Confederates, then take the walled towns and bridges on the Shannon before he could break into Connaught. The war in Ulster had its own dynamic throughout, partly because of terrain but mainly because Scotland played so large a role there. But the position had changed. Owen Roe O'Neill was dead, Monck was in Britain, the allegiance of the Scots in Ulster was strained and parliament had strengthened its position in the north. Between them, Coote and Venables had taken the walled towns of Ulster by late November, including the massive fortress of Carrickfergus, and the Scottish commander Monro now joined them.

Mixed loyalties dogged the royalists, whereas Ireton's officers were all Protestant – the English who accompanied him and Irish leaders like Coote and Broghill. Henry Cromwell, Oliver's second son, arrived in February 1650 at the head of a regiment of horse, and after his father left he stayed on to fight under Ireton, giving the family a sure hold on military command in Ireland which would continue through most of the following decade. The campaign of 1650 brought a string of successes for the parliamentarians. The Confederates chose Bishop McMahon as their commander in Ulster, but in June they were beaten by Coote at Scarrifhollis in Donegal; the bishop and Owen Roe's son were hanged. In July, Carlow surrendered and in August, Ireton took Waterford, giving him control of the whole eastern seaboard. Now he could concentrate on the Shannon fortresses and the west.

Henry Ireton.

Ormond's position continued to weaken. Many of his Protestant troops deserted him and increasingly he relied on the Confederates but the Catholics did not trust him to defend them. They looked to leaders from the old order, such as Bishop McMahon, who proved a disastrous commander in Ulster, and Ulick Bourke, Marquess of Clanricarde, from the great Anglo-Norman family in Connaught, but neither were a match for the English forces. Ormond, short of funds and armaments, tried to hold the royalist groups together as he retreated across the Shannon with his remaining officers. In August, however, he lost the support of his king. Charles, under duress in Scotland, gave in to the Covenanters and disowned Ormond's treaty with the Catholics. This made Ormond's position untenable and the king gave him permission to depart, but before he did, he tried to form a command structure to leave behind.

Ireton could concentrate his forces on the Shannon. He divided them, sending Waller to besiege Limerick while he and Coote attacked Athlone. Limerick Castle was a massive structure and the strategic heart of the west, where Ormond had appointed Hugh Dubh O'Neil as commander. Hugh had given Cromwell a tough fight at Clonmel; he might do the same to Ireton at Limerick. By October, Ireton realised he must concentrate on Limerick so he pulled troops off Athlone and led them to the river mouth, where he summoned the city to surrender. It was too late in the year to attack such a powerful fortress and a week later he withdrew to nearby garrisons to take up winter quarters.

Ormond had run out of options. He appointed Clanricarde as Lord Deputy and left Ireland on 6 December with Lord Inchiquin, Daniel O'Neill and many other royalist leaders. Abandoning their estates, and in danger of execution should they return, they sailed from Galway, bound for France and exile. This left the remains of the Catholic Confederacy to fight the English. Without military support from overseas, they faced almost certain defeat. They tried to enlist support from Charles, the exiled Duke of Lorraine, but without success.

As the war in Ireland progressed, the London government began planning civilian rule. Cromwell had initially been appointed as 'Governor-General and Commander-in-Chief' for Ireland,[2] but by the time he sailed, he was styled Lord Lieutenant, the old royal title with all the powers that entailed and the right to appoint a Lord Deputy in his absence. Now that Cromwell was commander in Scotland and Ireton was enlarging his territory in Ireland, some MPs worried about the power of both the army and its commander, raising the issue of his status in the House. The Commons decided that Cromwell should retain the lieutenancy and Ireton continue as Lord Deputy but they also appointed four commissioners to set up civilian government.[3] Cromwell wanted Edmund Ludlow as second-in-command to Ireton; the Council of State selected the others, choosing three MPs – Colonel John Jones, John Weaver and Miles Corbet – while parliament gave them their orders.

The Irish commissioners were all members of the new revolutionary elite. Ludlow's father was a Wiltshire landowner and fierce critic of Charles I; Ludlow himself was a Calvinist and a committed republican, who had fought for parliament, supported Pride's Purge and signed Charles I's death warrant. Jones was also a regicide and was propagating the gospel in Wales when he was called for service in Ireland. He saw ruling and planting Ireland as providential service, a 'strange worke' to which the 'lord hath led mee ... the forming of a commonwealth, out of a corrupt rude Masse, the deviding of the country amongst the servants of the lord'.[4] Weaver was an Independent and had refused to sit as a judge at Charles I's trial but was active in the Commons and on several committees. Corbet was a regicide and chairman of several parliamentary committees. With this

Bridget Ireton.

mix of soldiers and bureaucrats, the Commons planned for a godly government in Ireland.

In January 1651, the four commissioners travelled to Milford Haven in Wales to take ship for Waterford. With them was Cromwell's daughter Bridget Ireton, who had brought her eldest child and was going to join her husband, Henry. Bridget was Cromwell's eldest daughter and had his long face and air of robust energy. She had grown up during the war and had married her father's commissary general, now Lord Deputy. She had spent her life among the Puritan officers with their martial energy and spiritual calling; an Anabaptist preacher, writing to her father next spring, commented that Bridget had 'the power of God's grace in her soul, a woman acquainted with temptations and breathing after Christ'.[5] As wife of the Lord Deputy, Bridget had high status in the new regime and was now Lady Ireton. Coming ashore at Duncannon Fort, she and the commissioners travelled the short distance to Waterford to meet her husband. It was a warm reconciliation for the Iretons, but for the commissioners a worry. On 25 January, they wrote to the Speaker that 'we found the armye in worse condition and the enemie upon more daringe terms than we expected' and urged that more supplies be sent.[6]

The commissioners' job was challenging. Apart from supporting the army, they had to manage conquered districts and large numbers of defeated fighters. The Commonwealth had high ideals about justice and religion for Ireland, but land ownership was the key issue, with taxation close behind. Parts of the country were almost depopulated, with crops destroyed, cattle stolen and people driven away. Decisions had already been taken which would shape post-war Ireland: the Act for Adventurers and the terms for surrender agreed by army officers in the field were binding. The latter varied considerably from town to town; some fighters were transported to the Caribbean as penal labour and some were executed, but many were allowed to leave the country or move to the still-Catholic areas. This left Ireton and the commissioners controlling territory which was damaged, unproductive and sparsely inhabited.

There would be plantation by English settlers. Plantation had been government policy in Ireland under both the Tudors and the Stuarts, but this time specific terms had been set in advance by the Act for Adventurers, although the investors had as yet received no land. The costs of conquering Ireland were high, with soldiers' wages, armaments and transport all to be paid for, so government decided to use Irish land to meet those bills too. Confiscated land in England was also being used to pay the costs of war, but in Ireland plantation was an established policy and there was enormous scope for confiscation.

Despite the pressure of the military campaign, Lord Deputy Ireton was aware of these issues. Plantation would not just pay the bills but also bring more Protestants into Ireland. Cromwell was very keen to achieve that and the London government wanted to entice settlers back from America, but potential planters were dubious. Security weighed heavily on their minds; in 1641 there had been a bloody Irish revolt against the Ulster planters, and that might recur. Settlers in America had been attacked by indigenous people there – but was Ireland any safer? They were unwilling to move again. As for the Irish population, many had been displaced by war. Fearing attack, Inchiquin had expelled all the Catholic Irish from Cork city in 1644 while Ireton, fearful of guerrilla attacks and struggling for control, also tried to clear whole districts by declaring them hostile territory and expelling the remaining inhabitants. From these ad hoc and drastic measures enacted in war, the authorities began to move people in larger numbers.[7]

From the urgency of battlefield decisions, the need to end the war quickly, existing plantation policy and sheer muddle, the land settlement of Ireland gradually took shape. Its effect was far-reaching but some of its origins were mundane. London was demanding that tax be collected in Ireland but farms were untended and commerce decimated; Protestants pleaded poverty while Catholics fled to the west. Ireton needed a swift end to conflict. Offering moderate terms for surrender might hasten that, but if he was too lenient then too little land might be confiscated when he needed it for plantation. As for the terms for surrender agreed in the field, they had varied at first until a formula emerged; now the commissioners had to confirm them. All these factors influenced the final settlement.

Policies made in Ireland were sent for confirmation to London where other interests came to bear. As a result, the settlement of Ireland was designed over several years and was still being revised two decades later. It was appealed, contested and resisted. Known as the Cromwellian Settlement of Ireland and infamous to many, historians have analysed its construction and the extent to which it was Cromwell's by design or intention. His involvement fluctuated – as will become clear – but his responsibility for the settlement is much clearer. During its construction, he was Lord Lieutenant of Ireland, general of the army, the leading member of the Council of State, an Adventurer, a member of parliament and, from 1653, head of state. It would therefore be difficult to absolve him of responsibility, especially as he, his son and two sons-in-law headed the government in Ireland from 1649 until the Restoration, with a gap of only ten months. During those ten months, Cromwell's chosen commander of horse, Ludlow, had control. It seems fair to assign responsibility for the settlement to Cromwell, although Henry Ireton certainly shaped it and others finalised the details.

In his pamphlet *For the Undeceiving of deluded and seduced people...*, published in January 1650, Cromwell had indicated what the Irish should expect from parliament. Early in 1651, Ireton developed this idea into a scheme of qualifications for either pardon or punishment. Although he was taking cities and territory, there were still tens of thousands of Irishmen in arms, as well as tories in the woods and wastes; the population might rise in revolt again at any time, and Ireton still had to conquer Connaught. He wanted to speed up surrender and an end to war. By March he had drawn up his scheme. The most severe clauses would punish the active rebels of 1641, as well as the Confederate Catholic leaders and priests. Labourers, husbandmen and inferior people would be pardoned, as would soldiers who capitulated before a set date. Landowners would lose property depending on their military involvement. Ireton's text was sent to London for confirmation, but that April Cromwell was confronting Charles in Scotland while insurrection or invasion threatened England, so Ireton's qualifications seemed technical and were put aside. By the time they became law, their main purpose – ending the war – had already been achieved.[8]

Bridget was with her husband during the early months of 1651, but when spring came and the soldiers went out on campaign she returned to England. In June Athlone fell to Coote, but when English troops crossed the Shannon and surrounded Limerick the city rejected Ireton's terms and it was late October before the fortress opened its gates to the conquerors. Limerick proved fatal to Ireton. An austere and serious man, the Lord Deputy had neglected himself, working late and forgetting to eat. After the city capitulated he rode out in rain and snow to organise garrisons. When he became ill, his iron will pushed him on and still he went on working; the cold developed into fever and the purges of the doctors weakened him. Henry Cromwell was with his brother-in-law when Ireton died in his quarters outside Limerick on 28 November 1651. The news of his death shocked London. Ireton's body was brought back there for burial and his widow Bridget was awarded lands for her upkeep. Ludlow was left in charge in Ireland until new arrangements could be made. Captured at Limerick, Hugh Dubh O'Neill was sent as a prisoner to London but was released as a Spanish subject. In April 1652, Galway capitulated and that spring the remaining field armies surrendered: in official terms, the war in Ireland was over.

The war in Scotland had taken a very different shape. In Ireland, the English were avenging a violent Catholic rebellion, whereas in Scotland they were subjugating a previously friendly Protestant nation. The difference in outcomes between the two countries was striking.

A few days after his extraordinary victory at Dunbar, Cromwell rode into Edinburgh unchecked. The royalists had moved north; Leslie and his army of about 4,500 were high in the valley of the Forth and the Committee of Estates was at Stirling. Charles was at Perth; between him and Cromwell lay Fife and the wide Firth of Forth. To the north of Charles, Highlanders were joining forces to repel the English but Cromwell had support from the navy, which controlled the North Sea. It was only two years since Cromwell had last marched an English army into the Scots capital and here he was again, making himself comfortable in a fine townhouse in Canongate belonging to the royalist Countess of Moray. Edinburgh Castle held firm against him but it was cut off, so not an immediate threat. While his men attempted to mine their way in, Cromwell did his best to win over the citizens of Edinburgh and the Lowlands, inviting preachers to return to the city and merchants to continue their business. The discipline of his troops and their habit of paying for supplies made his army an unusual occupying force.

The defeat at Dunbar had not brought the Scots together. The more extreme kirkmen saw it as God's judgement for supporting an impure king. Less fervent Scots blamed the intransigence of the kirk and their purges of the army. For the royalists the defeat was a major loss, but it did give Charles more royal status and command. The Scottish elite remained split and new differences burst open. In the south-west, where Presbyterianism was most zealous, extremists tried to raise an army separate from Leslie's, known as the Western Association. Charles too began to look beyond the Edinburgh leaders and when the Committee of Estates banished members of his household he decided to rouse his own followers. He made a muddled move and later was found hiding in humiliating circumstances: 'The Start' was a dismal gesture but it warned the kirk that they were alienating the young king. From then on, he was given entry to their meetings and a greater public role.

That only enraged the purists of the Western Association. They published a Remonstrance, emphasising the 'sin of the kingdome' in giving power to the Stuart kings who opposed genuine reformation; they became known as the Remonstrants.[9] The Western Association attacked Lambert at Hamilton in December but was routed, which broke up its forces but did not alter the minds of its leaders. To the kirk, the religious Independency of the English was heretical and they railed against these 'sectaries'. The Scottish parliament had a broader view, believing that Scotland needed all the men it could get to beat the English. They began a general levy of men and published *Public Resolutions*, encouraging all Scots to enlist whatever their previous allegiance, and aiming for twenty-five new regiments. Members of this movement became known as the Resolutioners but they were deeply obnoxious to the strictest kirkmen. The Remonstrants allied with other disgusted parties to form the Protestors, who flirted with joining Cromwell. The kirk was hopelessly split, its moment of power over. Now the nobility coalesced around Charles and the wider Scottish nation rallied against the English.

Cromwell had brought 16,000 men to Scotland but losses were high, both in battle and from tough conditions, so he begged parliament for 8,500 more recruits. Leslie could remove food and fodder from the advancing English but Cromwell had superior firepower and support from the navy, which shipped up military supplies and food. After the losses of Dunbar, Leslie had to recruit again, whereas there were still substantial forces in northern England whom Cromwell could call on and a new Militia Act was raising thousands more. But costs were increasing; in the spring of 1651, the London parliament faced a bill of over £2.5 million for the army and navy.[10] The tax base had been widened to cover everyone with property or goods worth £10 a year or a capital value of £100. Such heavy taxation was risky, but Charles Stuart, a member of the 'previous family', was in Scotland and royalists everywhere might rise; the Commonwealth mobilised all its resources to crush him.

With troops in all three kingdoms, Cromwell's officers were widely spread. Charles Fleetwood had fought at Dunbar and had joined the Council of State; now a lieutenant general, he was recalled to London to command the militia. Harrison took a militia force to the north-west to meet any invasion from Scotland. Milton, now secretary for foreign tongues, burst into print as a journalist, condemning the

Scots and English Presbyterians. The Commonwealth spy network was effective and that spring two royalist agents were captured. Interrogated in London, they named English conspirators and their locations. One of the agents was executed and a spate of arrests followed, of Presbyterian ministers and other suspicious persons. So, England was primed and ready when military action began again, but in spring 1651 there was only desultory action because the Scots were still recruiting and the English general was ill.

Cromwell had had bouts of ill health throughout his career; in early 1647 he had a 'postume', or swelling, in his head and an equally severe bout occurred in Ireland in 1650 when he had dysentery and malaria. In Scotland, he was out in a snowstorm and refused to stop work. He described himself as 'a little crazy', meaning weak and shaken, when he held a planning meeting with his officers in late February. In April he seemed better but in May he was ill once more.[11]

He had suffered from depression as a young man, something his religious conversion seems to have alleviated, but all through his life he had periods of manic activity, especially on his military campaigns when, despite being in his forties and early fifties, he covered long distances sometimes by coach but often on horseback, moving swiftly with his armies over difficult terrain and in action with his men when they went into battle. Between these periods of intense physical activity, he would often succumb to illness, assaulted by infection, minor wounds, the scourges of dirty water and campaign food, then overcome by exhaustion. But Cromwell had a nervous temperament which swung into deep spiritual gloom, fired into sudden rages and lifted into real exaltation. This volatile disposition sat alongside the steady and practical gifts which make a good commander, with excellent organisational abilities, a farmer's attention to horses and livestock, and impatience when others would not address urgent practical needs. He held clear principles, such as concern for the poor and weak, care to minimize casualties among his own men and an iron discipline which prevented his troops from terrorising civilians.

But Cromwell could dither and prevaricate, especially when big political choices loomed or when he had not mastered a moral dilemma. Those crises of direction usually dovetailed with his own ambitions. He was a risk-taker – joining the parliamentary army had been a risk from the start, but he had been uncompromising, taking actions for which he was unlikely ever to be pardoned and pushing for total victory in the war. That driving energy had led him to full command as general of the English Commonwealth's army and it would be his fate to hold that army together and on course for the rest of his life. With such responsibility weighing on him, a middle-aged man constantly at war, it was little wonder that he became incapacitated by illness which, while physical at root, also had its emotional and spiritual component.

His adversary was at Perth, with Argyll attending him as chief minister, and it was Argyll who placed the crown on Charles's head when he was at last crowned King of Scotland at Scone on New Year's Day 1651. Argyll suggested a marriage with his daughter but Charles referred the decision to his mother, who said it would need English approval and so squashed the matter.

The Scots were still squabbling and no Scottish parliament sat during the spring, which made organising the army more difficult, but by May Leslie commanded about 18,000 men at Stirling. The Scottish parliament had made Charles commander-in-chief; he oversaw the fortifications on the banks of the Forth and went north to Aberdeen to talk the ministers into recruiting.

The English were south of the Forth estuary and the only bridge was at Stirling, where Leslie held the neck of Scotland. North of the great waterway was 'royal Fife' with its grainland, then Perth and the fertile eastern seaboard with its wealth. To break into this area the English must cross the Forth, either higher upstream to the west of Leslie or by boat across the firth. When Cromwell took the field again, he probed at the Scottish defences but they were sound. So he used boats and a feint. Cromwell took part of his forces west, while Lambert crossed the Firth of Forth by boat with about 4,000 men. Leslie had to split his army but the force he sent against Lambert was cut to pieces. The young commander was able to establish himself on the promontory of Inverkeithing with 4,000 men, which allowed the English to pour their troops into Fife. Once established, and without haste, the English marched north and on 2 August Cromwell took the surrender of Perth.

Cromwell had been determined to move Charles out of Perth and had succeeded; the king joined his army near Stirling but was now cut off from his supporters to the north. Cromwell and Lambert had made a clever tactical move. Overall the English outnumbered the Scottish royalists but they had left only eight regiments south of the Forth, who could not block Charles in that direction. Cromwell was determined that his men would not suffer another Scottish winter. If he flushed the royalists out southwards, that would suit his plan. But it was risky and

John Lambert.

he wrote to Lenthall to excuse and explain himself, because if the king crossed the border, 'it will trouble some men's thoughts'.[12]

As expected, Charles and Leslie, with the Scots army, took the road south into England. They had few illusions but hoped that English royalists would join them. This hope was not realised, as the leaders had been arrested and the English had already suffered heavily in blood and treasure supporting the king. What were the chances of a royalist victory? They hung back. The recurrent invasions of the Scots during the 1640s had been hard on northern England, where people now saw them not as liberating royalists but as a dreaded enemy.

Monck was left to hold Scotland while Fleetwood defended the approaches to London. Hard behind the royalist army came Lambert with 3,000–4,000 cavalry, while Cromwell followed with the infantry and Harrison brought troops from Newcastle. Fairfax came out of retirement to hold Yorkshire against the king and rode for 3 miles in Cromwell's coach – a chance for the old comrades to discuss tactics. Charles, with the Scots under Hamilton, moved south through Lancashire, while by mid-August Lambert and Harrison had joined forces behind them at Preston. They shadowed the Scots but it was

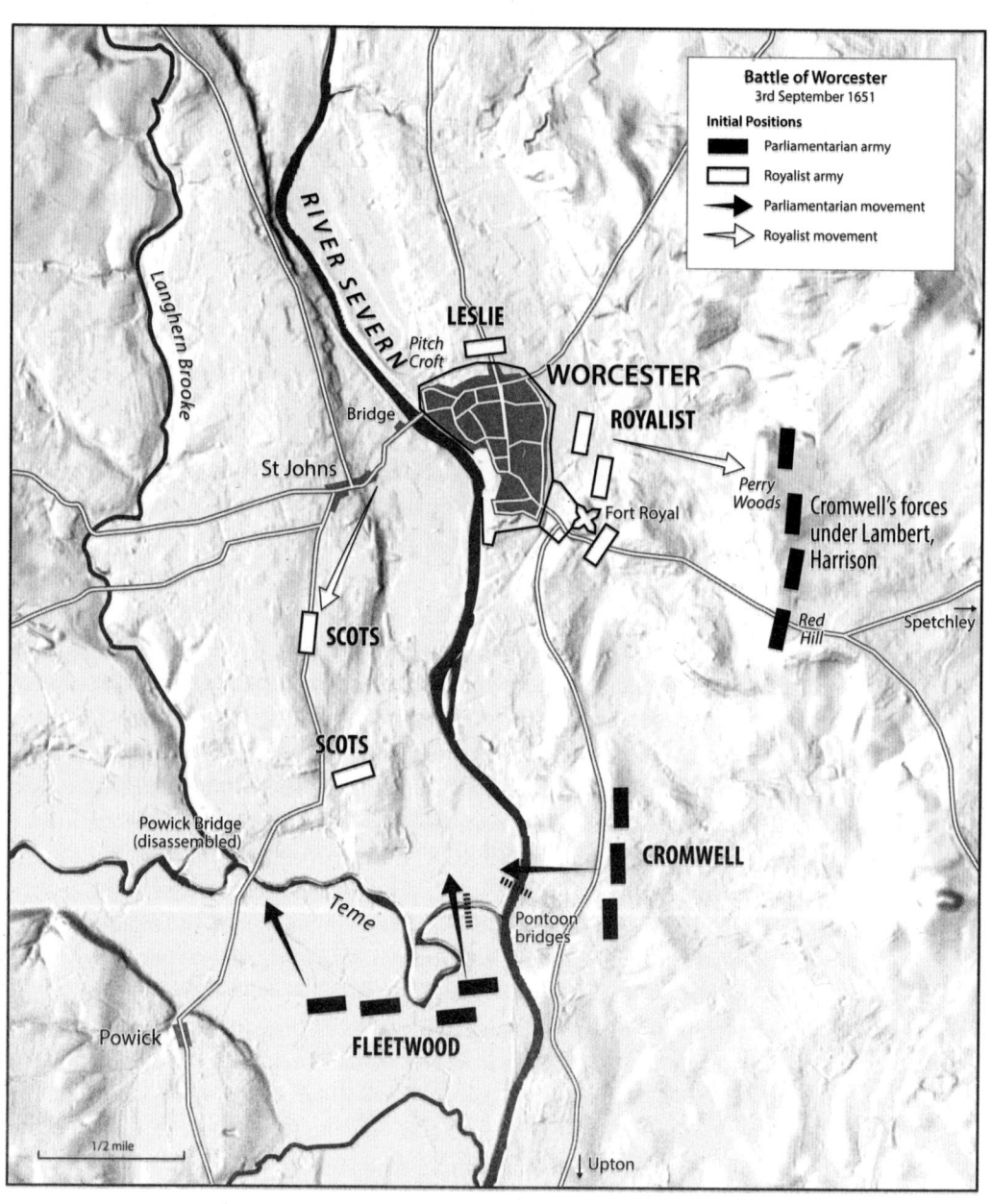

Battle of Worcester
3rd September 1651
Initial Positions

- Parliamentarian army
- Royalist army
- Parliamentarian movement
- Royalist movement

RIVER SEVERN

Langhern Brooke

LESLIE

Pitch Croft

WORCESTER

Bridge

ROYALIST

St Johns

Fort Royal

Perry Woods

Cromwell's forces under Lambert, Harrison

Spetchley

SCOTS

Red Hill

SCOTS

Powick Bridge (disassembled)

CROMWELL

Teme

Pontoon bridges

Powick

FLEETWOOD

1/2 mile

Upton

The Battle of Worcester, 3 September 1651.

awkward terrain for cavalry and in a short encounter the royalists saw them off. No recruits flowed in to swell the royalist army but on 23 August Charles led his army into Worcester, where he was warmly received and proclaimed king. Meanwhile, Cromwell met Fleetwood at Warwick. The Commonwealth forces began to close in. When all his regiments were assembled, Cromwell commanded 31,000 men.[13]

If Charles's upbringing had been patchy regarding administration, he had had plenty of experience of war. He had aimed to reach London but he was effectively trapped at Worcester, an old and well-defended city. To the west was the River Severn and to the south-east Fort Royal was a stronghold built into the city walls. Charles ordered the destruction of several bridges and had fortifications reconstructed. Cromwell commanded two bridges – one north of the city and one south – so could move his troops at will, but Worcester was secure and Charles was bound to put up a serious fight.

In Scotland, one of his nobles had suggested that Charles negotiate with the Commonwealth, resign his claim to England and hold Scotland. The king had rejected this furiously, determined to avenged his father and retake his birthright. Yet both countries were exhausted by war and violent politics; property owners feared further losses and only good pay would tempt recruits. So Charles had inferior numbers, but this was a desperate stand and unlikely to be repeated. For Cromwell, allowing the king to march into England was a risk but he calculated that one day the Commonwealth would have to fight this battle and it was better done while his forces were at full strength and Charles had only a modest Scottish army. If the Commonwealth beat him now, in England, he would stay beaten.

Cromwell had been on campaign for two years, had assaulted Irish towns and fought a pitched battle at Dunbar. He was fifty-two and had been seriously ill. Of his senior officers, Lambert was the more dynamic and ambitious, Harrison a religious visionary while Monck was stolid and capable. Charles Fleetwood was the son of a senior official and although he was competent with serious principles, he was not charismatic or decisive. Under Cromwell's leadership, these men ran an effective campaign but even with an army twice the size of the king's, Worcester was a tough contest and took all day. Charles, who was fighting for father, kingdom, honour and his life, was everywhere in action, urging on his men until there were none left to drive on.

Cromwell planned not to storm Worcester's massive defences but to fight on the land south-west of the city, between the Severn and the

Teme, using boats as a bridge to get his men across and drawing the Scots out of the city. Fleetwood brought his troops up the west bank of the Severn while Cromwell's moved up from Spetchley to Perry Wood. It took from before dawn until gone noon to get the men into position. Charles, watching from the tower of the cathedral, revised his plan as he saw the Commonwealth soldiers form up. Leading his troops himself, they charged Fleetwood's left wing as they crossed the Teme, while the Scots infantry fought hard against the right wing. The forces struggled in the hedged fields of the plain, until the parliamentary musketeers drove the royalists back into the city. The Commonwealth forces had succeeded in taking the land between the rivers; now the royalists regrouped on the city side of the Severn.

To the east of the city, the royalists initiated an attack on Cromwell's forces near Perry Wood. Leslie's cavalry had held back in Pitch Croft, but now they led the charge as the royalist horse and foot thundered out of the city gates, with Charles and the Duke of Hamilton commanding, and drove back the parliamentary forces. Three hours of close fighting ensued. As Cromwell's men pursued the Scots back towards the city walls, they came within range of the cannons in Fort Royal, which caused butchery among the advancing troops, but still the men fought on. Cromwell himself shouted offers of quarter but the royalists only shot at him. Gradually, the king's men were forced to withdraw behind the city walls.

It was sundown when Cromwell threw all his troops against the city. The Essex militia took Fort Royal with its heavy guns but savage fighting continued in the streets. Leslie and the Scottish horse were afterwards criticised, but it was Charles who was in the thick of the fight, urging his troops on with what royalist observers described as suicidal courage. Royalist leaders William, Duke of Hamilton and John Middleton were wounded and by 8 p.m. there were no royalist troops to lead back into battle. Hurriedly, the king's commanders made their decision: a desperate charge held the enemy back while the king and a lifeguard of six hundred men rode out of the only gate still open to them. The fighting continued into the night. Harrison wrote, 'What with the dead bodies of men and the dead horses of the enemy filling the streets there was such a nastiness that a man could hardly abide the town.'[14]

The victorious parliamentarians took more than 6,000 prisoners, herded them into the cathedral and locked them in. Cromwell's soldiers found any royalists in hiding and dragged them out, while others picked over the city for loot. Among the prisoners was

Sir Thomas Urquhart, the author and translator of Rabelais, who lost all his papers.[15] Escaping Scots had a hard road home, hated by the surrounding English for launching yet another invasion and eruption of war. Hamilton died of his wounds soon afterwards, while Leslie and Middleton were imprisoned indefinitely. Some soldiers were sent abroad as penal labour, and some finally reached home. Of the 'Worcester fight', Cromwell said it was 'as stiff a contest for four or five hours as ever I have seen'.[16] It was his last battle – from now on he would send men to war but not lead them.

The king was on the run, a fugitive in Commonwealth England. With a price of £1,000 on his head, Charles and two retainers dressed themselves modestly as they made their way between safehouses trying to reach the coast. Often it was Catholics who sheltered him; for one whole day Charles hid in an oak tree while below him soldiers searched the wood; and he rode to Bristol disguised as Jane Lane's servant but found no ship there. He and his companions made their way south through Somerset and Dorset; twice they thought they had agreed their passage, first from Lyme then from Charmouth, but one owner lost his nerve and the captain of the other was locked in by his wife. At last, a ship's captain at Shoreham agreed to take them to France. They landed at Fécamp in Normandy, whence they travelled to Paris. Charles was only twenty-one but when he rejoined his mother, he was leaner and quieter than before. The defeat seemed likely to be a lasting one. Yet the story of his adventures grew in the telling and as he related them to the young ladies of the French court he became noticeably more cheerful, although now his prospects in England were bleak.

On 12 September, Cromwell returned to London and was lionised. The Council of State came out to meet him, the streets were lined with shouting crowds, and when he arrived in Whitehall cannons and muskets were fired. Parliament needed his advice about the large numbers of prisoners and the reduction of the army. The militias were disbanded almost immediately and, with the claimant to the throne soundly beaten, parliament decided to reduce the forces in England by one-third. Scotland, however, would have to be garrisoned while George Monck continued the methodical process of reducing strongholds there. Cromwell had taken most of those south of Edinburgh, now Monck turned to the walled towns of the east. Using artillery, he broke into Stirling and gained control. At Dundee the storm was followed by looting, which continued for two weeks. The Scottish Committee of Estates was captured by Monck's men. At Aberdeen and on Loch Tay remnants of the Scottish government gathered, but as they attempted further meetings no quorum was even present. On 15 October, Argyll wrote to Monck suggesting negotiations. By the end of the year, English forces were in Aberdeen, Elgin and Inverness. All the Scottish Lowlands and eastern seaboard were in the hands of the conquerors. Argyll went back to his ancestral seat at Inveraray Castle and nursed the failure of his plans.

The Commonwealth of England had beaten the armies of Ireland and Scotland, taken their walled towns and fortified buildings; the two kingdoms were theirs to command. Resistance continued in the Highlands of Scotland and in the wild, uncultivated places of Ireland but the leaders were dead, imprisoned, exiled or quelled. The claimant to the throne had been driven out and the General of the English forces believed that the victory at Worcester was 'a crowning mercy'. In his letter to Lenthall reporting the battle, Cromwell wrote, 'The Lord God Almighty frame our hearts to real thankfulness, which is alone his doing.'[17] A day later, he humbly begged that their victory should always be seen as a favour from God, that it should 'not occasion pride and wantonness, as formerly the like hath done to a chosen nation; but that the fear of the Lord' might keep people 'humble and faithful; and that justice and righteousness, mercy and truth may flow from you, as a thankful return to our gracious God. This shall be the prayer of ... O Cromwell.'[18]

It was up to the rulers of the English Commonwealth to answer that prayer.

7

The Commonwealth Sets
Its Course

In sharp contrast to its position two years earlier, by the autumn of 1651 the Commonwealth seemed secure. The man who had achieved that was General Oliver Cromwell MP, under whom the army had secured domination over the three Stuart kingdoms for the new regime. Famous and feted, in November Cromwell topped the poll for the Council of State. He was a man of enormous influence.

Two days after Cromwell's election success, Henry Ireton died of fever at Limerick. His body was carefully embalmed before it was sent to England. Bridget, blonde and bright-eyed, with a straight back and vigorous air so like her father's, was now a widow with five children. She was given an award of £2,000 a year by parliament, for Lord Deputy Ireton had been at the heart of the revolution. After lying in state, he was buried in London the following February. Ireton's funeral gave London a sight of Commonwealth symbolism and pomp. His body was escorted to Westminster Abbey by a magnificent procession of cavalry and infantry regiments, the new Commonwealth arms of England and of Ireland marking his status. 'Thus in grave pace, drums coverd with cloth, souldiers reversing their arms, they proceeded thru the streets in a very solemn manner,' said John Evelyn, who saw the event.[1] At first Bridget was inconsolable but, living in her father's milieu, she was soon courted by another army officer and that summer she married Charles Fleetwood, a fair and slender man very unlike her first husband. Through marriage, Bridget stayed at the heart of her father's public affairs.

The victory at Worcester meant that power was centralised in London as never before. From Westminster, parliament made its decisions for Scotland and Ireland which were enforced by the troops

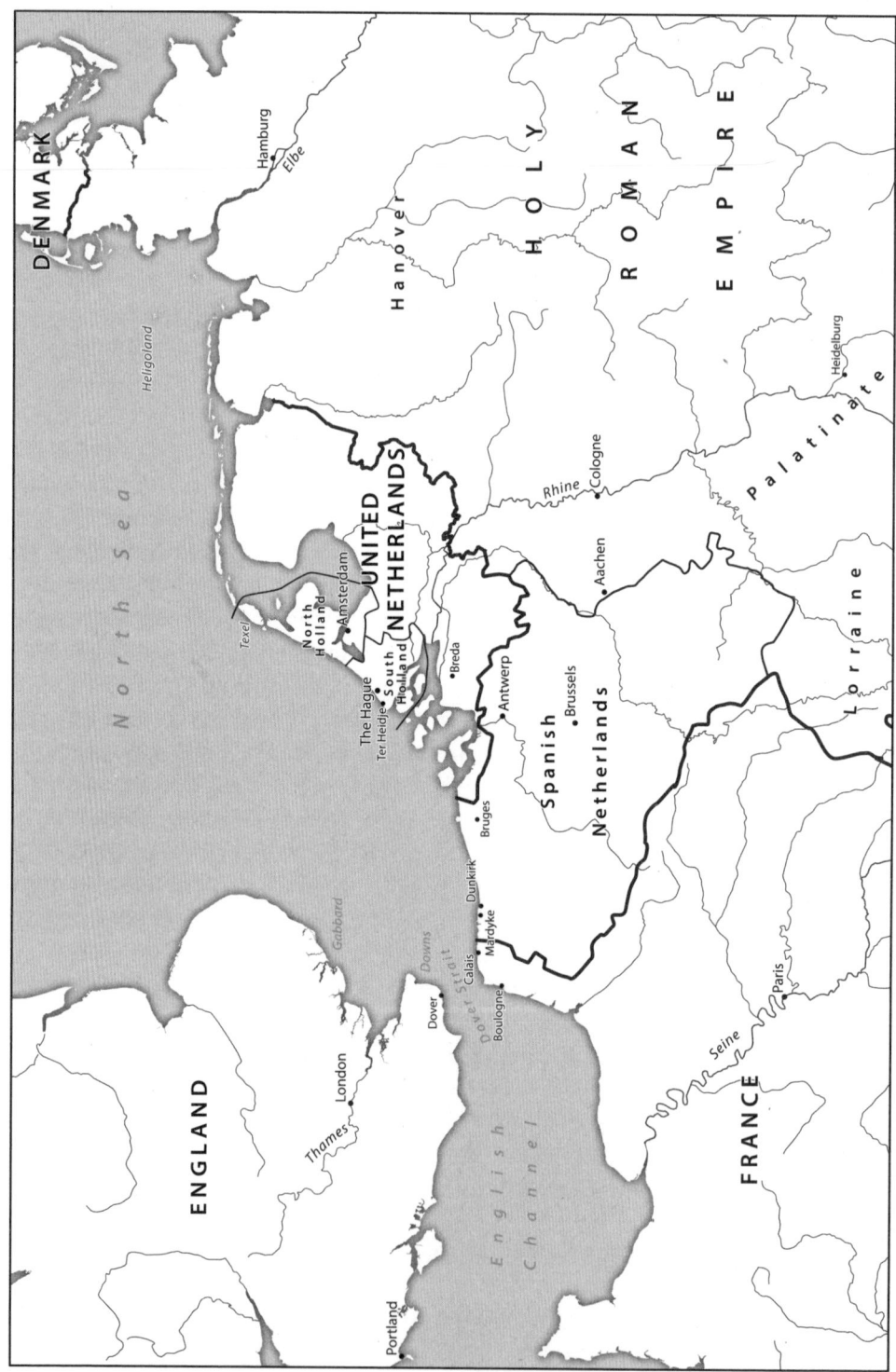

DENMARK

Hamburg

Elbe

HOLY

ROMAN

EMPIRE

Hanover

Heligoland

North Sea

UNITED NETHERLANDS

Rhine

Cologne

Amsterdam

North Holland

South Holland

Texel

The Hague

Ter Heidje

Aachen

Breda

Antwerp

Spanish

Brussels

Netherlands

Bruges

Gabbard

Downs

Dunkirk

Mardyke

Calais

Dover Strait

Dover

Boulogne

Palatinate

Heidelburg

Lorraine

Paris

Seine

London

Thames

ENGLAND

English Channel

FRANCE

Portland

England, the Netherlands and France, 1650s.

stationed in both countries. The army officers met at St James's and the Council of State had meeting rooms in Whitehall Palace, while Cromwell had the use of the Cockpit nearby and also Hampton Court outside London.

A short distance downriver from Westminster, a second centre of power lay in the City of London. With its concentrated wealth, the City had been parliament's principal funder during the war and so had political influence. Several influential merchants sat in the Commons and had business dealings with other MPs. As they built up capital, merchants bought landed estates and mingled with the landed gentry who dominated the Commons, but it was their overseas interests which influenced government – the City men had a hand in creating important trade policies.

During the 1640s, as warring factions rose and fell, so merchant groups had competed in the Common Council of the City.[2] When the Commonwealth was formed, an ally of the new rulers became Lord Mayor – Thomas Andrewes was a devout Puritan and a judge at the king's trial. Andrewes proclaimed the abolition of monarchy outside the Exchange in May 1649 and arranged a City banquet for the government and army officers to give thanksgiving 'for this wonderful blessing against the Levellers' when they were defeated at Burford.[3] Initially, Andrewes and his colleagues traded goods in the Americas but soon they also invested in plantations. Probably most influential with government among this group was Maurice Thomson, who made a substantial fortune trading in America, the West Indies and West Africa.[4]

Many parliamentarian leaders in the 1640s had a financial interest in America and many of them were still MPs in the 1650s with investments in international trade. Sir Henry Vane had been governor of Massachusetts while Haselrig had invested in Connecticut, as had Lord Saye and Sele, who was a leader in the Providence Island project in which Cromwell's colleagues and relations had taken shares.[5] The Earl of Warwick and Thomas Scot were related to Owen Rowe, a regicide and tobacco trader who became deputy-governor of Bermuda. These men were concerned about enterprise generally, but especially in the Americas. Their Puritan beliefs blended naturally with their entrepreneurial vigour.[6] It was they who pushed an active trade policy up parliament's crowded timetable.

During the two years since the king's execution, the Commons had been busy. It had to cement its control over officials, stabilise its finances and start work on the reform agenda, while the Council of

State managed the war and sent diplomats to European states. Among the urgent business of the Commons, the most fundamental was its own composition. It was a decade since a general election had been held, the constitution had been radically altered and the numbers in parliament had only been topped up at by-elections. It was generally felt, but especially by the army, that elections must be held and a new parliament formed. Before Cromwell returned to London, a bill for elections had been introduced into the Commons, 'a work much tending to their own honour and the satisfaction of the People' according to the government newsbook.[7] Meanwhile, the government was working on hearts and minds; *Mercurius Politicus* opened every week with opinion pieces denigrating rule by monarchy and clergy, arguing for republics and often referring to the Roman Empire.

Although Ireland and Scotland were being subjugated, the Commonwealth had yet to assert itself over the American colonies and was still building up its navy. During the war, sailors had shown mixed loyalties, so after 1649 the navy was purged and new captains appointed. Overall command was given jointly to Blake, Deane and Popham, former army colonels. Blake proved an exceptional sea commander; under him the navy supported the campaigns in Ireland and Scotland, and retook the Isle of Man and the Channel Isles. Prince Rupert still had a small royalist fleet and tried to tempt defections, but after 1649 the navy stayed loyal to the Commonwealth. In 1650 Blake chased Prince Rupert's privateering fleet from Portugal into the Mediterranean and then effectively broke it up, although Rupert – as dashing at sea as he had been with his cavalry – continued privateering off the African coast, taking ships to support the royalist cause.

As for the American colonies, the Commonwealth urgently needed to subdue royalism and assert control over all England's dependent territories. Both government and the London merchants were determined that colonial development should enrich England, not foreign states. All the colonies held charters containing vital clauses, so when the Council of State announced that all charters must be replaced, the colonists reacted badly. They feared losing their commercial freedom and new trade networks. Resentment was brewing, so the Commonwealth decided on a swift naval expedition to quell any resistance. Admiral George Ayscue sailed for Barbados in October 1651. The young settlements could not mount resistance to the Commonwealth forces, and by January articles of agreement had been signed. The colonists would not be taxed without the consent of their Assembly but must trade according to the

Admiral Robert Blake.

Commonwealth's laws. The other islands followed suit and by March 1652 Maryland had signed her agreement. Soon, resistance by the colonies to Commonwealth government had ended.

Trade was a high priority for the Commonwealth because of its precarious finances. Capital sums were raised by the sales of confiscated property but they took time. To bring closure after civil war an Act of Oblivion offered pardon, but it included many exceptions because government needed money. A new round of confiscations began in England, under which several hundred people lost their estates. Reinvigorating the economy was essential, so attention quickly turned to trade, but in the City the balance of commercial interests had altered. The Merchant Adventurers, who traded woollen goods into northern Europe, were no longer supreme. It was the East India Company, which imported spices, silks, fruit, dyes and saltpetre into England, and the Levant traders who now had the expanding trade.

Men like Maurice Thomson did not limit his interests to one region but traded tobacco and sugar from the Caribbean and Virginia, furs from Canada and saltpetre from the East. He took slaves to his plantation on St Kitts and cornered the tobacco market in London. He had raised funds for parliament during the war and they turned to him, as an experienced war contractor, when conflict began with the Dutch.[8] No wonder that, when the Commonwealth debated their commercial policies, merchants like Thomson and Rowe, MPs such as Oliver St John and civil servants like Benjamin Worsley joined the relevant committees.[9] The Venetian ambassador remarked that 'merchants and trade were making great strides as government and trade are ruled by the same persons'.[10]

But what was government policy on trade to be? Charles I had run a state-sponsored capitalism, offering charters to merchant companies, with joint-stock companies growing up to fund new enterprises. The crown had been active, awarding franchises to aristocrats, promoting key industries and driving forward a plantation policy in Ireland and America. It aimed for growth at the top, while the Elizabethan poor law should provide a safety net for the poorest.[11] The policy had been 'haltingly pursued' and as his rule collapsed, restrictions on trade weakened, giving new opportunities to Puritan entrepreneurs. With their ethos of hard work and probity, they were alert to new opportunities, both in England and overseas. Much would be revealed about the priorities of the new government when they published their trade policy. The name 'commonwealth' referred to the communal well-being of the nation, whereas the Puritan ethic focussed on individual endeavour. Which would government favour? How would it treat the monopolies and merchant charters about which the Levellers complained? High taxation was unpopular and slowed commerce; when would it be reduced?

Men like Thomson wanted a complete rethink on trade. The monopoly system had been awarded for single regions, whereas Thomson was building complex trade routes across both continents and sectors. In the evolving mercantile world, it was not merchant companies which required trade protection but the whole nation.[12] The merchants urged an assertive policy for England and her colonies because already other European states were trading in those waters. Of these, the most prominent was the United Provinces of the Netherlands, with Holland leading its sea trade. Here was a dilemma; for English Puritans, the Calvinist Netherlands was a natural ally, but to the merchants they were arch competitors. For government, the glaring problem of Holland was its connection to the Stuarts.

Princess Mary was in The Hague with her infant son, William, Prince of Orange. While Charles was in Scotland, Mary's husband had attempted to seize control of Amsterdam but his failure to do so had weakened him politically and he died shortly afterwards, leaving Mary a widow. She was not popular in The Hague; she was considered awkward and brittle, and she squabbled with her mother-in-law over control of her child and the family's wealth. Mary was utterly unlike her aunt Elizabeth of Bohemia, with her exuberant hospitality, disorganised finances and colourful family, but both were Protestants and royal Stuarts. After the defeat at Worcester, Charles had not returned to the Netherlands but had joined his mother in Paris. His youngest sister, Henriette, was there and his brother James was an officer in the French army. For the Commonwealth, the Stuarts remained a threat and their situation as exiles in France and Holland, where they were relatives of the ruling families, influenced Commonwealth foreign policy. The new government was struggling for diplomatic recognition by its European neighbours, so resident Stuarts complicated their efforts. For European statesmen, plagued by religious conflict and competing over trade in a fast-changing world, the plight of Charles Stuart was a consideration but not a priority.

Gradually, the Commonwealth's diplomatic position improved. The French government under Mazarin made overtures but there were protocol problems with London; it was now a republic with no designated head of state. On military matters foreign ambassadors would visit General Cromwell, but for trade or foreign policy they had to apply to the Council of State whose president changed every month. In confusion, the first French address was sent to '*les gens du Parlement de la Republique Angleterre*' – parliament returned it unopened as improperly addressed.[13]

Relations between England and the Netherlands were crucial. The Dutch ports were emerging as the trading hub of northern Europe, a growth area. Since independence from Spain half a century before, the Netherlands had become a leader in European trade, its new wealth creating a Golden Age, not just of art and material culture but in literature and philosophy. Amsterdam had become a banking centre and trade hub. The Netherlands had an agreement with Denmark giving them passage into the Baltic, but the Rump was more concerned about the English Channel and the Atlantic. The members opened negotiations with the Dutch, initially offering partnership;

Strickland and St John left for The Hague in spring 1651 to explore trade terms and offer a 'confederacy perpetual', a form of union. They were received with proper ceremony by the States-General but their mission was unsuccessful; the English set stringent terms regarding the House of Orange and the Dutch feared being drawn into England's wars. Suggestions of union only perplexed and alarmed the Dutch. In June the English envoys left. In September Cromwell beat Charles II at Worcester, and in October the Rump passed the Navigation Act, which defined its trade policy and posed a serious challenge to the Netherlands.

The purpose of the Act was to restrict the trade of all English territories to English ships. This would prevent the Dutch merchant fleet from carrying goods from England and her colonies. It would promote English trade but also stem the outflow of bullion from England. It would encourage merchant shipbuilding, which the navy could call on when necessary, and enhance England's sea power. In The Hague, news of the Act caused alarm. It was a threat to the carrying trade and the enormous commercial interests which had built up in Dutch ports, in the stacked warehouses and finely furnished townhouses. The intention was clearly aggressive and the States-General swiftly sent a high-level delegation to London for further negotiations. But the following year conflict broke out at sea.

Promoting trade in the island nations went hand in hand with security. Piracy was rife in the seventeenth century: travellers were frequently robbed at sea or taken captive for ransom. Algerian pirates roamed close to the shores of Britain and Ireland, seizing ships and raiding villages for slaves. A government which could protect its shipping would gain respect at home and abroad. Henry VIII had spent heavily on the navy and Charles I had levied an illegal tax to build up the fleet. The Commonwealth carried on where its predecessors had left off, and within three years the navy doubled in size. In Deptford, Woolwich and Portsmouth, carpenters were hard at work on new hulls and masts, while hemp was in demand for rigging and sails. Naturally, the costs were high.

By spring 1652, Commonwealth policy had led to war with the Netherlands. While the Dutch envoys were in London, naval aggression was escalating. When England asserted her sovereignty over the British seas, the Dutch fleet was expected to dip their flags as they sailed through the English Channel. When they did not, the English shot at them. Then Denmark closed The Sound to English shipping, and so blocked entry to the Baltic, cutting off valuable trade. In February

1652, as Admiral Tromp escorted the Dutch wine fleet home from Bordeaux, he met the English navy under Blake off Portland where a fierce battle ensued in which Blake was seriously wounded. Tromp had to get his merchant ships into port and managed a brilliant escape but left the battle with the English ascendant.

From now on the Dutch fleet, whether fishing in the North Sea or sailing through the English Channel, was threatened by the English. The Commonwealth was asserting itself as a military and commercial powerhouse. While parliament built ships, government propaganda tried to sway English opinion against the Dutch and in favour of conflict – with some success. In July war was declared and all through the summer repeated attacks and naval engagements made the Channel a place of conflict. Ayscue wreaked havoc on the Dutch fleet in July but in December Tromp shattered Blake's fleet off Dover, giving the Dutch command of the Channel. The monthly assessment rose by a third, part of it now diverted to the navy, and in February 1653 the English had the better of the Dutch off Portland, leaving them with command of the Channel once more.

The merchant interest was pleased with government policy. Some resented controls on the American colonies but generally the Navigation Act was welcome. It bolstered British sea trade at a vital moment in European affairs. The policy outlasted Cromwell and was strengthened by later governments. Among the population, however, there were mixed reactions to the Dutch war; merchants supported it but most people resented the cost. The army disliked a war against fellow Protestants and lamented the neglect of law reform and godly revolution. They pressed for dissolution of parliament and new elections, but without success. In the council of officers, there was a range of views but they all feared that, without social reform, the soldiers might become restive; with troops stationed in all three nations, they reasoned, trouble might boil up anywhere.

Parliament made a start. Matthew Hale's commission on law reform made regular proposals but legislation was slow to follow as the lawyers in parliament warned that law was complex and could not be altered piecemeal. The legal process was changed from Latin to English, which helped those too poor to pay for translators, but efforts to reform Chancery and the plight of debtors foundered. Radical legislation to create godly reformation was unpopular with the people, as the Rump passed Acts against swearing and non-observance of the sabbath. Adultery now carried a death sentence, although records show few court cases and no executions. The draconian Blasphemy

Ordinance of 1648, modified in 1650, was applied and in the army, at least, punishments were savage: in 1652 Bulstrode Whitelocke, now a rising star of the Council of State, records that 'one Boutholmey, a quartermaster, was tried by a council of war for blasphemy, and sentenced to have his tongue bored through with a hot iron, his sword broken over his head, and to be cashiered the army'.[14]

But what were the religious rules of the Commonwealth to be? Expectations that the kingdom of Jesus was close excited the Fifth Monarchists and over a hundred 'gathered' congregations of millenarians sprang up, mainly in London. To them, spiritual revolution was imminent, heralding the thousand years of Christ's kingdom. The Fifth Monarchists, who did not intend to wait for it, made strident demands in church and in print for a government composed only of the godly. But Independency naturally led to a proliferation of sects and the gathered congregations were not of one mind; they had a range of views and forms of worship. The Seekers were new, the Baptists dated from the reign of Elizabeth but became more vocal, and the new sect emerging under the leadership of George Fox was egalitarian, pacifist and opposed to the swearing of oaths. 'Tremble at the name of the Lord,' Fox exhorted the judge who tried him, and the man mocked him as a Quaker – the name stuck. Inner conviction was important to Puritans but the Ranters took this to extremes, maintaining that 'swearing, drunkenness, adultery and theft were not sinful unless the person guilty of them apprehended them to be so'.[15]

In religion, England and Scotland were different; the former had a church ruled by parliament, the latter had an independent kirk. The Presbyterian service which had been agreed when they were allies was now dropped. Instead, the Commonwealth drafted legislation for the English church but never made a firm decision. Charles I had been unable to agree church policy with any of his captors; now the Church of England had lost its governor and its liturgy was banned – anguished discussion continued among churchmen over what was legitimate.[16] Matthew Wren, Bishop of Ely and uncle of the architect Christopher, was strongly anti-Puritan. Imprisoned in 1641 for eighteen years, Wren advised using no liturgy at all rather than bastardise the one in which he had been ordained. The Commonwealth aimed for a regulated national church but failed to define it. Most people were Presbyterians or Anglicans and had sworn allegiance to the king, so they remained a threat.

If there was to be a national church, how were the clergy to be paid? The existing system of tithes was an additional tax on the poor and a constant source of grievance. Often, tithes were paid to patrons of the living, who considered them a form of property, and there were many owners in the Commons. Which interest would prevail? In 1650, the Toleration Act softened the compulsion to attend the parish churches. This gave the sects greater freedom and they used it. However, the Roman Catholic mass was not permitted nor the *Book of Common Prayer*, although evidence suggests that, in rural areas, it was quietly used as before. With the king's death, other institutions like the church courts had also been closed. When the catechism was discontinued, Puritans realised that their cherished aim of rousing people by preaching was hopeless, as congregations had no basic Christian knowledge. The government heard that religious teaching was non-existent in Wales, leaving people as good as heathens. That stung them into action. An Act to propagate the gospel was passed, leading to a vigorous campaign headed by Vavasour Powell, a vocal and highly motivated preacher. His programme probably underlies the strong dissenting and low church tradition of modern Wales.

Rising to the top of the agenda was the enormous question of how the three kingdoms were to be governed and what the constitution should be. The soldiers had published their ideas in 1647, and Ireton had moulded the Agreement of the People with the Levellers in 1648-9, but other officers had watered it down and the Commons had shelved it. Parliament was now a fraction of the original body, yet London controlled Ireland and Scotland as well. How would the three nations be ruled and what was the future of the current parliament?

The bill for elections, introduced after Worcester, posed problems. If voting rules were not changed, there was every danger of a royalist chamber. Equally, conservative MPs feared the election of more soldiers. The Fifth Monarchists, impatient for the rule of the saints, wanted the 'gathered congregations' to be the only electors. The franchise varied between constituencies but if it was altered, MPs feared for their seats. Gradually, the Rump decided on the redistribution of seats and to have biennial elections, but who was to vote and when was the first of these elections to be held? The house decided on 5 November 1654, three years away. That gave MPs plenty of time to reorganise the seats, decide about the franchise and try to win the support of their electors. For MPs with special interests or afraid of losing parliamentary privilege, it gave ample time to reorganise their affairs. The subject of elections did not go dead – it appears from time to time in the Commons Journals over the next two years – but it drifted down a busy agenda. Immediate elections might destabilise a fragile situation, and the form of government for Ireland and Scotland had to be decided, so at first the army officers did not protest at the delay in choosing a 'new representative'.

The structure of government was preying on Cromwell's mind. Power now lay in a parliament with one chamber. There were no other institutions to challenge it and its processes were too slow for the issues it faced. Concerned about these problems, in December 1651, not long after his return from Worcester, Cromwell called a meeting at the house of Speaker Lenthall, to discuss the constitution. Army officers and lawyer MPs attended; Bulstrode Whitelocke, Commissioner of the Great Seal and a member of the Council of State, was there and kept a note of what happened. The question was whether England would be a pure republic or return to a mixed constitution with some element of monarchy in it. The lawyers preferred the latter but the army officers were strongly against any form of king. According to Whitelocke, Cromwell prevaricated and suggested 'that a settlement with somewhat of monarchical power in it would be very effectual'.[17]

Henry, Duke of Gloucester was the person proposed as king, exactly as Charles I had warned the boy at their last meeting. Henry was still being held by the government, although he was agitating for greater freedom. Did Cromwell envisage the boy becoming king? If not, whom did he have in mind? Under what terms or constitutional arrangement would someone have 'somewhat of monarchical power'? A second meeting with Whitelocke the following year suggests how the General's thoughts were running.

8

The Cost of Government

Coming to power at the end of civil war, with the country depleted by many armies, the Commonwealth was left to settle the debts. The prolonged conflict, followed by the garrisoning of Ireland and Scotland, enormously increased the budget. Figures for the early years of the Commonwealth make the point forcefully; since 1641, government expenditure had roughly multiplied by three. Even with the proceeds of the ship money tax, Charles I had revenue of about £800,000 a year, whereas in 1650 the budget total was £2.75 million, the bulk of which was military spending.[1] The Treasury was in a chaotic state, with money held in multiple accounts at various halls and offices, supposedly for specific purposes but drawn on erratically. The Commonwealth's main form of revenue, the assessment, was never controlled by the Treasury but went straight to the army. The government began to settle its debts by selling confiscated land in all three nations but in Scotland the final amounts were small compared to those taken in England and Ireland. In the former, the land had been taken from the church, the crown, members of the royal family and royalists. Retained in government hands, it might have brought them income but the financial position of the Commonwealth left it no choice – it had to raise whatever funds it could.

As part of the disposals, a sale of the king's goods was ordered. During the war, Charles had left Whitehall Palace and lost control first of London, then of Windsor and his country houses. Parliament became concerned that valuable artefacts were disappearing from those buildings and secured them, appointing trustees to make inventories of all the contents, especially the king's art collection which was known to be of the highest quality. Charles had bought from Italy and elsewhere, accumulating an unrivalled Renaissance collection, and had commissioned the famous Van Dyck portraits of himself and his family. He had supported the tapestry workshops at Mortlake and acquired the nine monumental canvasses of the *Triumph of Caesar* by Mantegna which were among the Gonzaga Collection, his earliest purchase. Increasingly knowledgeable, he had gone on to acquire smaller pieces too – famous works by Titian, Rubens and others, as well as drawings and sketches kept in his cabinet. Visitors to the royal palaces saw the quality of the collection in every room. A few pieces were to be held back to decorate government buildings, but the Puritan government viewed much of this work with distaste; besides, the urgency to raise funds was more important.[2] The Act ordering the sale acknowledged their value 'by reason of their Rarity or Antiquity', although the authors of the Act thought 'for particular men's use in England they would be accounted little worth'.[3] They were not to Puritan tastes. So, one of the great early modern art collections was dispersed, much of it to European collectors.

Parliament owed money to the merchants and bankers of the City of London who had given loans, to the Adventurers who were owed Irish land, and to military suppliers who had sent in their invoices. The soldiers' pay was late, even as more became due. Now naval expansion created substantial new costs. Sir Henry Vane held many commanding positions but of them all, his role on the Naval Commission was vital. With his long, lugubrious face, limpid brown eyes and shoulder-length hair, Vane had the look of an intellectual and idealist – something he certainly was – but as the son of a career diplomat, he had useful skills as an administrator, and practical ones; he got ships built and was even credited with inventing the frigate. No wonder he became such an influential member of the Rump. As a young man in Massachusetts, Harry Vane had taken the side of the Independent preacher Anne Hutchinson, which had cost him the governorship there and led to his leaving New England with Mrs Hutchinson's brother-in-law Richard. Now Vane appointed Richard deputy treasurer at the navy, and when business pressures became too great Hutchinson took over the Treasurer's job himself, running the Navy Board throughout the decade.[4] Unfortunately, in an office which handled large sums, Hutchinson was never as forceful as Vane in controlling the funds.

Vane's politics and religious outlook were all of a piece. Opposed to the execution of the king, once it was over he accepted it as God's providence, rejoined government and worked hard to produce a republic based on English liberties and religious tolerance. Over the latter, he and Cromwell were in sympathy – both opposed a compulsory state church, both supported freedom of conscience and worship, but Vane wanted wide-ranging freedom whereas Cromwell was a social conservative and more cautious. They were not often in parliament together in the early years of the Commonwealth, as Cromwell was away on campaign. When he returned, Vane left for Scotland, so it was 1652 before they were both settled in London – and tensions between them soon arose.

Before raising funds for the navy, the Commonwealth first had to clear its debts. In all, the sales of confiscated land in England were on a scale comparable to those enacted in Ireland but the terms were entirely different. As early as 1646, parliament sold the land of bishops to pay the Scots army to hand over Charles and leave England. After 1649, when parliament had sole power, it felt free to dispose of far more. Over the next three years, the government sold lands belonging to the deans and chapters, the crown, Henrietta-Maria and the Prince of Wales. Some property was awarded by parliament for service: Cromwell, Skippon and Bridget Ireton were all generously provided for, and the Duke of Buckingham's estate went to Fairfax. Royal lands were disposed of to meet the arrears of soldiers' pay, but often the troops were given chits for small amounts of land and sold those to their officers, who could then claim sizeable holdings. Only a fifth of the crown lands went to civilians, while the bulk were purchased by 499 army officers.[5] The large royal properties were not useful to their new owners and several were demolished – for example the palaces of Richmond and Oatlands, the country houses of Theobalds and Holdenby.[6] Their new owners cut trees, drained land and transformed parks into agricultural holdings.

The complaints of pamphleteers and newswriters that bishops' lands had fallen into the hands of parliament men and City merchants was largely correct, since they had given loans and got land in return. Commonwealth land grants were not in the old feudal forms but in 'free and common socage', with a small ground rent payable to the state. Unlike feudal ownership, this property could be freely sold. Land tenure was being transformed from one based on military or agricultural service to individual ownership, which could be let or purchased on the open market. This gave prosperous tenants scope to buy. Merchants made useful purchases of potential industrial property where docks and warehouses might be constructed. John Lambert bought a nice property of Henrietta-Maria's in Wimbledon and acquired others in Yorkshire and Scotland. Colonel Philip Jones, governor of Swansea, accumulated such a large estate in South Wales that gossip persisted. Edmund Prideaux, who became Postmaster General and died a wealthy man, bought Forde Abbey on the Devon–Dorset border and modernised it handsomely in the style of the time. Sir Arthur Haselrig won himself the title of Bishop of Durham for the large landed estate he amassed there. His properties were purchased but he was accused of corruption and dishonesty in his methods. As the Lilburnes held land in Co. Durham, it is no surprise that John Lilburne became one of the angriest of voices raised against Haselrig, whom he accused of unjust sequestering.[7]

Crown and church property was disposed of immediately but it was 1651 before private land was sold. Perhaps the government was unsure how to treat the defeated royalists; it certainly had no intention of vast social change. At first they were fined, which brought in useful funds, but in 1651 the lands of 'delinquents' (i.e. royalists) began to be sold, although only that belonging to the most prominent, whom parliament blamed for the war. In fact, the main purchasers of royalist land were royalists themselves, either buying back their own properties or buying on behalf of relatives, minors or friends. [8]

Confiscated land in England was disposed of, either by sale or transfer, to clear debt, but the government also needed ready cash. For its day-to-day needs it relied on customs, excise and other small taxes but it wanted to prise more loans out of bankers and savers; hence the various schemes for 'doubling'. The procedure had been used to increase funds for the Irish reconquest and was later offered for confiscated English land too. If investors advanced more cash, they got better returns when they were paid. In Ireland, this meant twice as much land for 25 per cent more money, which complicated the settlement calculations. In England, security on a confiscated property was offered in return for doubling the loan. Almost all the confiscated institutional land – from bishops, deans, chapters and crown – was used to repay obligations in one way or another. The total value of the land disposed of in England was over £5 million but it brought little cash into the Treasury; most of it simply got debt off the books.[9]

Charles I's inability to fund his government had been one of the causes of the war; he had resorted to dubious methods, causing outcry. Parliament had the legal right to raise tax but it now ran three nations and carried a large standing army. Every month, army and navy commissioners sent in their demands. In September 1651, the commissioners in Ireland were demanding £2,500 a month to pay the troops and that more men be sent over, 'as your horse here being very much worn out and the foot being too few to carry on'. In November, they wrote to London that 'we have not one penny of money in the treasury; ... unless we have considerable supplies from England within very few days, we shall not be able to pay the soldiers upon their next muster'.[10] There were 35,000 men in Ireland but the mortality rate was high from both combat and disease, leaving widows and orphans as a significant drain on state finances.[11]

The numbers of troops in Scotland was lower – about 12,000 in 1651 – but in England the army payroll comprised 45,000 men. In March that year, the Commons was given a budget update: the army in the three kingdoms cost almost £2 million a year, the navy about £590,000, whereas civilian government was budgeted at £200,000.[12] To meet the army bills the Commonwealth relied on the monthly assessment, which was collected by county committees and sent to the Treasurers at War to pay the troops.

Naturally, parliament was keen to re-establish government in Scotland; the English Puritans saw the Scots as religious allies, if only they could be freed from kirk strictures and encouraged to think for themselves. Cromwell took a printing press to Scotland, both to publish ordinances but also to sway people's minds.[13] Parliament aimed to win Scottish support rather than rule by subjugation and late in 1651 made proposals for government. A declaration was printed announcing London's intentions. There would be religious toleration and freedom to preach, crown and royalist property would pay England's war debts, and clansmen who had gone to war under their chiefs would be pardoned; but, to weaken the hold of the lairds, new forms of tenancy would be instigated. Eight English commissioners were appointed to negotiate with the Scots; four were already in Scotland while the others set out from England in December, clattering north by coach along the winter roads, Vane and St John among them. For the Scots, Vane was a mixed blessing; he promoted union which offered English liberties and free trade, but whereas Vane believed in broad religious toleration, Presbyterian Scots viewed the proliferation of sects with horror.

It took the rest of the winter to agree the terms for union. To win over the Scots, confiscations and punishment were limited to the elite, but raising funds in Scotland to pay for government was a challenge.

On his march through the Borders, Cromwell had seen how depleted the local people were after years of war. All the same, tax was levied; the English followed the Covenanters and raised it through parishes and Presbyteries. Within a year, tax had multiplied by two and a half. If it was unpaid soldiers took free quarters from the people, but this burden was clearly too heavy and the rate was subsequently reduced.[14]

If Scotland had been drained, Ireland was devastated and depopulated. All the principal armies had used scorched earth strategies and people had fled their homes. Ireton said he had ridden for 30 miles without seeing signs of life. William Petty, the mapmaker and social analyst, thought that Ireland's population fell from over 1.5 million before the wars to 850,000 – a drop of over 40 per cent.[15] Others calculate population loss of 15 to 20 per cent; certainly it was on that scale.[16] Death, disease, famine and transportation out of the island were high. Crops had been burned, cattle stolen, much of the land was untilled and overgrown. Communities had dispersed and the social fabric was fragile. By 1651, some tax was being collected along the eastern seaboard but recovery was weak; in a demonstration of the depletion of the Irish economy, its revenues could not pay the commissioners' salaries, which had to be sent over from England.[17]

With Ireton dead, a decision had to be taken about overall command. Cromwell was still Lord Lieutenant of Ireland with Ludlow acting as commander, but a permanent appointment had to be made and Cromwell suggested Lambert for Lord Deputy. Parliament agreed. Major General John Lambert was still only thirty-three but had proved an outstanding officer at Dunbar and in Fife. When the appointment was made, he was parliament's head commissioner in Scotland but he returned to London in February and was due to leave for Dublin in May. Lambert was the son of a minor gentry family from Yorkshire, had trained as a lawyer and, through his marriage, had come into the orbit of General Fairfax. He and his wife were considered ambitious; the deputyship meant leading the army, holding court in Dublin Castle and acting as de facto head of state. They set about buying new clothes and equipment which would suit the style they meant to keep up there. Lucy Hutchinson, who wrote her memoirs when she was embittered against both Cromwell and the monarchy, describes Lambert as collecting 'a very proud train' of other officers 'so that too soon he put on the prince, immediately laying out five thousand pounds for his own particular equipage'. His wife Frances seems to have been very insensitive about her promotion. When she met Bridget Ireton, who was walking in St James's Park having recently lost her husband and therefore her position in Ireland, Mrs Lambert made the young widow feel very clearly who was now the Lady Deputy. This preening by Frances Lambert hurt Bridget, according to Lucy Hutchinson, who said that Lady Ireton, 'notwithstanding her piety and humility, was a little grieved at the affront'.[18] However, it was not long before the position was reversed once more.

Ireland was to be treated very differently to Scotland. There had been recurrent rebellion against English rule in Ireland and plantation was the established response of the London government. The Adventurers Act of 1642 was based on the same concept. Investors had 'adventured' money to subjugate Ireland and would be paid with specific amounts of confiscated Irish land. Paying the English soldiers stationed there by the same method was now official policy. By 1652, as the conquest wound up, the authorities were anxious to begin this process but the Act stated that the Adventurers had to be paid first. As Irish armies capitulated and territory came under the commissioners' control, decisions about the settlement had to be made. The Act was specific; in each province the value of land per pound sterling loaned had been set out but, on the ground, awarding land was not so easy. Whose land was to be confiscated, which land and where? How was it to be allocated? What was to happen to the population, many of whom had been displaced by war? The soldiers needed paying off but that could not be done until the Adventurers had their land.

Conditions on the ground and decisions made by Ireton months before his death shaped what followed. As Ireton had worked his way westward, he had sometimes cleared districts where enemy action still threatened.[19] When he captured strongholds and agreed terms of surrender, he often demanded that citizens leave. So, many Irish people had been moved by war and conquest before any blueprint for plantation was drawn up. As for whose land was to be taken, Ireton had sent to London a list of qualifications for penalty or pardon but when he died in November 1651 nothing had been decided. While Lambert assembled grand clothes and equipage in London, Ludlow and the commissioners in Ireland were under pressure to start the settlement and drew up a proposal for plantation. In it, land in sixteen counties, four in each province, would be used to pay the Adventurers and soldiers and, for greater security, they suggested a new pale of settlement, bounded by rivers and the east coast. They sent their scheme to parliament and the Adventurers were called into the Commons for discussion.[20]

By now, the mood of the Adventurers had turned sour. They had put up money a decade earlier, much had been diverted to war in England, and even now Ireland was not fully pacified. That April, they sent a petition to parliament with full calculations, showing that they had invested a total of £356,874, which they calculated entitled them to 1,308,232 acres in English measure. But their reluctance to plant was apparent; they even suggested they receive cash payment with interest rather than land. The idea was promptly quashed but their demands for better conditions were harder to refuse – they wanted all their land together and tax concessions. Their petition described Ireland as 'the land of desolation ... a wilderness abounding with nothing but wants and dangers'.[21] They said they would get better terms in America.

This negotiating ploy was not wholly inaccurate. When Sir John Perceval, whose family had received land under the Tudor plantations, returned to Kilkenny that September, he wrote to his cousin:

Such is the miserableness of this place, I can compare it to nothing but the first chaos ... or as Justice Cooke called it, at the late meeting of the officers (where was much exercising), a white paper. Indeed poor Ireland has lost much blood and I cannot wonder it shall be pale-faced now, and it may be called paper in that it may be quickly set on fire with faction, but that 'tis white paper ready to have anything writ in it that the state shall think fit, that is denied by some ... The great McCarty Reagh is apprehended, and to be tried at Cork for murder. Col. Wat. Bagnall, the Lord Viscount Clanmaliere, and a daughter of the Lord Mount-Garrett are prisoners here on the same score, and like to partake of the same fate intended to all murderers, which is hanging.[22]

His mother warned him, 'I hope you will lay out no money on stock until the Tories and wolves of all sorts are rooted out and destroyed in Ireland.'[23]

Ireland must be settled but parliament passed the problem on to the Council of State, who passed it to a committee. They suggested a single-block plantation but insisted the Adventurers must plant within three years or forfeit their land. That caused an outcry from the investors, who insisted on their rights under the Act with passionate indignation.

While proposals and draft legislation made their way through Westminster committees, the Irish commissioners were dealing with the aftermath of war. When Galway surrendered in May, the last city in Connaught fell to the English. The terms of surrender were important, both at the time and later. Often officials used Ireton's qualifications as their basis, but army officers in the field tended to be more lenient. Ultimately, the settlement would be made in London but the commissioners on the ground had influence. Their attitudes swerved from clemency to severity, but to fortify themselves the commissioners went back to the depositions which the Protestant settlers had made after they fled the rebellion. Tales of savagery by the Irish rebels chilled the commissioners' hearts and stiffened their resolve. They sent on to London their abstract of those reports, noting that it had prevented 'any aptness to lenity' among themselves and hoping it would do the same in parliament.[24]

How the settlement might have turned out under Lambert we can never know, as an eruption of republican sentiment in parliament that May abolished his job. Some say Haselrig was the instigator, others that rivalry between parliament and the army for control in Ireland put paid to Lambert's ambitions. Whoever raised the issue, parliament agreed that a Lord Lieutenancy was incompatible with a Commonwealth and Cromwell's job in Ireland was abolished. That meant the position of Lord Deputy went too. Whitelocke blamed Cromwell himself, which seems illogical, but Lambert was furious and when a lesser position was offered he refused to take it. Cromwell used part of his salary to defray Lambert's grand outlay, which Lucy Hutchinson heard amounted to £5,000.[25] In June, Bridget married Charles Fleetwood and under Cromwell's influence his new son-in-law was appointed head of both the army and government in Ireland, so Bridget returned as first lady. Henry Cromwell was still there, so the family would retain a firm hold on the western island.

Conditions had worsened in Ireland. The commissioners went sturdily about their work but plague had invaded Galway and Limerick, then Dublin, so the commissioners held their meetings in Kilkenny. They reported to parliament that 'it is a sad thing to consider what vast numbers of men have perished in Ireland by the hardship of the service, cold (through want of clothes) and diseases of the country'. They believed that 'one third part of the recruits you sent over last year are not now alive', and asked that more be sent swiftly.[26] During that summer, they wrote to parliament that they were unable to hold trials for murder because in some counties 'there are no inhabitants at all, the counties laying waste, and there cannot be juries had in any county but such as are Papists and Irish, and such as have had a hand in Rebellion and no ways to be trusted'.[27]

Ireland could not feed the army, as the commissioners made clear in their letters to London: 'In our last from Waterford we presented to your Lordships the present sad condition of this country for want of bread ... and do humbly desire ... your Lordship's ... ordering competent and seasonable supplies for your forces here.' They said they had only enough to feed their 35,000 men for six weeks, enclosing a list of the precise required quantities.[28]

However, parliament was making progress with the Irish files; they were calculating the arrears due to the Irish troops and they put a proposal for the Adventurers' settlement to committee for discussion. Ireton's qualifications had lost their original purpose of hastening surrender but in August parliament used them anyway when it framed the Act for Setling [*sic*] of Ireland. In the preamble, the Irish were informed:

> It is not the intention of the Parliament to extirpate that whole Nation, but that Mercy and Pardon, both as to Life and Estate, may be extended to all Husbandmen, Plowmen, Laborers, Artificers, and others of the Inferior sort, in maner as is hereafter Declared.

After this, penalties were set out for higher ranks. But when the Act arrived in Ireland, it was leaked, causing consternation.[29] Under its provisions, eight classes of people would be penalised; five classes would lose their life and land, while three more would lose up to two-thirds of their property and might be banished unless they could prove 'good affection' to parliament between 1641 and 1650, which was almost impossible.

The number of people likely to fall foul of this Act was enormous; one historian calculated that 100,000 people would be condemned to death by it and far more would be dispossessed, as few Irish Catholics could prove good affection.[30] When it was published in Ireland, there was general alarm. The commissioners, who now saw their job as quieting the country and re-establishing order, worried that the legislation would cause panic. 'We have received lately the Act of Qualifications,' they wrote. 'We know not what disturbance it may breed by those who now see their condition desperate.' Clearly, the qualifications would contradict some articles of surrender and, in the regular courts, it was now unclear what constituted murder; several trials were suspended until the new commander arrived – hopefully with more instructions from parliament.[31]

In September, the commissioners were relieved to hear that Lieutenant General Fleetwood had come ashore in Ireland. Ludlow was still in Ulster but as soon as he came south, senior officers were to meet their new commander in Kilkenny. The commissioners were concerned about costs. Irish combatants were leaving; Clanricarde had a pass to 'go beyond seas', and throughout the autumn and early winter thousands of Irish soldiers boarded ship, many for Spain and most taking up military service overseas. Shipping was being pressed into government service to remove them but the government had to pay for that too. Bills were mounting up; it was essential to disband English troops as soon as possible. In Kilkenny, the officers urged that land grants be made swiftly to soldiers, without waiting for the Adventurers' settlement, but London insisted that the law gave the Adventurers precedence.[32]

The Act for Setling Ireland was radical but it did give the authorities a formula for beginning the confiscations. Luckily, it also gave some discretion because 'proving good affection' was open to mild or severe interpretation. However, the aim was plantation and there was still no plan for that. Parliament had not finalised the soldiers' accounts but it was already clear that confiscation would be extensive. Had the Act for Setling Ireland been the only instruction, land would have fallen to government wherever the guilty owned it and been awarded – but that was not the final outcome because transportation was also envisaged.

Colonel Algernon Sidney now chaired the committee in London which was drafting the plan for plantation. He was the son of the Earl of Leicester and combined a high-handed aristocratic temperament with strong republican beliefs; later he became an influential political writer. He had been in Ireland during the war so knew something of the conditions. His committee sent a first draft for plantation to the Irish commissioners in October but they were unhappy with it and Fleetwood sent three representatives to London to discuss issues of 'some concernment to the army and affairs in Ireland'.[33] Sir Hardress Waller, Colonel Richard Lawrence and Dr Carteret, the Advocate General, made a verbal presentation in London, with the army in mind. The officers wanted the soldiers to start settling straight away and, having seen the country, they made suggestions for apportioning land. The scheme which evolved late in 1652 was neither a sixteen-county nor a single-block plantation but a ten-county scheme and used only three of the four provinces. The army wanted to be paid at the same rate as the Adventurers, which would be a good deal for the soldiers. On 4 January 1653, the new scheme was reported to parliament and accepted. Sidney's committee was ordered to draft a bill on this basis and 'to bring it in with speed'.[34]

By March, the qualifications were being contested in Ireland because they conflicted with previous agreements. Not only terms of surrender given in good faith but even Charles I's commissions to his now defeated officers were being brought forward in evidence.[35]

Meanwhile, the Irish commissioners, who could not leave houses empty and land uncultivated indefinitely while parliament delayed, began to lease out various properties. For security reasons, by April they had shifted a few convicted rebels to Connaught and some troublesome Ulster Scots, who were preaching against the government, were to move to poor land in Leinster. In effect, they were making a start on the settlement.

London however, had not completed its consultations. The bill to satisfy the Adventurers was debated in parliament over five days in early April, as new amendments were discussed and revisions made.[36]

Then, on 20 April 1653, a cataclysm descended on the Rump parliament.

Ireland – the scheme for settlement.

9

The Dissolution of the Rump

A single-chamber parliament with a rotating executive was an experiment and in 1653 it ran into trouble. It was criticised as ineffective, unmotivated, corrupt and self-serving, some of which may be accurate, but it had a huge burden of work. The Rump now had to rule three nations, there was a constantly changing executive and the country was at war. Its decisions on Ireland were late, radical and ill-informed but over Scotland it was more proactive. Within months of the victory at Worcester, the *Declaration of the Parliament ... concerning the Settlement of Scotland* announced union with England, and by the following spring sheriffs had been appointed, local government restored and inspectors appointed for the universities. Until the new court system was set up, the army dispensed a fairly rough justice. Merchants were not to be dispossessed – the Commonwealth needed commerce and tax revenues.

Technically, the Scots were to be consulted over the future of government but they had little impact on the outcome. General Monck told Cromwell that the Scottish delegates had come 'to receive such commands ... as the Parlt Hath ordered',[1] which was probably more accurate. The Scots were told to send a small group to London to hammer out the details of union, men of 'good affection', preferably from modest backgrounds rather than the nobility. The Commonwealth leaders were confident that they could radically alter society in all three countries by side-lining the old elites, creating better institutions and promoting their own religious goals. Time would show that, although modernisation was necessary, the enduring habits of all three nations were hard to mould.

The kirkmen had snatched a decade of self-government from the crown but they were now split and vanquished. The Marquis of Argyll had returned to his fiefdom and was pondering his future at Inveraray Castle. Having allied with both Cromwell and Charles II, he now negotiated with Monck for Scottish self-government. Monck let the commissioners do their work while he concentrated on subduing Scotland. Tall and strongly built with a square head to match his massive body, Monck was not a man to cross. Coming from a modest gentry family in Devon, he was a younger son who had made his way as a soldier. Blunt in speech and capable in action, he had fought doggedly for the crown until captured, then served parliament in both Ireland and Scotland. Cromwell had recognised his qualities and quickly promoted him to lieutenant general and military governor of Edinburgh. Left in charge, he captured the assembled Estates at Alyth. During his storming of Dundee, eight hundred Scots were killed. It was unwise to pester or underestimate Monck, who took a dim view of Argyll's protestations, but in February he was taken ill and retired to Bath. He did not return but joined the Dutch war. Major General Richard Deane was left in command in Scotland. When Argyll kept propositioning the commissioners, Deane marched on Inverary – soon afterwards Argyll agreed to the union.

By the spring of 1652, England controlled the Lowlands of Scotland and their commissioners returned to London to finalise the settlement. The mood in Scotland was mixed. When union was declared in Edinburgh, the soldiers cheered but the Scottish crowd was silent; occupation was irksome and rule from London worse. If the burghs agreed to union, they could elect their own magistrates and councillors, but London controlled most appointments and officials had to take an oath of loyalty to government which offended religious principles. Soldiers were collecting high taxes, but at least they were disciplined. Union meant free trade; customs were no longer collected at the English border but that might work both ways. In reality, Scotland was under military occupation. The delegates in London had little influence. They could present 'Desires', so they pleaded for maintenance of the kirk, the removal of sequestration, an Act of Oblivion, lower tax, the removal of troops and the release of Scottish prisoners in England. On trade, Scottish views diverged as some hoped to export freely to England and some hoped for investment and skills from England while others feared competition and wanted border tariffs. There were arguments about fishing rights.

In the Lowlands, political Scotland was hopelessly riven. Remonstrants and Protestors refused to co-operate with each other. The Kirk thought the English Puritans scandalous, with their ad hoc sects and preaching. The General Assembly of the Kirk produced warnings to be read in church against the occupying army's views and threatened extreme censure on anyone who collaborated with the English.[2] For the Kirk, Scotland's defeat was a judgement for sins which they had to rectify, but more to be feared were the 'dark dungeons of error' which now threatened, as the English seduced people from their Covenant with God towards the 'impious monster of Toleration'.[3] Determined to weaken the Kirk, the English brought in preaching ministers from the south but it was the occupying soldiers who most scandalised the Scots, with their extempore prayer meetings; horrifyingly, they even took over important Scottish churches. Nonetheless, religious striving had its effect; in villages and small towns, soldiers and locals exchanged views, often in public debate, and some Scots turned to Independency. The army viewed the Kirk as warmongers; the Scots had invaded England repeatedly under the banner of the Covenant. Actually, both the kirk and the English Puritans verged on theocracies, claiming power as a right from God.[4]

The Highlands were a different problem for the English as they started to move into the hill country and found conditions there difficult and unpredictable. Argyll might have accepted union and troops on his territory, but when Deane came ashore with those troops, violence broke out. William Clarke, secretary to the army, was horrified at the conditions in the Highlands – the poor hovels of the people, their primitive clothes and lack of modesty, their wild ways. But the Highlanders were vigorous; like the tories in Ireland they could mount sudden attacks and they knew the terrain as no English soldier ever would. With effective leaders, the endemic lawlessness of the Highlanders could swiftly become revolt and the English suspected Argyll of provocation. They were wrong – not Argyll, but several Highland chieftains, roused by the 'condicion of Scotland' under occupation, contacted Charles II in Paris while other Scottish leaders mobilised.[5]

For Charles, the war between England and the Netherlands offered a new opportunity. Could he ally himself with the Dutch and then liaise with Scottish royalists? Charles appointed Lt General Middleton as commander for Scotland, a professional soldier from Aberdeenshire who had fought for parliament, then for Charles I in 1648. Having been humiliated by the Kirk, he nursed an abiding hatred for them and had fought with Charles II at Worcester. In 1652, he was at St Germain trying to raise money but was as yet unable to fund an expedition to Scotland. In the Highlands, attacks continued against the English, who uncovered caches of weapons but were unsure they could contain a full uprising.

There were going to be confiscations in Scotland, and five army officers had already been given grants of Scottish land, but generally the Commonwealth policy was for mercy. They had trouble selling royalist land in England and looked for other assets to sell. A plan was hatched to demolish the cathedrals and sell the building materials but parliament took fright and overruled the idea. In December, the assessment was raised by 25 per cent. The Dutch war was causing hardship, interrupting trade and pushing up the price of coal in London. Nor had the increased tax paid off the army, as so much of it went on new ships. More troops were disbanded and a salary cut for the soldiers was mooted but complaints alarmed the government, which backed down.

So, 1652 was an increasingly difficult year for the Commonwealth. The army was slowly disabling resistance in Ireland and Scotland, but in both countries guerrilla warfare persisted and even though troops were gradually disbanded, meeting the military costs was proving hard. The reform agenda was only pursued spasmodically while the army and Levellers fulminated. Some issues seemed easy to tackle but proved resistant. In 1647, Christmas had been abolished as pagan but the ban was hard to enforce. Although services could be prevented by the locking of churches, they were still held in private houses until soldiers broke them up. To set an example, the Commons sat on Christmas Day but members had thinned out. It was impossible to force the shops to stay open. Fines were imposed but still Londoners closed their businesses and had a good plum pudding. Despite the best efforts of parliament, there were constant reports of feasting and wassail cups, 'bellows and bag-pipes'.[6]

Naturally, prostitutes were targets for the Puritans. Legislation condemned them to be branded and whipped but more commonly they seem to have been gaoled. Some bawds were shipped to the Caribbean, but at the end of the decade there were still brothels running in London which had been there in 1652 and 'the Queen of Morocco', despite imprisonment, was back in business.[7] The people were proving less pliable and more resistant to godly reformation than the Puritans had hoped. Inspired by spiritual effort and now with power in their hands, still they were unable to enforce their will or inspire others with their own ideals. They laboured on.

Religious policy was crucial. The collapse of Charles I's dictatorial church policy coupled with Puritan experimentation had led to extremist congregations springing up. Of all the attributes ascribed to Oliver Cromwell, the one principle we know he held dear was that people should find their own path to God. 'I had rather that Mahometanism were permitted amongst us than that one of God's children should be persecuted,' he is quoted as saying.[8] When he became Chancellor of Oxford University, he appointed John Owen as vice chancellor, hoping to reshape the curriculum to Puritan ideals. Owen, like Cromwell, was an Independent but he believed in a state church with a salaried clergy; that meant tithes. He enforced core beliefs and condemned those who rejected the Trinity or the divinity of Christ.

It was the effect of preachers, in the army and in the gathered churches, which stirred the population to spiritual excitement, especially in London where All Hallows the Great and Blackfriars became hothouses for Fifth Monarchist expectation. Radical religion was linked to radical politics – that was the danger for government. Much of the army had a godly outlook; they had trained under a regime of sobriety, regular fasting and prayer. Chiliasm – the expectation that God's kingdom was imminent – ran through the army in glowing threads; the rule of the saints must be established, which would initiate the kingdom of Jesus on earth. Among officers, Major General Thomas Harrison was the most fervent of the Fifth Monarchists and by 1652 was emerging as leader of the millenarian faction in the army. Exultant over the death of Charles I, the Fifth Monarchists expected England to spread the godly revolution to other lands, to root up monarchies and install the Lord's justice. After Worcester, they increasingly saw the Rump as part of the Fourth Monarchy which must be swept away. 'The Sword of the Lord' was to be 'sheathed in the sides of all kingdoms', wrote one of their members. 'England, thou hast begun to drink blood,' he wrote, threatening more in a millenarian crusade.[9] Their attacks on 'scandalous ministers' bore fruit. Parliament set up the Triers and Ejectors to test the faith and learning of parish clergy; many lost their livings. Official policy was for toleration but where were its limits?

For parliament, the end of armed conflict spelled danger. As troops lingered in garrisons, their attention reverted to politics. Used to swift decisions and actions, they had little sympathy for the complex parliamentary systems by which law was made. Now, restless in their quarters, the energy of the warriors turned towards reform.

Disbandment reduced the troop numbers but the officer corps was permanent; it was these men who increasingly urged religious and social change. Cromwell had promised John Lilburne 'to make the people of England the most absolute free nation on the earth', but Lilburne had been banished for libelling Haselrig and was in Amsterdam.[10] The general called for 'justice, righteousness, mercy and truth' but what was needed were specific policies with decisions and legislation, whereas parliament was fighting a foreign war while trying to re-establish government in three nations. Progress on reform was slow.

Another goad angered the army when the Act of Articles was renewed. Articles, or terms of surrender, were agreed by officers fighting in the field, so when parliament tried to alter them, the army's honour was in jeopardy.[11] Officers in the Commons resisted but could only partially influence the Act. Grievances were building up. The army petition to parliament of August 1652 was a sign of their growing impatience. As so often before, they held prayer meetings 'to seek the Lord and to speak of the great things God hath done for this Commonwealth', before they finalised their ideas. Then they penned their demands: the propagation of the Gospel, an end to tithes, law reform as recommended by Hale, that those in positions of authority should not be 'profane or scandalous persons' but 'men of truth, fearing God and hating covetousness', that soldiers should be paid their arrears, that articles of war to royalists should be fulfilled, and 'that a new representative be forthwith elected'.[12] This last – the demand for dissolution and a new parliament – came to embody all the other demands and aspirations. To the officers, the Commons seemed jaded and depleted; God had given to the army great victories and they were at the threshold of the promised age of godliness – to usher it in, new rulers must be elected. But parliament's responses were muted and the council of war became increasingly restive.

At sea, the Commonwealth was gradually asserting its strength, not only against the Netherlands but between France and Spain, who were vying for control of Dunkirk. France held the city, Spain was besieging it; in September Blake attacked a French flotilla sent to relieve Dunkirk and captured French warships. To get them back, France would have to negotiate, which meant recognising the Commonwealth and sending an ambassador to London, something that Mazarin now realised was inevitable.

Internally, however, the future of the government remained unresolved. In his memoirs, Bulstrode Whitelocke recounts how he was walking in St James's Park that November when he was accosted by the General. They went on together as Cromwell unburdened himself of his worries. It was not only parliament's neglect of reform which weighed on his mind, but the way they formed cliques and awarded themselves property and positions, while among them were men of scandalous living – Henry Marten might be a committed republican, for instance, but he lived openly with his mistress. In short, the parliament was entirely unworthy of the power it had received from the army's great victories, yet since the statute of 1649 no one had the power to dissolve it.

Never a man to mince his words, Cromwell blurted out, 'What if a man should take upon him to be king?' During their last discussion, there had been talk of putting one of Charles I's sons on the throne but now Whitelocke was under no illusion who the 'man' in question was. As a lawyer, he gave a measured answer. The general already had both power and honour; the war had been fought to promote liberty and the victors cherished the Commonwealth they had created; to re-establish monarchy would antagonise them, said Whitelocke. Besides, it would re-open the question as to who should

BULSTRODUS WHITELOCK
Eques Aurat Windforij Proconſtabularius
Scaccharij Commiſs: dudum magni Sigilli
Cuſtos: nuper ad Sueciam Legatus extraordinari
R. Gaywood fecit: P. Stent excud

Bulstrode Whitelocke.

be king: a Cromwell or a Stuart?[13] Cromwell was displeased. He had already emphasised how restive the army was and, although he said he could contain mutiny, the officers' demands were becoming strident. He pressed Whitelocke to suggest a solution but when the lawyer advised reinstating Charles II, who had the legal right to be king, Cromwell was aggrieved. Whitelocke pointed out that Charles was abroad, dependent on others and with scant resources: the Commonwealth could set their own terms. The two men parted. Afterwards, Whitelocke felt that Cromwell was cooler towards him. At Christmas, as if to prevent any move to install the teenage prince, parliament ordered that Henry, Duke of Gloucester be sent overseas. In February, the fourteen-year-old was released from Carisbrooke Castle, put on board ship and sent to the Netherlands to stay with his sister Mary, before joining his mother and brother in Paris. No royal Stuarts remained within the Commonwealth's territory.

In the army, discontent was building. Meetings for fasting and prayer became more frequent at St James's. The French ambassador heard that Cromwell might lose his position and that parliament might bring Fairfax back as commander. London was rife with such rumours. Parliament even made moves to go on with the sale of Hampton Court, which had been Cromwell's reward for his great victories. As taxation rose and the cost of living increased, discontent was widespread. The Dutch war strengthened England's trade position, but elsewhere the Rump was losing support, while in the radical London churches preaching produced red-hot emotions and unruly spirits. However, the bill for a new parliament was put in hand. From February, it was to be debated weekly with Thomas Harrison in charge of getting it through parliament; he seems to have neglected this role, for Henry Vane took over.

Also in February, Blake had an important sea victory over Tromp but was wounded and out of action until the summer. Monck and Deane had both left Scotland and been promoted as naval commanders. That summer, decisive engagements gave England victory and the Netherlands sued for terms, but by then the regime in London had been radically altered.

Tension between the army and parliament was growing. Precipitous action in 1649 had left the Rump with sole power but many of its supporters were disillusioned with the Commonwealth. The officers believed the fault lay with MPs; a new parliament was essential. If only the current one would legislate for dissolution and elections all might be well, but issues were building up. Arrears had not been paid and the settlement of Ireland was being debated intermittently, despite so many soldiers having a vested interest. The army, however, was not of one mind; there were factions among the officers and differences throughout the army. The troops were concerned about pay but some wanted social reform while others were hungry for godly revolution. The great moment might be missed, sinfulness subverting the nation's trajectory towards its exalted inheritance. God had shown his providence in battle and victory – now was the moment to consummate that promise.

The Fifth Monarchists and radical churches looked to Thomas Harrison for leadership and it was he who led the group which pushed Cromwell into acting. Harrison came from Newcastle-under-Lyme in Staffordshire, where his father had been a butcher who became mayor. The son had been a clerk in a London lawyer's office before joining the parliamentarian army where he rose quickly, serving in Fleetwood's cavalry regiment, one of the most religiously radical. Harrison had openly declared that Charles I was a 'man of blood', assigning the blood guilt of the war to the king. It was he who had escorted Charles from his last prison into London and he had been among those who signed the death warrant. A successful army commander, a sitting MP and a member of the Council of State, Harrison had been promoted to major general in 1651 and led London troops who fought at Worcester. He had commanded in Wales where he was severe and pressed for education in the Gospels. He was not only a vigorous army officer but passionate about purity in religion. With the war won, that urge for godly completion became urgent, relentless.

In London, pressure was increasing. Early in 1653, the officers held daily prayer meetings to win back God's providence. At All Hallows, prayers for a new representative were heard. Far more pervasive was a letter, written at army headquarters – either St James's or Windsor – and sent to every regiment in all of the three nations, as well as being available to the public in London. It opened portentously, announcing that Satan had been very active, that the army must repent of its sinfulness but that corruption in parliament required correction. They repeated their demand for a new representative of 'men of truth, fearing God and hating covetousness'.[14] Their primary demands were for law reform, liberty of worship and a ministry paid for by the state. Replies came back from the regiments; a few have survived, echoing the officers' self-reproach and their fervid hopes that the ungodly might be removed so that there might emerge the pure state promised in the Bible and won by the sword.

Rumours swirled through London that the soldiers could make a move against parliament; civilians were alarmed. Newsbooks advised calm, reminding the military that their cause would not be served by might alone. Parliament had already chosen 3 November 1654 as the date for dissolution, but now it brought that forward a year. Gradually, week by week, they decided on the constituencies and on the franchise, which would be standardised but still based on property. Ireland and Scotland were to send members but the Scottish union still required legislation. By March 1653, these issues had been decided but more dangerous ones were still in discussion. Qualifications for the electors and elected were highly sensitive; if elections were held without them, Presbyterians and royalists might flood the chamber. Cromwell wanted strict qualifications to be set for both electors and members. There would be gaps between parliaments, of course, and who would rule then? The officers became increasingly concerned.

For many years, sitting MPs had controlled who joined parliament, ejecting royalists and managing the recruiter elections held to fill those vacancies. It was the army, however, who had purged parliament late in 1648. After Charles was executed, power flowed back to parliament while the army stood back and went about its military business. But with elections looming, a sense of insecurity returned. The government was young; a dissolution would create grave instability, and how would the new intake be controlled? Some MPs thought that current members should stay on and only hold recruiter elections for vacant constituencies. The army viewed that strategy with dismay – the whole point was a thorough cleansing of the Commons. Without a king, who would call elections and rule between parliaments? If the Council of State was to fill that gap, who would choose the councillors? And who would set qualifications for the MPs? The army had run into a problem; they had fought for the rights of parliament but elections might produce a government they deplored. Parliament was equally concerned; would they be re-elected or lose control of the revolution? The constitution was inadequate and the revolution in jeopardy.

Officers were congregating in London, some from Ireland and Scotland. Cromwell was at the Cockpit, guarded by his own regiment of foot. Around him were colleagues and family; Charles and Bridget Fleetwood were in Ireland but his son Henry had returned to England. Cromwell's brother-in-law John Desborough, his cousin Edward Whalley and Whalley's son-in-law William Goffe, as well as John Barkstead, who commanded the Tower of London, were often with the General. He had his own views about parliament but his priority was unity of the army so he stayed close to Harrison and his faction – men like Colonel Pride and Nathaniel Rich. John Lambert's views were less religious and more like Ireton's; he favoured a constitutional republic and leaned to Cromwell, not Harrison.

In the Commons, Haselrig was the arch enemy of the army and may have been behind moves to sack Cromwell, but when he took charge of the bill for the new parliament it moved more swiftly through its stages. During March and April, Cromwell was seldom in the house or at meetings of the Council of State but he stayed in touch with sympathetic MPs – Whitelocke among them – and had discussions with Henry Vane. In March, Cromwell met the City clergy and asked them bluntly to agree to the army dissolving parliament. Mr Calamy said it was 'unlawful and impracticable'. Cromwell repeated an earlier argument that it was for the 'safety of the nation'. Calamy said that nine out of ten people would be against it. 'Very well,' said Cromwell, 'but what if I should disarm the nine and put the sword into the tenth man's hand, would not that do the business?'[15]

A newsbook dated 1 April, copied out by Clarendon and left among his papers, shows the pressure that Cromwell was under. If he worked with MPs, the godly officers suspected him – his position seems to have been under threat from several directions. 'Our souldiers resolve to have speedily a new representative, and the Parliament resolve the contrary. The General sticks close to the House, which causeth him to be daily railed on by the preaching party, who say they must have both a new Parliament and the General before the work be don; and that these are not the people that are appointed for perfecting of that great worke of God which they have begun.'[16]

The bill for a new representative was pulled from debate on 6 April. The following day, the army petitioned for swift action and more rigorous qualifications for voters, to keep out royalists. The house complied with this request, but when Cromwell attended he was shouted at, some saying it was time for a new general. Cromwell then offered his resignation to his officers but they gave him their support. Now, several issues came before parliament which were highly sensitive for the army. First, MPs did not renew the Committee for the Propagation of the Gospel in Wales and attempted to restrict the extempore preaching so beloved of the army.[17] Highly sensitive too was the settlement of Ireland, which would pay the soldiers and entrench Puritan ideals in that papist nation; but, despite debate, it was not finalised. The bill for the new representative was the most explosive issue, but as preaching and Ireland moved through parliament, it was already lighting a smouldering fuse.

In the bill for the new parliament, all the unsolved problems of the constitution came face to face with the real issue, which was the power struggle between parliament and the army. Parliament was small and unrepresentative – probably fewer than 220 members had returned after the execution of the king and generally there were only about 60 members in the house. So the charge made by the army, that parliament was not really dissolving but only recruiting, was misleading; even if they only filled the empty seats, the resultant body would be very different.[18] In reality, the army was waking up to the danger to itself. If, as they feared, parliament was flooded with royalists and Presbyterians, it might well sack General Cromwell, and possibly promote Lambert or bring back Fairfax, neither of whom were radical enough for the officers. Were that to happen, would other officers be sacked, would the army be paid, would they even be secure? Cromwell, in a speech made months later, summed up the fears of the officers: 'Thus, as we apprehend, would the Liberties of the Nation have been thrown away into the hands of those who had never fought for it.'[19]

Members of parliament, however, believed they embodied the revolution. They, who had resisted the ship money tax, been harassed or imprisoned by Charles I, run a war against him, survived the tumults of mobs and finally created a republic, believed that the aim of the revolution had been to secure the rights of parliament. Now it was achieved, they reasoned, it was they who owned it. Besides, in legal and constitutional terms, they alone had a claim to rule.

By early April, the shape of the bill was becoming clear. The army had persuaded parliament to include stringent qualifications for MPs. Only two issues remained – the nature of the council which would rule between parliaments, and whether elections were for the full chamber or only recruiter elections to fill vacant seats. As regards the council, Cromwell 'humbly proposed that parliament should devolve power to a new group of persons of honour and integrity that were well known, men well affected to religion and the interest of the nation'.[20] The army did not want the existing councillors to remain in charge.

Whitelocke left an account of those hectic days in April, when the tensions reached a crisis point. On 19 April, he was at a meeting of army officers and sympathetic MPs called by Cromwell at the Cockpit. Whitelocke and Widdrington argued against a sudden termination of the current government. Cromwell and his associates were determined that parliament should be dissolved but had not decided on what terms. The bill was due back in the Commons the following day but the officers had been assured it would not pass before their concerns were met. On the morning of the 20th, the Cockpit meeting reconvened for further discussions. Whitelocke was worried about the interim council, which he feared he would be asked to join but which he thought would be in a 'desperate condition' with 'exorbitant power', once there was no parliament. News reached them that the bill was back in the Commons and might imminently be passed. The MPs present left the Cockpit and hurried to the House, where Whitelocke 'found them in a debate of an Act … which would prolong their sitting'. So, it would not be a full dissolution after all, only recruiter elections; the officers would be incensed. Colonel Ingoldsby rushed back to warn Cromwell.[21]

The general was not dressed to go out but, unheeding of everything, he called a troop of soldiers and rushed to the chamber where the bill was still being debated. At first he took his place, sat and listened, but then he got up and put on his hat – a sign of disrespect – before beginning a long oration, at first polite and complimentary, then increasingly angry. Once Cromwell became enraged, he was reckless and his mind closed to argument. Pointing often at Vane and Whitelocke, he railed against their slowness, lack of dedication, corruption and bad living – Henry Marten was the object of Cromwell's scorn in that respect.[22] Whitelocke's description of Cromwell is vivid:

> In a furious manner bid the Speaker leave his Chair, told the House that they had sat long enough, unless they had done more good; that some of them were Whore-masters, looking then towards Henry Marten and Sir Peter Wentworth. That others of them were Drunkards, and some corrupt and unjust Men and scandalous to the Profession of the Gospel, and that it was not fit they should sit as a Parliament any longer, and desired them to go away … Some of the members rose up to answer Cromwell's speech, but he would not suffer none [sic] to speak but himself. Which he did with so much arrogance in himself and Reproach to his Fellow members that some of his Privadoes were ashamed of it.[23]

Having worked himself up into a rage, the General turned to Thomas Harrison, who was among the MPs in the house, and told him to 'call them in', at which a troop of musketeers came into the chamber. Cromwell ordered them to remove the Speaker, who was pulled from the Chair. Algernon Sidney, who was sitting beside the Speaker, tried to resist but the soldiers took him by the shoulders and he gave in. Cromwell went over to the mace, symbol of parliament's right to sit, and ordered the men to remove it – 'take out this bauble' – which they did. He then snatched up the bill under discussion, thrust it under his cloak and, ordering the door to be locked, strode away. What was the final form of the bill? It was never seen again, making it impossible to verify or modify Cromwell's claims about its contents.

That afternoon, Lord General Cromwell completed his work. Taking Lambert and Harrison with him, he went to the chamber where the Council of State was electing its next chairman and closed that too. He told the members they could only meet as private persons, not councillors, because parliament had been dissolved. Bradshaw contested that assertion, telling Cromwell plainly that 'no power under heaven can dissolve them but themselves; therefore take you notice of that'.[24] However, resistance proved hopeless.

'There was not so much as the barking of a dog,' Cromwell remarked about the dissolution of the Rump.[25] The Rump had not been popular and the Venetian ambassador thought that Londoners were pleased at the dissolution, while royalists hoped the revolutionary party was breaking up. One thing was certain: the army ruled. Revolution had rolled over once more – now it was complete and had ended up where many revolutions arrive, with the army taking charge.

Thomas Burton, later MP for Westmorland, said that 'a petition, the day after the Parliament was dissolved, from forty of the chief officers, the Aldermen of the city of London, and many godly divines … besought to have that Parliament restored. But the Protector [Cromwell], being resolved to carry on his work, threatened, terrified and displaced them; and who would, for such a shattered thing, venture their all?'[26] The Long Parliament was finished.

'Thus was this great parliament,' wrote Bulstrode Whitelocke, 'which had done so great things, wholly at this time routed by those whom they had set up.'[27]

10

Rule without Parliament

'There was not so much as the barking of a dog.'

Cromwell may have been right that comment and resistance were both minimal when the parliament was dissolved, but newsbooks were restricted by licensing laws and people in all three kingdoms were cautious about antagonising the army.[1] Or was Cromwell justifying his actions because he felt disquiet? His biographers suggest he never reconciled himself to what he had done, never rested easy. He was an MP himself and had been hired by parliament to fight for its rights – now he had closed it down. As for the rest of the country, the evidence suggests that the Rump was not well-loved; but dissolving it caused consternation, and there were rumblings of dissent from the City of London and from within the army itself. The group which Cromwell had certainly alienated was the MPs themselves, especially the committed Commonwealthsmen, some of whom were vocal and influential.

The views of this group were mixed and still in debate. The Levellers talked of natural rights and of all men having an equal voice in elections, but the leaders of the Commonwealth had other views. The word 'democracy' was seldom used in the seventeenth century and 'republican' only sparingly; the word republic harked back to the *res publica* of Rome and throughout the Interregnum, several leading parliamentarians aimed for forms of oligarchy, for Plato had prescribed the rule of philosopher-kings. The Commonwealthsmen had rejected rule by a single monarch and, to form a theoretical base for their state, some explored arguments made by Bodin and Grotius about the nature of sovereignty, but widening the franchise was not a central aim – they expected the state to be governed by educated men like themselves. For some, the key issue was religious belief; the profane could not rule. When Cromwell closed the Rump, this group of clever men from elite backgrounds not only lost power but saw their principles trampled on and overturned.[2] They proved tenacious and formidable enemies.

Cromwell may have acted in haste, putting the aims of the army before the rights of parliament, but once it had been dissolved, he had to inform all three nations and establish control. Troops were sent to the City of London in case of trouble, but when the Lord Mayor offered his resignation Cromwell told him to keep his post.[3] Soldiers also took up positions in the parliament chambers, to make sure the members could not reassemble. For Londoners, the soldiers were now a familiar sight; they had first marched into Westminster in 1647 to assert their position, they had purged parliament in 1648 and had overseen the king's execution in 1649. Their headquarters were in Whitehall and the officers met at St James's, so the army was already highly visible at the centre of government.

On 22 April, two days after the dissolution, the *Declaration of the Lord General and his Council of Officers* was published. This carefully worded document recounted the army's expectation that parliament would 'give the people the harvest of all their labour' and 'settle a due liberty', and noted that little progress had been made, despite Cromwell's personal exhortations to MPs and polite petitions from the officers. The *Declaration* accused parliament of wanting to perpetuate themselves 'in the supreme government' and of recruiting 'similar persons to perpetuate their own sittings'. The officers had wanted parliament to hand power over to a group of 'known persons, men fearing God', but it was clear to the army that MPs were determined to continue in parliament. They had agreed to delay legislation for elections but the following day the bill was underway in the house once more and the officers knew they had to end the sitting. They were now preparing to call together 'persons of approved fidelity' to take up the reins of government and, promising further explanations, they confirmed all law officers and public servants in their positions.[4]

The *Declaration* was advertised and published in all three nations. It took several days to reach northern England, Edinburgh and Dublin, but by 29 April the reply of the Judge Advocate of Scotland had reached London, assuring fidelity, and the *Declaration* was published on the same day in Dublin, with a letter signed by the parliamentary commissioners saying that 'we hold it our duty to publish the same' and reminding all public servants to act diligently 'that the common enemy may not have advantage'.[5] They exhorted 'all good people ... into special fervent wrestling with the Lord', and appointed two days to be set apart for prayer. All four commissioners signed the letter, although Ludlow was to become one of Cromwell's most virulent critics. His memoirs, however, were written later so do not chronicle the hardening of his distrust into hatred, which seems to have taken place towards the end of the year.

The navy held firm with the army. Blake was against the dissolution but was talked round; Monck and Deane signed a letter stating that they had no politics and this, in turn, acted as an order to Penn. The navy was fighting a war against the Dutch and had little attention to spare for parliamentary problems. Cromwell's enemies saw the dissolution as part of the General's plan to end that war, as it allowed him to make an early peace with the Netherlands. He was certainly unhappy about fighting the Dutch but in fact peace was only made later, after the navy had triumphed.

The question remained – who was to govern the three nations and on what basis? In the 1650s, the philosophy of government was developing rapidly in the hands of intellectuals but it could hardly keep up with events. Perhaps the journalist Marchamont Nedham had come nearest to the mark when he published *The Case of the Commonwealth of England Stated* in May 1650, which argued that those who took power by force had the right to wield it. He was greatly criticised and Hobbes's *Leviathan*, published in 1651, dealt in scholarly fashion with the difficulty of reconciling right with the force required to control the state. All the same, the New Model Army had deposed the King, Lords and Commons, as well as conquering Scotland and Ireland. Like many revolutionary armies since that time, it now threw aside the politicians and theorists to make the revolution its own.

Having disbanded both the Rump and Council of State, Cromwell and his officers chose a small new council of thirteen men to rule until they could decide how to enact the godly reformation. Nine were army officers, of whom four – including Cromwell – were generals. Three councillors were religious radicals, one was a merchant and two were on the commission for law reform. It was clearly a body of military men but there was a balance of interests and beliefs. Its first president, in place for one week, was Lambert.[6]

A few days after the dissolution, fortuitously, coal boats arrived, bringing down the price of fuel. The Commission for the Propagation of the Gospel in Wales was renewed, placating the godly, and

Cromwell prevented a group of prisoners from being hanged, forbidding further hangings in London except for murder. These were popular developments, pleasing important constituencies. All the same, Cromwell had no legal right to rule; he only did so as commander of an army which had taken power by force. However, he took up 'that power that I thought was devolved on me', and made decisions about a new government.[7] The council of officers was disgruntled that a separate executive council had been chosen, while the soldiers were unsure that they were not being swindled in some novel way, but the army leaders assured the public that a new government would be put in place in due course.

Though it became clear later, it was not spelled out at the time that the arguments over the Rump had turned the army against new elections. They were unhappy about recruiting into the existing parliament, but full elections were bound to bring in royalists and 'neuters', i.e. Presbyterians. The officers thought that elections should wait until the country was ready for them, which might be a few years. Instead, the new council debated how to assemble a trustworthy group to replace the Rump. Lambert, practical but ambitious, favoured a small council, while Harrison wanted a 'sanhedrin' of seventy, as in the Bible. Some expected a king but 'a man after God's own heart'. Could this mean Harrison, who was such an inspiration to the godly?[8] Or was Cromwell the new Moses, soon to be anointed king? Royalists dreamed that without the usurping parliament, Cromwell might recall the Stuarts, or even marry his daughter to Charles.[9]

What he actually did was rule by ordinance for three months while he and his colleagues hand-picked a parliament of the godly. 'Men of good affection' from all three nations were to form an interim assembly. The gathered churches were at the heart of the Puritan movement; now they sent petitions begging for godly representatives. These churches, in turn, were tapped for nominations. The new parliament was to make the reforms so longed for by the Puritans and army. Those chosen were mainly lesser gentry, with some artisans and a few peers, many with university experience or legal training; their views and backgrounds reflected Cromwell and his officers. They were from the congregations but included very few Fifth Monarchists. There were to be 128 representatives for England and Wales, plus 5 for Scotland and 6 from Ireland, to reflect population size and tax take.[10]

The representatives for Scotland were lawyers and Presbyterians who were willing to collaborate with the Cromwellian regime; of these, two later became Quakers. Of those for Ireland, four were soldiers, including Henry Cromwell; one was a Dublin alderman; and another, the planter Vincent Gookin, was later a famous pamphleteer. None, of course, were Irish or Roman Catholic. Among those invited for England were Fairfax and Henry Vane, both of whom declined and remained at their country estates. It took time to work up the list but on 6 June 1653, a summons was sent to 140 people by 'Oliver Cromwell, Captain General and Commander-in-Chief of all the Armies and Forces raised and to be raised within this Commonwealth', to attend the council chamber in Whitehall on 4 July.[11]

The three-month interval from April to July 1653 was the first in which Cromwell indisputably ruled. One of the first issues taken up by his council was the Act of Articles; the officers altered it to honour the terms of surrender and, as a result, some royalists regained property. Bear- and bull-baiting were banned and an enquiry launched into the post office, while efforts were made to rationalise the Treasury and one of the debtors' prisons was investigated.

On 20 May, the leaders of the City petitioned for the return of the elected parliament. Their petition was written in complimentary and submissive language but its message was clear: they felt bound to comment on 'the sad condition of this nation, which seemeth as on one day to be deprived of its ancient liberty, to wit being governed by Representatives chosen by themselves which in all ages since England hath been civilised the people have been so constantly addicted unto'. They considered this 'so ancient and so useful a privilege, the birthright of the nation'.[12] Cromwell rounded on them and had three of the councillors dismissed.

Another well-known voice was heard again that summer when John Lilburne returned to England. The Rump had pronounced his attacks on Haselrig as treasonous and banished him on pain of trial as a traitor should he return. In exile, Lilburne had befriended the Duke of Buckingham while intriguing with exiled royalists, for he now spoke of Cromwell as 'the grandest tyrant and traitor that ever England bred'. However, when the Rump was dissolved, he thought his banishment might be annulled and, longing to go home, he did not wait for legal process but sailed for England and petitioned for clemency. He was picked up, and Cromwell referred his case to the council, which had him incarcerated in Newgate. As usual, Lilburne managed to create a storm of publicity as he awaited trial.[13]

The five representatives to be sent from Scotland to the Nominated Assembly had little influence on events, whereas the increasing unrest which was spreading in the Highlands greatly concerned the government. After Deane followed Monck south late in 1652, Captain Robert Lilburne was left in charge. A less effective soldier than the indomitable Monck, Robert Lilburne had skills as a politician but not the demagoguery of his younger brother John the Leveller. He was up against a difficult enemy; from early in 1653, there were reports of men gathering for meetings and then that MacDonald of Glengarry had created a flying army. His territory was near Fort William among the other restive MacDonalds of the western seaboard. Argyll, their ancient foe and leader of the Campbells, was behaving like a government loyalist, but Robert Lilburne had little faith in the marquis. A host of other angry clans became active, easily roused into attacking the English invaders but also hoping to improve their finances.

During the period of Cromwell's personal rule in England, the unrest in the western Highlands blew up into a full-scale revolt. Charles's commander for Scotland, Middleton, was still abroad but the Earl of Glencairn emerged to lead the rising. Riven by rivalries and lacking the support of many significant but cautious noblemen, Glencairn's men nonetheless posed a serious threat to the occupiers because of their tactics. Acting in dispersed groups, flying columns attacked the English wherever they seemed vulnerable but held back from a full offensive until Middleton or, as some hoped, King Charles himself should arrive. By late summer, Glencairn had between 7,000 and 10,000 men.[14] They could coerce local populations to support them and by so doing deprive the English of assessment, strengthen themselves and then send positive reports to Europe encouraging more support.

The English had a firm grip on the Lowlands but Scottish people began escaping into the hills to join the insurgents, after which royalists mounted flying raids into the Lowlands. Gradually, they infiltrated Galloway, while Argyll's son Lord Lorne helped the royalists get a foothold in his father's territory. Other grand men of the Highlands including the young Marquis of Montrose, whose father had died so bravely for the Stuarts, came out for the royal cause.

They had the sympathy of the Scottish people but physical support was less forthcoming and they were weakened by constant rivalries and disagreements. Landowners in the Lowlands were vulnerable to English reprisals if they showed disloyalty or failed to pay tax. So, they were cautious; in Perthshire, the powerful Earl of Atholl hung back. The English, whose strategy had been to win the allegiance of the Scots, were now torn between retribution or leniency. On the whole, Robert Lilburne chose leniency – he rewarded loyalty with some rebates of tax and he offered protection against reprisals by Glencairn's men. But royalism was strong in Scotland and mild treatment of the Kirk by the English had not won over the religious factions. Tax was being collected to pay an invading English army – that fact enraged most Scots.

The Marquis of Argyll had not succeeded as a soldier, a politician or a kingmaker, and the war had cost him dearly. Heavily in debt and at bay in Inveraray Castle, he now fell out with his son as, in earlier times, he had fought with his own father. While Lord Lorne joined Glencairn, Argyll stayed in correspondence with Cromwell and his commanders. The marquis did not openly inform against his son but they were estranged, while his collaboration with the English left Argyll open to retribution when Cromwell was no more. Somehow, for all his power and wealth, Argyll could not win trust, leverage his position or even safeguard himself. Yet, during this vulnerable period, he lured his nephew Lewis Gordon, heir to the Huntly estates, to a meeting and bullied him into signing over his estates, giving Argyll a brief financial reprieve. Like all his manoeuvres, this later backfired.[15]

For the English, conditions in Scotland deteriorated throughout the summer of 1653. Neither of the kirk parties would co-operate. They lauded the Scottish people's bond with God and saw their constituency as the Scottish nation, whereas the Independents represented the elect of all three nations. English soldiers promoting their ideas in towns and villages antagonised the kirk leaders even more. Nor had rule under the English army made any improvement in Scotland's Treasury; instead it was bleeding it dry. The cost of the garrisons was over £250,000 in 1654, of which Scotland contributed only £45,000. The rest was made up from England or by accumulating debt.

Robert Lilburne had to meet the brunt of Glencairn's offensives on his own initiative. He received no help from London, indeed his letters to Cromwell seem to have gone unanswered. Scotland had a long and complex coastline, vulnerable to shipping from Ireland or the Netherlands, but Lilburne had few ships. He managed to get control of Lewis but the three ships he used in the western seas were subsequently wrecked.[16] Highland leaders who had fought the English before, many angered by sequestrations, were joined by men of the next generation such as Lorne and Montrose. Until Charles or Middleton sent reinforcements, Glencairn's forces relied on guerrilla tactics, took horses and cess (tax) due to the English and drove further into the territory they controlled. Colonel Lilburne considered the kirk a dangerous enemy and when a General Assembly was called in Edinburgh, he broke it up. The rising was slow to reach a climax because Middleton delayed in France. Nor did the Cromwellian regime send reinforcements. Without parliament they had no legitimate right to raise tax for more troops, the Dutch war was not finished and the council was not confident it could hold London.

Over all these issues loomed the problem of finance. In Ireland, the commissioners still had thousands of enemy combatants to transport abroad but lacked money to hire ships.[17] Supplies were slow to arrive by sea and exorbitantly expensive within the island. A little tax revenue was being raised in the east and some order was being brought to Ireland. The Cromwellian regime was a centralising and homogenising one, moulding three kingdoms into one Commonwealth, but Scotland was to retain its own laws, whereas English laws were introduced into Ireland for managing beggars, punishing bastardy, swearing and drunkenness, as well as relief for the poor.[18] Establishing order and initiating production was a challenge.

Ulster was a particular problem. It was here that plantation had been most intense, here that rebellion had broken out in 1641 and here that the links to Scotland were strong: the Ulster Scots shared beliefs with the Presbyterians, while Gaelic Catholics were related to the clans of the Western Isles. Glencairn sent an agent to Ulster, looking for support. The English appointed special commissioners to run Ulster but they reported to Fleetwood and Ludlow that 'there is no visible expedient to preserve these parts in safety, but by transplanting all popular Scots into some other part of Ireland'. The most dangerous of them should be moved immediately; their antagonism to the Catholic Irish might be useful elsewhere. Venables made a list of Ulster Scots who were to be transplanted from Ulster to Wexford.[19] The concept of moving people was now established, whether transported overseas or within the country. Confiscation and plantation were government policies, the rates of land to be paid for loans had been spelled out, categories of guilt had been legislated for, so all the commissioners needed was a clear blueprint to start settling men on the land.

Charles and Bridget Fleetwood had been in Ireland for seven months when Cromwell ejected the Rump. Fleetwood may have been a better soldier than Ireton but he was a less impressive head of government. He showed favour to religious factions and was severe when leniency would have won support. When parliament was dismissed, there was disquiet among the rulers in Ireland but the work of stamping out resistance and setting up government had to continue. Officials were frustrated that no orders had arrived; parts of the country had been more or less abandoned. 'It is humbly offered and presented to the Commissioners, on behalf of the small number of inhabitants now remaining in County Clare that the said county ... is now totally ruined and deserted,' it was claimed on 3 June.[20] The poor were 'swarming everywhere'; 'occasioned by the devastations of the country, and the habits of licentiousness and idleness, which the generality of the people have acquired in the time of Rebellion, insomuch that frequently some are found feeding on carrion and weeds, some starved in the highways, and many times poor children, who have lost their parents or [been] deserted by them, are found exposed to, and some of them fed upon by ravening wolves and other beasts and birds of prey'.[21] It was imperative to provide relief for them, put vagrants into houses of correction and get the land farmed. The officials were taking subscriptions from persons of substance to boost their funds.

Once parliament was dissolved, the council could expedite the Irish land settlement. A bill had been drawn up from which they could work. Henry Scobell had been clerk to the House of Commons and managed its paperwork. John Thurloe, a lawyer and capable administrator, had been appointed secretary to the Council of State in 1652 and retained after the dissolution. The two men had considerable expertise. On 5 May, Thurloe ordered Scobell to bring all the papers on Ireland, together with the bill which parliament had been debating, to the council.[22] Colonel Clark and Mr Scobell were to read through the papers and iron out any discrepancies, to avoid later legal challenges. On 17 May, a small committee was formed to finalise the text, so that the process of settlement could start. When the Nominated Assembly convened, it could pass the necessary legislation.

Lambert led the committee; the others were Colonel Phillip Jones, Colonel Bennett, Mr Scobell and Mr Thurloe. They were to confer with whoever they thought fit and then send draft instructions to the council.[23] Meanwhile, the council ordered that, in allotting land to soldiers in Ireland, those disbanded first should be first to receive their portion.[24] On 1 June, another committee was formed to scrutinise the Adventurers' claims. A week later, the council ordered that five Irish counties should be set out for the first allocations to the soldiers. It took the rest of June to agree the Adventurers' claims; then the soldiers' rights were tackled. In Ireland, the commissioners ordered

John Thurloe.

army officers to decide how and where disbanded soldiers 'may be fixed to plant'.[25] The Cromwellian regime was in a hurry to reduce troop numbers and get the men off their books.

The settlement was getting underway. In London, arrangements were made for the Adventurers to draw lots for their land, while officers in Ireland began a similar process with their disbanded men. By June, the ten-county scheme had been formalised; both Adventurers and soldiers were to be planted together in a band of ten counties stretching across eastern Ireland from sea to sea.[26] The formula for calculating the Adventurers' land was already fixed, but for the soldiers, only their arrears of pay had been calculated, not how much land that would buy. On the confiscation side of the account, qualifications determined who would lose land. Lists of men had been made when they surrendered but their fate rested on when they had fought, so clarifying whose land should be confiscated was a complex task. The government needed to know how much of it there was and where. This had to done quickly, so at the end of June the council ordered Fleetwood to commission a survey of all the rebels' land in the ten counties: Limerick, Tipperary, Waterford, King's and Queen's counties (Offaly and Laois), East and West Meath, Down, Antrim and Armagh; also any crown lands or those belonging to bishops, deans and chapters – all of which were now forfeit to the state. If anyone had a claim to mercy under the Act of 1652, they must register it with the commissioners within forty days of their land being surveyed. The instructions went out in the name of 'The Keepers of the Liberties of England, by Authority of Parliament'.[27]

The counties had been chosen, the accounts were being finalised, rebel land was being surveyed and those with claims to mercy were lodging them. So how were land allocations to be made? The Irish committee and the council made a radical decision. It was motivated by fear of further unrest and it ordered a forced movement of much of the Irish population. On 2 July, 'Further Instructions' were issued to Fleetwood and his fellows, setting out the plan. Anyone who had the 'right to Articles, or to favour or mercy', would not retain their own land but must remove to Connaught by 1 May 1654, where land would be allotted to them. Meanwhile, English or Protestant loyalists who had land in Connaught could move to the plantation counties and claim land there.[28] The details of this order had to be worked out on the ground in Ireland, which clearly would be extremely difficult, but the intention was clear – Irish Catholics with any claim to land were to move west of the Shannon, while incoming English Protestants would settle in Munster, Leinster and Ulster. The *Further Instructions* allowed for most of the Catholic population to be sent to Connaught if necessary.

The *Further Instructions* were signed by Thurloe 'at the Council of State in Whitehall' and despatched to catch the packet boat in Wales. At last, Cromwell and his council had given orders for Ireland; this was probably the issue they most wanted to settle before they relinquished control.[29] Certainly, they now handed the government of the Commonwealth over to other hands; the Nominated Assembly convened in London two days later. The *Further Instructions* was not a long document but it ordered a movement of people which would entirely alter the settlement pattern of Ireland, although carrying it out as envisaged proved impossible. When the order was sent, Cromwell had undiluted power as general of the army and the leading member of the council. He had been very careful to keep

Ireland under the control of his family and close associates; now the ten-county scheme and the transplantation were enacted when parliament had been dissolved and he ruled unopposed.

The Irish commissioners had discretion over implementing the instructions and the power to clear enormous amounts of land. On the other hand, only ten counties had been allocated for the Adventurers and soldiers. Until the land was surveyed, it was unclear whether the ten counties would provide enough. There were other debts to meet; the English Treasury had paid most of the cost of the Irish war and was owed £2.5 million.[30] There were bills outstanding to arms companies and suppliers, which also had to be met from confiscated land but, for these, other counties were set aside. The island contained roughly 20 million acres in English measure, of which the Adventurers claimed just over a million. Of the thirty-two counties, six were reserved for the Irish Catholics. There were 35,000 soldiers expecting to receive land. Difficult calculations still lay ahead.

11

Rule by the Saints

At last, Cromwell had assembled a government of the godly. On 4 July 1653, the chosen representatives gathered in the privy council's old chamber in Whitehall Palace. The room was not large and contained the table once used by the king's councillors, so when 140 members crowded in on a warm July day, it was soon stuffy. Cromwell stood by the window with 'as many of the officers of the army as the room could well contain' clustered near him.[1] He said he would speak briefly, as he and the officers had drawn up an 'Instrument' which would enlarge on the members' duties. In fact, Cromwell spoke for about two hours. He seemed glad to hand the burden of government over to the Nominated Assembly; he certainly wept freely.[2]

He reminded the members of the great successes which God had given the army 'and in civil matters too. Bringing of offenders to justice and the greatest of them. Bringing of the state of this Government to the name of a Commonwealth. Searching and sifting of all persons and places. The king removed, and brought to justice; and many great ones with him. The House of Peers laid aside. The House of Commons itself, the representative of the people of England, sifted, winnowed, and brought to a handful; as you very well remember.'[3] He then rehearsed why he had closed down the Rump – its failure to enact reform and its intention to perpetuate itself by holding recruiter elections only.

His text from scripture was 'Judah yet ruled with God, and is faithful with the Saints'. For 'the Saints' was clearly how Cromwell saw the new assembly, a meeting called by God. 'And you are called to be faithful with Saints who have been somewhat instrumental to your call.' He told them, 'I confess I never looked to see such a day as this, when Jesus Christ should be so owned as He is, at this day and in this work.'

The millenarian in Cromwell asked: 'And why should we be afraid to say or think, that this may be the door to usher-in the things that God has promised, which have been prophesied of; which he has set the hearts of His people to wait for and expect?'[4]

He told them that the army in all three nations consented to the assembly and to their authority; then he produced a document appointing them as the Supreme Authority of the Commonwealth. Their sitting must end by 3 November 1654, and three months before their dissolution they were to choose others to succeed them who should not sit longer than a twelvemonth and must decide on their successors.

Subsequently, the Assembly met in St Stephens Chapel, where the Commons used to gather.[5] To confirm their status, they voted to call themselves a parliament, chose Francis Rous as speaker and invited Cromwell, Harrison, Desborough and Tomlinson to sit as members. They decided on a Council of State containing thirty-one members, which included Cromwell.

In terms of reform, the Nominated Parliament showed considerable promise, but among the members were religious radicals with links to millenarian congregations who won the assembly the name of Barebones, after one of its members, a London councillor and lay preacher called Praise-God Barebones. He was not an extremist but his name conjured up the growing exhilaration of the wilder Independent congregations. During the autumn of 1653, their voices became more excited and insistent, especially in London where St Anne's Blackfriars held Monday prayer meetings led by Christopher Feake. He was an organiser, while others were more incendiary. Similar views were heard among the Fifth Monarchists in parliament and Thomas Harrison's faction in the army. Over the life of the Barebones parliament, these voices reached a crescendo and greatly contributed to its downfall. Many members were from gentry backgrounds and initially its aims were not radical; its first *Declaration* promised to be 'tender of the lives, estates, liberties, just rights and properties of all others as we are of ourselves and posterity, whom we expect still to be governed by successive parliaments'. But its religious hopes were high: 'Many, if not all of the people of God in all the world, are in a more than usual expectation of some great and strange changes coming on the world, which we believe can hardly be paralel'd with any times ... that in peace and joy we may all wait, expect and long for his glorious coming, who is king of kings, and Lord of Lords, our hope and righteousness.'[6]

For the Fifth Monarchists, being tender of estates was tepid stuff. The most militant expected the removal of the existing law and church as 'out-works of Babylon'. Others wanted to destroy the army which prevented 'true monarchy', and many opposed the assessment.[7] They had both power and ambition: councillors could purge local officials and some radicals talked of bringing in God's kingdom by violence and of attacks on European states.[8] By organising, the radicals could achieve more influence than their modest numbers in the House suggested.

Which group would be uppermost in the Assembly, diligent reformers or millenarian idealists? Cromwell, who havered between conservative and millenarian, had high hopes. The Nominated Assembly got off to a busy start and during its short life it passed thirty pieces of legislation. As Cromwell and the officers had hoped, its immediate concerns were tithes, the relief of poverty, advancement of learning and law reform. Committees were set up and legislation prepared. Cromwell seems never to have sat in Barebones. Feeling squeamish about the dissolution of the Rump and having assembled a new parliament, he stood back. Nonetheless he retained his power. Now that he was a famous figure, ambassadors visited him and newsbooks reported on his activities, while he lived and worked at the centre of the army's quarters in London.

His other erstwhile colleagues, the Commonwealthsmen, had dispersed. Vane, Sidney, Neville, Marten and the group of about twenty MPs who had formed the republican core of the Rump and argued for its sovereignty had not been called to Barebones or had not accepted. Vane retired to the country for religious contemplation, Neville was banned from London by Cromwell and Marten was hounded by creditors. The republicans had lost power and the army had chosen others among the elect. Barebones was the highest expression of the Puritan revolution, with its aspiration for godly rule and its hopes for the coming of Christ's kingdom.

The mace was found – it had been stored in Colonel Worsley's house – and with its return the parliament's traditions and procedures were reinstated; debates began and committees set to work. First they tackled tithes, as members wanted a paid ministry but also to relieve burdens on the poor. Tithes were supposed to be one-tenth of produce and rural people often paid them in kind. Property owners would block their abolition but paying ministers another way was difficult, so the tithes problem was sent to a committee for investigation. Barebones was diligent, much more so than its predecessor; attendance was high in those first weeks and the assembly sat six days a week, whereas the Rump sometimes only managed four mornings. Nor were the members inexperienced: eighteen had sat in the Rump and many had served in local government. Yet the parliament only lasted for five of its expected eighteen months. Part of the problem was the otherworldliness of the religious fringe, but the issues they tried to solve were difficult and even the more experienced Rump had struggled with them. The funding of government was still a constant threat, with military bills coming in regularly for settlement. Like the Rump, Barebones held all the power but had no permanent executive or head of state. They acquired a reputation for incompetence but, all things considered, made some important decisions. Fatefully, it was Barebones which finally passed the legislation for the land settlement in Ireland.

They met against a background of continuing warfare. Ireland was in horrible post-conflict dearth, but in Scotland armed insurrection against the English was increasing, while at sea the naval contest against the Dutch was building up to a climax. Peace had not come to the Commonwealth. At home, public opinion was stirred up when John Lilburne came into court at the Old Bailey on 13 July, charged with treason. For four days, while his trial lasted, there were crowds of several thousand, among whom were many women who always appeared when Lilburne was performing, and meanwhile, pamphlets by Lilburne and his supporters argued his case. The trial created great excitement.[9] A newsbook asked: 'And what, shall then honest John Lilburne die? Three score thousand will know the reason why.'[10] The Rump's heavy-handed actions and the doubtful nature of the government were pitted against Lilburne's popularity. However, due process of law was being observed. The jury took its own line and refused to convict him 'of any crime worthy of death', so he was removed to the Tower 'for the peace of this nation', and the public uproar subsided.[11]

The new parliament had been sitting for almost a month when the Dutch war reached its climax. Negotiations with the Netherlands had broken down because England's demands were high but the Dutch ambassadors returned to London early in July, when they met new officials from Barebones, whose conditions were just as exacting. Cromwell was still dreaming of a union of the two Protestant nations but the Dutch thought that restrictive and refused to consider it.

On 31 July, Admiral Tromp tried to break Monck's blockade of the Dutch ports, which led to a major naval engagement off the Texel. It was a punishing encounter, in which Tromp himself was killed. Monck ordered all enemy ships sunk or burned, as guarding them would weaken his fleet. The Dutch lost twenty-six ships to England's two, while the loss of men was in a similar proportion. It was a resounding victory for England but they had to abandon the blockade and sail for home ports, so extensive was the damage. The Fifth Monarchists in Barebones railed against the Netherlands for its ambitions in wealth and trade but negotiations continued. In September a perpetual Protestant military alliance was suggested, with free trade, shared fisheries and possibly including France. In their enthusiasm, the English suggested a partition of the whole globe, with Asia for the Dutch and America for England. The Dutch commissioners understandably thought this scheme dangerously ambitious.

Reality dawned in October when unpaid sailors mutinied. One party surged into Whitehall where the men were only checked by the intervention of Monck and Cromwell. When the seamen returned the following day, they were stopped by infantry, then checked by cavalry. One ringleader was hanged, another flogged, but a proclamation was issued promising pay.

The possibility of a Dutch alliance hurried the English into decisions over their other European relationships. France, Spain and Portugal were now exploring alliances with the Commonwealth, in either trade or defence. But England's revolutionary government was inexperienced at diplomacy and the frequent government upheavals played out badly. London became notorious for its gauche reception of foreign delegations. Men of modest status were now hosting aristocratic professionals who were accustomed to royal audiences. The Commonwealth prepared reception rooms decorated with some of the king's pictures and furnishings, but the English officials caused confusion and offence with their plain manners and lack of protocol. The Puritan regime had to shed its wilder ideals and learn new skills but the increasing volume of millenarian rant made the English government seem extreme.

Charles Fleetwood had been elected to the Council of State but it was an honorary position as he remained in Ireland. Under him, the business of disbanding the troops and awarding Irish land was beginning. The Boyles were once more ascendant and Lord Broghill became a commissioner for the land settlement. His brother Richard, Earl of Cork had recently regained his estate and owned Cork House, the family's Dublin residence, where the Boyles stayed when in the capital but which increasingly was used for government business; Broghill held meetings of the transplantation and trade committee there.[12] Having fought for king, parliament and under Cromwell, Broghill continued his skilful navigation of changing political water and his career prospered.

The settlement was getting underway. In July, work began on the survey to make inventories of forfeited land.[13] Soldiers leaving the army were given debentures showing what they were owed. The Adventurers had begun organising themselves to draw lots in June although the actual land could not be allocated until it was surveyed and legislation was passed. This was to be an enormous transfer of property and it was important to get the legal details correct. Over a decade had passed since the Adventurers had put up funds; since then, some had died and some had sold their debentures, so the claims of heirs and purchasers had to be confirmed. Money had been raised by several Acts, with doubling and special rights, so checking all the calculations took time.

At the same time, the Catholic Irish had to make their claims to property. Under the *Further Instructions* of 2 July, 'for the better security of all those parts of Ireland which are now intended to be planted with English and Protestants, and to the end that all persons in Ireland who have right to articles, or to any favour or mercy held forth by any of the qualifications', those people were ordered to transplant to Connaught by 1 May 1654.[14] Some part of their estate might be exchanged for land there but they must now gather their evidence and make their claims. Then the transplantation could begin.

It was late September before the Nominated Parliament brought forward what was called the Act for the speedy and effectual Satisfaction of the Adventurers for lands in Ireland, and of the Arrears due to the Soldiery there, and of other Publique Debt, and for the Encouragement of Protestants to plant and inhabit Ireland. The purpose of the Act was to pay the soldiers and Adventurers the land owed to them; it confirmed the transplantation to Connaught and formally instigated the ten-county scheme. The Catholic Irish were to be removed to an area bounded by water, which would restrain them. Even in Connaught, they were not permitted to live in any port, town or garrison nor on a strip of land adjoining the River Shannon, but if they settled peacefully they 'shall be pardoned of offences' (except murder) and 'shall be no more molested', though the pardon did not extend to priests, indicating how dangerous they were thought to be.[15] Furthermore, none could bear arms.

For the Irish, the Cromwellian settlement was a gross injustice, since they were guilty unless they could prove their innocence, and a tragedy as they lost their homes and property. It had a catastrophic effect on the social fabric of Ireland as all the family links, traditions and obligations of an old society were torn apart. But for some of the English officials, the total reorganisation of a nation offered a glimpse of a bright future. They believed that populations could be re-designed, numbered and sorted. Ireland was finally to be anglicised and civilised according to English Puritan standards, the wild Irish could be contained on a moated province where they could not rebel or delay development. Behind the religious ideals of the 1650s, scientific concepts were emerging with which Puritanism had a strange resonance – that nature could be counted and harnessed, that mankind was perfectible and that energetic endeavour brought both spiritual purity and economic development. In particular, the scientists in the Hartlib Circle, a European network of learned individuals centred on Samuel Hartlib, took a great interest in Ireland, for which they had utopian plans.[16]

First, however, the Irish land settlement had to be enforced. The Act was passed in London and proclaimed in Dublin. The surveyors completed the Gross survey, which was a crude first attempt. On 16 December, the Commissioners in Ireland wrote to London to say there would not be enough land. The 'total acreage returned in the surveys of the ten counties appointed for the satisfaction of the Adventurers and Soldiers', with Co. Louth to top it up if necessary, added up to 2,148,403 acres.[17] The Adventurers had invested £356,874 and therefore claimed just over 1 million acres. That meant the soldiers must be satisfied with 1.15 million acres.[18] However, the latter were owed £1.5 million and were supposed to be paid at the same rate as the Adventurers. It now looked as though they would get far less land for every pound they were owed, probably a third of the Adventurers' rate.[19] On top of that, the Irish administration had debts of £200,000. There was more forfeited land, about 500,000 acres, but it had been reserved for government use.

The army officers in Ireland had already flagged up this problem. In November, under pressure, they agreed to a rate for the soldiers which was considerably less than that of the Adventurers, while attention turned to the quality of the land: clearly good arable land was more valuable than bog. The soldiers had now been in Ireland for several years; they wanted to stay near their garrisons and friends. For those stationed in Cork city, the government chose several baronies east of the city and it was here that soldiers were first allocated plots.[20] Throughout the early months of 1654, the troops who had subjugated Ireland moved into the farmhouses, repaired the damaged buildings and began to farm their allotted acres.

The Irish population, some of whom were great landowners, some of whom were small proprietors and some labourers, reacted in different ways. Many of the great landowners had already left the country, men like Ormond, Inchiquin and Clanricarde. Some attempted to fight confiscation by legal means or personal contacts. Others accepted confiscation of their family estate and acquiesced to transportation, calculating this was their best hope of retaining property somewhere. Others stayed where they were and waited to see how the English might deal with them, developing ways of thwarting the conquerors by subtle means. Some sold what they had retained to the new capitalists emerging in rural Ireland.

It was beyond the strength of the Irish to resist any further, but the Scots could still fight back. The Scottish armies had not been sent overseas and although Scotland was depleted, there are not the descriptions of depopulation and waste that were reported from Ireland. Throughout the autumn of 1653, Glencairn's men became more daring, attacking as far south as Falkland in Fife. Sir Archibald Johnston of Wariston's house outside Edinburgh was plundered, in December parties of armed men were roving in Dumfriesshire and Galloway, and horses were even seized near Berwick. Robert Lilburne, many of whose officers had left their posts and gone south, offered concessions to the Scots while demanding reinforcements from England but none would be sent until peace was made with the Netherlands. Without support and with the forces against him strengthening, Lilburne hung on through the winter and well into spring.

Further south, negotiations with the Netherlands dragged on. Cromwell led the English delegation who were still demanding stringent terms. He had dropped his hopes of union in favour of a defence treaty and free trade, but was still demanding supremacy in the British Seas – Dutch ships must lower their flags in deference and pay for fishing. Also, the young Prince of Orange must be barred from any public office. The Dutch rejected these terms and prepared to leave London. It was February 1654 before they reconvened, by which point the government of England had changed once more because the Nominated Assembly, despite working diligently throughout the autumn and early winter, ran up against the same army dissatisfaction which had proved fatal to the Rump.

The Nominated Assembly was expected to tackle those reforms which the Rump had neglected and it came close to achieving its aims, but it faced similar problems to its predecessor. Fundamentally, social reform challenged the interests of lawyers and property owners who were still influential in parliament, the army and the City of London. The members of Barebones probably lacked diplomatic skills and their impatience led to blunt decisions, where more nuanced ones might have worked. They alarmed English property owners, of whom Oliver Cromwell was the most prominent. But having called Barebones into being, he was careful about not interfering with it. He sat on the Council of State and negotiated with foreign representatives, but he did not meddle with the assembly; he left that to others, as he had during Pride's Purge.

The Nominated Assembly was having a side effect – it was arousing royalist activity. The Rump had had some legitimacy, whereas the new assembly had been nominated by the army. In the public mind, Cromwell had created Barebones. Those who had given the Rump the benefit of the doubt now began to look to the legitimate king. For the Fifth Monarchists, however, Barebones was wasting time; they wanted to be guided by the Bible and establish Mosaic law. For them, modest reforms of law and tithes were derisory. It was not long before chasms of belief split the assembly, as moderate Puritan gentlemen tried to improve the law and prison system while radicals pushed for God's elect to rule and the property of the ungodly to be confiscated. They wanted to promote trade and did not condemn usury but they planned to upset the social order and ignore elections. Millenarian belief was a spectrum but the extreme position was deeply shocking to English public opinion. Those who had grudgingly accepted the Commonwealth were horrified by Barebones.

As autumn became winter, attendance in parliament fell, leaving the radicals dominant. They set up a committee to reform law by harmonising it with the law of God, looking to Massachusetts for their example. Common law, on which so many English liberties had been built, looked threatened. By late August, Cromwell was worried about his parliamentary creation. A Fifth Monarchist prophetess named Anna Trapnel, who was a compelling preacher and public performer, was denigrating the General while Thomas Harrison, who had collaborated with Cromwell in assembling Barebones, now drew away from him. Cromwell was in a bind because if he rejected the godly assembly he would lose Harrison's faction, whereas moderate opinion everywhere blamed him for the wild direction the country was taking.

Scotland was riven with factions and rivalries but the one thing which united the Scots was their loathing of English occupation and a determination to eject the English army. Ireland, on the other hand, was in a more complex position. Now in garrisons with leisure time, the soldiers were developing divisive religious opinions, some leaning Baptist while others took up more radical Quaker ideas. Among Irish landowners, the Old Protestants were coming together to protect their property and position. Before the war they had gained power, and now that Catholicism was overcome they hoped to take official roles, but large numbers of new planters were moving in who might become influential. To the native Irish population, England's intention to dispossess and marginalise them had become shockingly clear. Some resisted eviction as feelings of despair grew into intense hatred for the Puritan regime and increasing bitterness at the curse which Oliver Cromwell had laid on Ireland. The numbers of tories and their attacks still plagued the Irish government.

In England, opposition to Cromwell grew. On 14 September, John Lilburne's followers printed a broadside accusing the General of high treason, not for dissolving the Rump but for calling a new parliament without holding elections. There was strong public feeling against the Fifth Monarchists too – one of their preachers was attacked by apprentice boys in St Paul's Cathedral.[21] In foreign affairs, at least, Cromwell's strategy looked promising: Bulstrode Whitelocke had been sent to Sweden to negotiate a treaty with Queen Cristina, and the council chosen in November favoured peace with the Dutch. In the assembly, however, the radicals were gaining ascendancy. At Blackfriars, preachers predicted the downfall of 'parliament, army, Council of State, and all now in power'.[22] Radicals talked of abolishing English law and substituting a simple form based on the law of Moses, while instead of reforming Chancery, Barebones planned to abolish it. Worried about extremism among juries, moderate MPs passed a bill for a new High Court of Justice to bypass them; but conservative opinion was increasingly alarmed.

Among Cromwell's officers, the idea of a written constitution came back into play. They looked at the Heads of Proposals and the Agreement of the People. Those documents had been designed to constrain the king; now the officers realised that parliament too could become tyrannical without a balance of power. A new formula was needed and this time it was John Lambert who set out to create it. Harrison and Cromwell were increasingly at odds, but the Commonwealth could not afford splits in government when royalist insurrection was growing in Scotland

and English royalists might take up arms once more. Unknown to them, that November a secret committee calling itself the Sealed Knot was formed to organise royalist conspiracy in England. The army was right to be alarmed about security.

Among the Fifth Monarchists, the urgency of their vision was growing. There was talk of deposing Cromwell as head of the army and installing Harrison. Cromwell called the most virulent preachers to a meeting with the Council of State and warned them against giving succour to enemies of the Commonwealth, but Feake retorted by accusing Cromwell of 'assuming exorbitant power'.[23] The preachers said their words were inspired by the Holy Spirit and could not be repressed. They were dismissed but not quelled.

Lambert and his colleagues were working on a new constitution and seem to have consulted Cromwell, but the General was cautious; he did not want to plot his own ascendancy to power. Lambert saw that parliament could not rule alone and took up the old formula of king, lords and commons while using new institutions. While the officers plotted, parliament was taking bold decisions. In November, they voted to abolish tithes and ordered a bill to be drafted but then moderated their proposal and failed to pass it. The godly were aggrieved that no provision was made for ministers, and the radicals that tithes continued. This was an important issue among the crescendo of problems in Barebones which brought the Nominated Assembly to a premature end.

On 12 December, following an arranged plan, the moderates arrived early to take their seats. They chose a Monday, when many extremists were at the Blackfriars prayer meeting. One by one, the moderates got up to denounce the radicals for threatening the church by rejecting the tithe bill, for threatening to discontinue the assessment which supported the army, for undermining the law by trying to abolish Chancery and proposing an entirely new body of law, and for threatening property by abolishing patrons' right to tithes. Speaker Rous was in on the plan and only allowed moderates to speak, who proposed that the parliament should abdicate. Speaker Rous left the chamber with the moderates, which effectively closed the session. Once more, soldiers arrived to eject the disgruntled members who remained. Rous led his group to Whitehall Palace where they signed a document resigning their power back to Cromwell, who had given it to them. Cromwell claimed to know nothing of this scheme beforehand, which may be true – Lambert had probably kept the details from him. Cromwell did, however, know the main points of the new constitution which was now promoted.

Old London Reconstructed: The Palace of Whitehall *c.* 1680.

London seems to have received the dissolution of Barebones with relief, but Blackfriars resounded with Feake's bitterness and the preachers there railed against Cromwell and the army. Other sects reacted calmly: the Baptist leaders told their congregations not to resist the collapse of the Nominated Assembly since it had threatened to bring government itself into disrepute.

Charles I had claimed that he had been appointed by the will of God. The radicals of Barebones said something similar – that it was God's will that the Saints should rule. Equally, the army claimed that its victories showed God's providence and gave it the right to power. The Independent sects saw government as deriving immediately from God's written word. Despite the execution of the king and the efforts of the republicans, power was still seen as emanating directly from God. However, England had a well-developed body of law and parliamentary tradition. It was this, and the previous attempts at a written settlement, that the more worldly army officers considered when they drew up a new document by which the country should be governed. Experiment had shown that to settle the three nations and achieve stable government, a structure would have to be created with a head of state, a strong executive and an orderly succession of parliaments.

It was under the Instrument of Government, on 16 December 1653, that General Oliver Cromwell was at last officially installed as head of state.

12

The Protectorate in England, Scotland and Ireland

Since 1647, hostile commentators had accused Oliver Cromwell of being ambitious for supreme office, so when he was installed as Lord Protector of England, Scotland and Ireland, it confirmed their long-held suspicions. Cromwell had certainly mused about becoming king or some similar position, but with his customary skill and perhaps genuine modesty he had held back while others promoted him. Whatever the suspicions of his detractors, the creation of the Protectorate was a genuine attempt to solve the constitutional puzzle after various experiments had failed. Unfortunately, many important groups were already enraged by the upheavals of the previous years. Pride's Purge, the execution of the king, the dissolution of the Rump parliament, followed by the Nominated Assembly and its closure had alienated parliamentarians, royalists, Commonwealthsmen, Levellers and radical Puritans. When the army wrote a new constitution and named its general as head of state, the worst fears of many were confirmed – this was unashamedly rule by the sword.

On the other hand, the Protectorate used tried and tested forms which were now modernised and improved. Power was to lie in a single person and parliament. The Protector had powers not unlike those of monarchs but he shared legislative power with parliament and executive power with his council, who were initially chosen for him and whose agreement he needed for action, so his power was contained. Parliaments must be called every three years and sit for a minimum of five months; elections would be standardised, with redrawn constituencies and a uniform property qualification for voters. Catholics could neither vote nor sit in parliament, nor could any Irish rebel, and those who had fought against parliament were banned for four parliaments. There were to be four hundred members for England and Wales, with thirty each for Scotland and Ireland. Oliver Cromwell was appointed Lord Protector for life, and when he died his council would choose his successor. Until parliament was called, Cromwell and his council had full control of the state. The official style changed: orders and appointments once issued by the crown and since 1649 by the keepers of the liberty of England would now go out in the name of the Lord Protector.

The transition to the new scheme had to be swift lest pockets of dissatisfaction coalesce. Cromwell was installed as Lord Protector only four days after the Nominated Assembly resigned. Westminster Hall, with its vast space and hammerbeam roof, had been used for Charles I's trial and was chosen for Cromwell's inauguration. The Lord Protector wore a plain black suit and cloak to take his oath of office, although, daringly, his hat had a broad gold band. The dignitaries who installed him were the Lord Mayor and Aldermen of London in their scarlet robes, the judges and law officers, and his army, all of whom formed the procession from Chancery Court to Westminster. The most senior surrounded his chair as the Lord Mayor offered him the Great Seal, the sword of state and the cap of maintenance – the old royal symbols. After the ceremony, the officials retired to the Banqueting Hall until salvoes of shot proclaimed the ceremonies finished. From now on, Cromwell signed documents as Oliver Protector or Oliver P; he was styled His Highness the Lord Protector.

For his inauguration, the streets were lined with soldiers. Observers say the crowds were silent and that it was only the troops or members of Cromwell's party who applauded the new head of state.[1] (A month or so later, when the Lord Protector was invited to a sumptuous banquet in the City, members of the City companies sat on benches lining his route. Cromwell was dressed in civilian clothes, a pale suit embroidered with gold, and repeatedly doffed his hat to them – but there was no response.) However his government turned out, he was a military leader installed not by heredity or election but by his army. He would have to work hard to overcome the resentment this aroused.

But if some were enraged by this new form of government, others were gratified, hopeful or peaceably resigned. Some thought that Cromwell had played his cards very cleverly. Ambassadors thought Londoners pleased to see the last of Barebones, the University of Oxford sent flowery congratulations and the army in Scotland expressed themselves relieved that after all its 'shakings' the state had been given firm direction. The Protector and his council had control of the armed forces and management of foreign policy, a parliament was required to meet by 3 September 1654, funds had been provided for a standing army of 30,000 men and any taxation beyond that required, as always, the consent of parliament. The new arrangement was a balanced one and it gave time to shape public opinion before elections were held. It confirmed in power Cromwell and his officers, relatives and colleagues who had become the inheritors of the revolution but who were unlikely to really disturb the social order. His council was half military and half civilian, with Worsley and Pickering joined by Anthony Ashley Cooper, who would be influential long after Cromwell's reign. There was bound to be resistance to the Protector's rule, but if stability could be achieved, men of property and the law, merchants, artisans and apprentices might all support the new order.

The radical sects and especially the Fifth Monarchists were too incensed to be mollified. They were a challenge that government would have to meet. Christopher Feake castigated Cromwell as the 'most dissemblingest perjured villain in the world' and identified him as the Little Horn or Antichrist of Daniel's prophecy. Vavasour Powell asked whether 'the Lord would have Oliver Cromwell or Jesus Christ to reign over us'. Feake and Powell were put in custody for four nights and released under orders to offend no more. When they did, they were imprisoned at Windsor Castle. Thomas Harrison was a more difficult problem. Having been the driving force behind Barebones, when asked to support the Protectorate he refused and was stripped of his army commission.[2] He would be imprisoned several times over the coming years and did not long outlive Cromwell.

Already, the Puritan revolution was having to limit its toleration of the sects. The Protectorate needed to protect itself, but as the law stood treason was defined as attacks on parliament, so Cromwell and his council acted swiftly to redefine it, issuing an ordinance which made any questioning of the Protector's position treason. The preachers could have been taken to court but were not, as a trial would inevitably lead to execution, igniting more fury. Sent home or put in custody, the religious extremists were quelled but not extinguished.[3]

The Rump had failed to tackle reform, while Barebones had been more energetic but too blunt and split to succeed. Would the Protectorate do better – in religious policy, in law reform, in managing the state's finance – and would it achieve the godly reformation of society on which its Puritan and military backers were determined? It actually spent considerable time managing itself, as its legitimacy was constantly questioned. It also had military challenges to meet, but its greatest impact was on religious policy.

The Protectorate government was certainly active. Its first parliament was not called for nine months but before then, the Protector and council issued eighty-two ordinances which acted as laws until parliament met. After that, the Protector's powers would be curtailed; he could delay legislation but not prevent it. Oaths of office were removed, cockfighting banned and Chancery modified, and a state church was to be maintained but attendance would not be compulsory. For the first time the three nations would have a single government, and for Scotland an ordinance of union was issued (although legislation was slow to follow), though nothing of the sort was forthcoming in Ireland.[4] This meant Scotland had free trade with England but Irish imports still paid customs, probably because Ireland was a competitor in agricultural goods, whereas Scotland was not. The Scottish monarchy and parliament were abolished, while feudal dues were removed. In the first months of the Protectorate, the hopes of the Cromwellians for a single vigorous government, modern and reforming, seemed likely to be rewarded.

As the English digested the latest eruption in government, news of the Protectorate spread to the north, into Scotland and west to Ireland. Public opinion was important but for Cromwell, the reaction of his own army was crucial, both officers and men. Ludlow was furious:

> The perfidious Cromwell having forgot his most solemn professions and former vows, as well as the blood and treasure that had been spent in this contest, thought it high time to take off the masque, and resolved to sacrifice all our victories and deliverances to his pride and ambition, under colour of taking upon him the office as it were of a High Constable, in order to keep the peace of the nation, and to restrain men from cutting one another's throats.[5]

Other army officers saw promise in the new regime. Nineteen men wrote from Limerick to 'Protector Oliver Cromwell' on 25 December to beg for greater efforts to promulgate the gospel in Ireland. 'Seeing that the Lord Jesus, whose right it is to rule nations, hath providentially made choice of you for his deputy under him', they hoped that Cromwell would strive to 'increase the Lord's kingdom by all means possible'.

'We, whom God hath brought out of a land of much light into a land of thick darkness, cannot but lament and bewail unto your highness the gross and great darkness, that the poor people of this land are under,' they complained. 'We have observed in our own experience, that where God hath sent among us godly, painful and able ministers, he hath made their ministry successful.'[6]

The officers thought the Irish would undergo a religious awakening if only inspirational preachers could arouse them. Unlike Ludlow, who was a committed republican and thought Cromwell a usurper, many officers were more concerned about the religious policies of government than its legal basis. Some were unsure. In January 1654, Colonel John Jones, one of the Irish commissioners, wrote to Phillip Jones in Wales that 'the suddenness of the late change, with the occasion and somewhat of the formality of it, doth amuse many previous saints in this land' – they were waiting to see how it turned out, whether the new government produced 'the fruits of Righteousness'. He warned his friend about seductions of power, urging him to 'guird your lynes with the strength of Christ' for 'we are here listening very narrowly what kinds of persons you call to your councell', whether they were 'sober zealous Christians' or 'carnall and persecuting spirits'.[7]

For a government resting on insecure foundations, intelligence was essential. Who was a serious threat and how capable were they of causing harm? John Thurloe, secretary to the council, became head of security and proved highly effective at hiring agents and intercepting communications. The Cromwellian Protectorate worked hard at keeping the respect of the powerful London merchants and the urban businesspeople. However, most people were rural and winning their confidence was harder, as they were conservative and among them was the settled core of royalist resistance. Many of the gentry had suffered fines and confiscation, but other rural dwellers were ambivalent about the changes, unsure how it might affect their lives.

The committed Levellers were a different problem, as they had intellectual arguments and a public profile. Crushed at Burford, their leaders regularly imprisoned, they nonetheless had a groundswell of support in London and among the troops. Now that the army officers and their colleagues ruled, the Levellers lost any lingering hope of representative government and some Leveller sympathisers were already plotting with royalists against the Protectorate. Edward Sexby, for example, had been a trooper in the New Model Army, then governor of Portland, and was known for his courage and ability. The Rump had employed him as an envoy to the Prince of Condé, but once Cromwell became Lord Protector Sexby turned his back on the regime. Soon he was communicating with disaffected republicans and not long afterwards he contacted the royalists. If the Protectorate was to survive, it was essential to stay vigilant over these shifting groups of adversaries.

In Scotland, news of the change of government was greeted with relief by Colonel Robert Lilburne, who was desperate for supplies. He blamed their lack on 'the late inconsistency in the Parliament'.[8] Conditions in Scotland made it impossible to collect the assessment; in fact Lilburne thought stronger hands than his own were needed. In January 1654, he was told that Monck would come north when he could be spared – agreement had been reached with the Dutch, but until a treaty was signed Monck was needed for the war at sea.

In February, a new protagonist came ashore in Scotland. Charles realised he would receive no funding from the Netherlands and ordered John Middleton to wait no longer but sail for Scotland. Glencairn could not prevent the incessant squabbling of his chiefs and lairds but Middleton might get control of them. He arrived at Tarbatness in the Moray Firth and met the royalist troops at nearby Dornoch. Middleton lacked the glamour of Montrose but he had the king's commission, so despite continued dissension among his officers, he took command.

The Protectorate did not send Robert Lilburne the funds he needed – when Monck arrived in April there was only £500 in their treasury.[9] Lilburne wrote to Lambert, 'Having bin a pure drudge almost these 4 yeares in Scotland, I should bee glad to know how his Highnesse intends to dispose of me.'[10] He was keen to leave but had to make sure the authorities appreciated his efforts. To the Protector he sent reports of his forces' minor successes, 'as the hand of God seems to appear as much for us against this wicked people, I doubt nott butt with the blessing of God and little more assistance an happy end may be brought to these troubles ... I heare General Monck is at Berwick this night, to whom I shall be readie to deliver the keyes of my Government.'[11] With relief, Lilburne handed over command. Monck had influence with Cromwell and once he arrived in Scotland military supplies were gradually provided, along with larger sums of money.

Monck was now head of both army and government in Scotland. The soldiers' pay was in arrears and Monck reckoned he would need £33,000 by the end of June. Patriotic spirit in Scotland was for King Charles and passionately against the English invaders but Monck reasoned that the lure of security might win some over. On 4 May, Edinburgh gave a banquet for him, a good opportunity to make the position clear. Two proclamations were read, one announcing the Protectorate and the other the union of Scotland with England and Ireland, including the terms.[12] The Protectorate had listened to Robert Lilburne; there would be clemency over confiscations and some softening towards the gentry, whose support the government needed. By the Act of Pardon and Grace, the Scots at last learned who would be punished and who pardoned. Twenty-four nobles lost their large estates and another seventy-three gentry were fined.[13] This was modest by comparison with England where 780 people had by now lost their land. The remainder of the Scottish people were pardoned, except those currently in rebellion, but Monck had the power to pardon those who surrendered, hoping to end the war quickly that way – the same policy attempted by Ireton in Ireland.[14]

Crown and noble lands would be forfeit but Argyll, having given assurances to the English, kept his vast territory. The confiscated land was used to reward army officers for their service and pay government grants, but first government wanted dependents of the owners to have a modest income and any debts attached to the land settled.[15] Aristocratic royalists were dispossessed, army commanders rewarded and the plain people absolved – that was the outline of the Scottish confiscation policy.

Some courts were working and cess was collected with the help of the army but, despite the commissioners' earlier efforts, civil government had not been properly reinstated in Scotland. Monck's first task was to quell the rising in the Highlands. A professional soldier for three decades, he had been imprisoned and changed sides but remained faithful to the Commonwealth having sworn an oath. In difficult circumstances in Ulster, he had developed more devious and tactical methods than he had used before. Promoted by Cromwell, who had a high opinion of him, Monck at last found himself in a winning army under an exceptional general and repaid that trust, working tirelessly under Cromwell in whatever campaign he was assigned.[16] Now, returning north to crush the rising, Monck became the 'hammer of the Scots'. He knew the guerrilla tactics of the Irish and had a strategy for countering similar attacks in Scotland. Lilburne had tried to seal off the Highlands but Monck had more resources and could penetrate the hill country. He sent his troops, with packhorses and food, in columns up the valleys and mountain passes, burning crops and killing cattle. Mercilessly, the English chased the Scots up through the glens and by autumn many were surrendering.

Middleton had come ashore in February, three months before Monck took charge, but when he arrived Glencairn's rising was already losing its vigour. Once Monck arrived in Scotland, he took his troops out to meet the royalists, consulting with Argyll on his way and then burning the land of the MacDonalds, Camerons and MacKenzies. Colonel Morgan was sent on to intercept Middleton himself; he caught up with the royalists at Dalnaspidal and in the ensuing engagement routed them. Middleton escaped to Caithness where he spent the winter, leaving Scotland the following spring. Monck had fulfilled his commission, flushing out the royalists and suppressing Highland rebellion; now the English could establish government in Scotland on their own terms. They identified able Scotsmen who would work with them and set about the task.

Monck's military campaign against the Highland lords had been relentless but he wanted to win the goodwill of the Scottish labourers and poor people. Most importantly, if the English could control the kirk and universities, their influence on educated opinion might bear fruit. Two years earlier, the commissioners had appointed ten men to regulate both institutions.[17] They had been cautious with the kirk but government now controlled both kirk and university appointments. Patrick Gillespie, who loathed the king and was an ambitious friend of Wariston, co-operated with government and was installed at Glasgow University; others were appointed for Edinburgh and St Andrews. The English turned to the anti-royalist Protestor party, who seemed more open-minded in religion, but dealing with the Scottish factions proved tricky for the English.

They might have used a similar strategy in Ireland, because the old Protestants were well-established and willing. Unfortunately, most had fought for the crown and might be liable for banishment and forfeiture.[18] In 1649, Cromwell had offered them good terms to change sides, but with Fleetwood in charge they felt vulnerable. The Irish commander was not his father-in-law; with his 'meek, condescending disposition, especially to those who were supposed to be godly', he was lenient with the Baptists but severe with the Irish and fearful over security.[19] As the English gained control of the island, they planned to re-establish courts, education and the church; there would be plenty of jobs. The Adventurers and soldiers had little experience of the country but they were not tainted by the war and government might hire them. The Old Protestants were worried; they needed sponsors. Into the breach stepped Lord Broghill, who had delivered the Munster ports to Cromwell, got his royalist brother reinstated, secured himself on important committees and gained the trust of government.[20] Cromwell had a keen instinct about hiring people; he had admired

Broghill's father who was a great entrepreneur and he valued the son's abilities. The General made sure that Broghill was well paid for his allegiance; parliament had awarded him Blarney Castle and a large tract of land.[21] Ambitious and intelligent, Broghill was now regaining the inherited estate he had lost during the war and building up his political position. Naturally, Old Protestants looked to the viscount for support. Landowners had multiple problems; apart from the threat of confiscation, rent had not been paid for years, high tax was being levied and they had debts from the war. Getting land back into production was hard enough without the uncertainty of Fleetwood's administration.

Ireland always held a central position in Oliver Cromwell's mind. He had both invested in and fought for its reconquest. Since his departure from the island, his family had taken command but reports reached London which worried him; there was a growing Baptist strain in the army which might lean towards Feake and Powell and repudiate the Protectorate. Fleetwood was sympathetic to the Baptists and unlikely to restrain them. So, Cromwell sent his younger son, Henry, to find out the temper of the army and discover Fleetwood's position. Leaving his new wife in England, Henry arrived early in March as the guest of his sister and brother-in-law. Dublin was a difficult base in 1654; the worst of the plague was over but Dublin Castle was badly damaged. Government business was being carried on in nearby Cork House and the Fleetwoods lived outside the city at Phoenix House, which stood among parkland and forest.[22] Here, Charles and Bridget Fleetwood could house their large family and entertain Bridget's brother.

Henry Cromwell came ashore on 3 March and, according to Ludlow, was brought immediately to the latter's house which was nearby, until Fleetwood could come down by coach to fetch him. Ludlow made it clear to Henry that he could not accept the creation of the Protectorate, would not serve as a commissioner under it and expected to be sacked from the army too. Diplomatically, Henry said he was sure that was unnecessary, but his report to Thurloe said the opposite, complaining that Ludlow took every opportunity to 'vent his venomous discontents'.[23] It must have taken all Henry's tact to manage this visit to his sister and brother-in-law. Sitting down for dinner and exchanging news, he would hear the Fleetwoods explain the problems of managing Ireland but formed his own judgement. Over two weeks, he spoke not only to members of the army but also to judges and officials. Before he returned to England two weeks later, he had a frank discussion with Charles Fleetwood about his position.

Henry Cromwell.

Henry reported to Thurloe – the letters between them are invaluable and show considerable sympathy and mutual trust. Henry's view was that, although some of the army was Anabaptist and aggrieved that the Nominated Assembly had closed, they were a small group. He thought the bulk of the army remained loyal. Ludlow was a different matter; Henry thought him a troublemaker, as well as John Jones, although the latter was subtler in his methods. Henry was scathing about the current Irish administration, which he thought 'does very little unless it be to make orders to give away the publique lands, of which they have given large proportions to each of themselves'. He criticised Fleetwood for being too close to the Anabaptists but speculated that his brother-in-law was not keen to remain in Ireland. [24] On 21 March, Henry was back in England and in the autumn he was elected an MP. His father's colleagues thought Henry capable, with more of the Protector's strengths than his elder brother Richard had, and suggested he be promoted further.

In Ireland, the problems and misery of transplantation were becoming apparent. The legislation was aimed at landowners; the Act said that 'pardon both as to life and estate may be extended to all husbandmen, ploughmen, labourers and others of the inferior sort',[25] but poor people were not exempt from transplantation. Those Irish Catholics who had claims to land under the qualifications had been ordered to present themselves at Loughrea in Co. Galway by 1 May 1654. When Henry Cromwell visited in March, that movement should have been in full flow but in fact, only a fraction of the Catholic Irish had got debentures and moved. They could not be given land until it had been surveyed and confiscated, which had not yet been done, so it was difficult for the officials to find places to send the transplanters. Meanwhile, the government was deluged with claims, appeals and petitions, as landowners tried to show 'good affection', press their rights under various Acts or under articles of surrender, or to point out the anomalies of their position under a set of instructions which, however precise and detailed, was unclear. Many people just did not move. They had been ordered away on pain of death but the only records of punishment for refusing to transplant were the few who were sent to Barbados instead.

By the due date of 1 May, about fifteen hundred heads of households had presented themselves at Loughrea to be awarded land, bringing with them their dependents, their families, servants, tenants and livestock, so that a total of 44,000 people had officially moved.[26] This was a tiny fraction of the Irish Catholic nation, almost all of whom could be forced to transplant if the Acts were strictly interpreted. All the same, those thousands of people with all their livestock and possessions had made their way across the country during winter and early spring.

The practical problems of farming were quickly outweighing the grand scheme to remake the nation. If all the Catholics moved and it proved difficult to attract settlers from Britain or America, who would mind the cows and till the fields? The soldiers were strong, practical fellows but even a modest farm might require a dozen men, while women were needed to milk cows, keep poultry and sow corn. Besides, the Irish knew the land and the weather; if they were all removed, the settlers would have to start clumsily from scratch. The Adventurers had been afraid of the Irish living near them; now they were worried that there would be no labourers. They wanted the dangerous Irish gentry removed but the tillers of soil retained. However, gentry, tenants and labourers formed communities and complex family groups; how were they to be dealt with? What had begun as a mixture of godly retribution and ambitious notions of social engineering evolved into a piecemeal allocation of land, under a blueprint which was difficult to interpret. Detailed records were kept both of those who transplanted and those to whom land was awarded but most of that paperwork later burned. Yet even in the records of the 1670s which survived, farms often have several owners, and family histories suggest that several proprietors made do among buildings which, anyway, had to be rebuilt. Among them, some of the original owners hung on but many were later forced to sell. In both islands, families lost their property not only by confiscation but by the losses of war and debt.

In Dublin the old forms of government were to be re-established. That August, Cromwell gave Fleetwood the status of Lord Deputy, with a council of six members. Instructions were sent from London which gave him power to reduce or dispense with transplantation, but Fleetwood was implacable. He wrote to Thurloe that 'these people are abominable, false, cunning and perfidious people, and the best of them are to be pitied, but not trusted'.[27] A second 'civil' survey of land was commissioned in June, which was based on records and local enquiries, not physical measurement; but it was a complex task.

While Fleetwood tried to hurry transplantation, the first soldiers were being disbanded and allocated land. Awards to the Adventurers had begun in London the previous summer with ballots used to match investors to counties and baronies. In 1654, actual farms were allocated and the Adventurers began arriving to take possession. As ownership was transferred, substantial proprietors lost their property but they had tenants and the surviving records show that many modest landholders were transplanted too.

Prendergast copied some of the records before their destruction; clearly the officials at Loughrea were very thorough and the debentures carefully made up. John Hore, for example, was described as aged seventy, with grey hair, tall stature, a freeholder owning ten cows. However, he arrived at Loughrea with 130 people which included children, servants and tenants, some of the latter with larger enterprises than Mr Hore. For example, Ellen Magner, aged fifty-seven, had three cows, twenty-six sheep and could claim for '4 acres of wheate and beare, and four of pease'. Thomas Butler, also a tenant, aged twenty-eight, had thirty-one cows, one hundred sheep, six oxen and claimed for '28 acres of wheate and beare, and four of pease'.[28] These were whole settlements on the move, with carts, household goods and livestock, who had to be found some useable land.

If they were not allotted land, they could not drift into towns, as the Irish were being removed from the larger urban areas. Inchiquin had driven them out of Cork city after a plot in 1645, so expulsion was not unknown. In 1654, the Irish were ordered out of Kilkenny, Wexford and Clonmel. The following year they were removed from Galway and Dublin. In Connaught, they were not to settle beside the Shannon or the sea, lest ships come ashore to support them. To many in the Puritan regime, the Irish natives were a terrifying threat and must be moved to a landlocked reservation where they could do no further harm.

While these caravans were on the move, the Old Protestants were trying to shore up their position. One important step came in June, when Cromwell honoured his pledge to the Munster Protestants and gave them indemnity for supporting Charles I, after energetic lobbying by Vincent Gookin.[29] This gave comfort to the other Old Protestants – they reasoned that if the Munstermen were safe, they too could be pardoned. John Perceval wrote to his uncle from London, 'As to the Act of Oblivion, I shall tell you the progress of it. Mr Gookin (who hath exceedingly laboured in that business) presented a petition to his Highness.'[30] Later, Protestants in other provinces were allowed to compound for their land on similar terms to English royalists. So, the Munstermen came off best but in fact, even the fines were not collected.[31] There had been such extensive destruction – the Old Protestants were estimated to have lost £2 million in stock and property – and taxes were high; if they were also fined, the land would remain unstocked and infrastructure left in ruins. The Protectorate thought it better to let the Old Protestants reinvest and get their farms going.

As they struggled to hold their land and re-establish their income, the Old Protestants were watching as jobs became available in civil government. Under Charles I this group had done well in both politics and placeholding, but now Fleetwood was in control. How were the Old Protestants to secure positions? John Perceval had been told 'that no man should have any office that should seek for it', but some men were making themselves useful and conspicuous if not actively lobbying for jobs; having a well-placed friend to speak for one was a great help.[32] The new Irish council appointed that August was chosen from Cromwell's circle and included two lawyers. These were the coming men whom place-seekers should court, but by summer it was known that a new parliament was to be called; MPs too would be influential.

In July, writs went out for the first elections under the Lord Protector. Once that body sat, Cromwell and his council could no longer rule by ordinance, so a great deal rested on the outcome. By the middle of August, the results were in. In Ireland, only Protestants were involved and the elections were carefully managed. Sir Paul Davys wrote from Dublin to John Perceval, 'I do not think that Lord Broghill can intend to come over suddenly, as he, Col. Jephson and Vincent Gookin are elected Parliament men in Munster.'[33] A new elite was emerging, composed of those the Protector favoured. Ireland was developing a new patronage system in which men like Broghill and Gookin had influence. This was a system which John Perceval, and men like him, could recognise.

In England, the elections produced more real contests and energetic jostling for position. Royalists could not vote but several republicans stood for seats. There would be challenges when parliament met but, as the new regime crystalised, men with influence or connections pressed forward. The key to any patronage system was always the man at the top – and he was not a Stuart but a Cromwell.

13

A Familiar Set of Problems

The date set for the first Protectorate parliament, 3 September, honoured Cromwell's two great victories at Dunbar and Worcester. The Instrument of Government had given the new regime nine months to establish itself before elections but a key question remained: which was more important, that parliament be freely elected or that it maintain the values for which the war was fought? The problem remains today in the debate over whether electors should be free to make a personal choice that overturns cherished values. Milton thought that religious and intellectual liberty were more important and lauded Cromwell as their champion, but men like Fairfax and Bradshaw thought the rights of a freely elected parliament were paramount.

During the nine months before it met, the Protectorate had set a style, made peace with the Netherlands, purged the clergy and tinkered with Chancery. An ordinance to suppress drunkenness and swearing had been published in June and the Post Office, which was increasingly important for merchants and a source for Thurloe's spies, was regulated. Yet only parliament could confirm the ordinances and award tax. Once it met, Cromwell would lose his power to legislate, so the elections were crucial. Two previous parliaments had closed suddenly without due process – would this one be more successful? The writs went out in June, causing considerable excitement.

During 1654, life had changed enormously for Oliver Cromwell and his family. The Protector had moved into Whitehall Palace and had the use of Hampton Court. His household staff was smaller than the royal one had been but included many of Charles I's servants who naturally ran the palaces in their accustomed way. As head of state, Cromwell entertained ambassadors and it was partly to satisfy their expectations that the rooms were decorated with Charles I's pictures and tapestries, kept back from the sales. The Protectorate was keen to win respect overseas, and so, even if it offended the taste of some of the elite, the government now conformed to certain rituals and standards of reception.

Nonetheless, the style of the Protectorate was Puritan. The clothes were more sombre and the utensils less glittering than the court of the king, and much had been sold, but the lifestyle of the Cromwellians inevitably recreated part of the earlier royal routine. Cromwell's wife Elizabeth adapted to this finery and state living to the best of her ability. Officials and servants from earlier days remembered the little French queen on her light feet, trained from birth to dance and hold court. Mrs Cromwell cut a more homely figure. She kept two cows in the park behind the palace to be sure of fresh milk, and once, when her husband asked for an orange to squeeze over his meat, she reminded him with alarm that they cost several groats. She was laughed at for her plain ways and she must have known it; in 1660 royalist journalists produced a pamphlet mocking her recipes using cheap cuts of meat and gossiping about her friends and behaviour.[1] Her unmarried daughters, however, enjoyed being princesses, especially when they were courted by young aristocrats from families who supported the revolution.

Elizabeth Cromwell.

Around them a court of likeminded people gathered, most but not all sharing Puritan ideals. The godly were deeply engaged with their inner spiritual worlds, while externally they were ambitious and commercially vigorous. This was reflected in their attention to art and culture: they wholly disapproved of art in churches and even in secular life seemed unresponsive to visual art. Some portraits were painted of the leaders but there is little evidence of an interest in painting generally. They frowned on lewd behaviour and drunkenness but allowed modest dancing, such as at the wedding of Cromwell's daughter. However, the Lord Protector is said to have loved music and, as Chancellor of the University of Oxford, was able to move the organ from Magdalen College to Hampton Court. Since it was only 12 miles out of London and on the Thames, he went there frequently, usually from Friday to Monday, often indulging his love of hawking and hunting.

About the Protector's person a layer of formality had arisen, partly because of his status but principally for security. He always had guards around him and visitors went through several anterooms to reach his presence. His safety had become a major issue since, without the consent of Charles, some royalists had launched an assassination attempt that May. It was incompetent, the leaders were arrested and two, Gerrard and Vowell, were executed. Cromwell was more carefully guarded thereafter and Thurloe strengthened his spy network.

The Protector's job was demanding. Foreign policy was a large part of his brief and at first Cromwell attended few council meetings, as his days were taken up with diplomats and relations with neighbouring states. Appointing officials and agreeing payments and procedures was wearisome for him, and foreign ambassadors reported that Cromwell 'looked utterly careworn' in the early days of the Protectorate.[2] He was now fifty-eight, an ageing soldier on whom the enormous task of erecting and managing a new state had fallen – no wonder he looked tired and harassed. Nonetheless, by the summer, alliances were taking shape. For English merchants, access to the Baltic and Spanish markets were paramount. Bulstrode Whitelocke struck up a good rapport with Queen Christina of Sweden, the diminutive daughter of the great Gustavus Adolphus, who confided that she disliked being queen and was planning to abdicate. Before she did so, a trade deal was struck. The treaty with the Netherlands, signed in April, pledged to block the four-year-old Prince of Orange from power and not to harbour enemies of the Protectorate.

With these treaties, which included Denmark, the Sound and Baltic trade were open to English shipping. This was important, but it was

Spain and France who were the key European powers and both were negotiating with England over military and trade benefits. Cromwell and his council were striving for commercial and colonial expansion for England; Scotland would benefit but Irish trade was disadvantaged by the Navigation Act. In all discussions, religious policy influenced the agenda, both sides complaining about persecution: of Catholics in Britain or Protestants in France and Spain. Cromwell leaned towards an alliance with France, which had now stabilised under the young Louis XIV while run by Mazarin and was beginning a period of expansion. As a sweetener, Mazarin offered Dunkirk to Cromwell should France take it from the Spanish Netherlands – that would strengthen England's hold on the Channel.

Charles was still in Paris and was living with his mother in the Louvre. At first, his privy council included her courtiers, but over the three years which Charles spent in France the royal Stuarts split into groups. Henrietta-Maria was very changed by her husband's death; the spirited and art-loving queen was now a sad little widow who wore black, frequently retired to her convent, found consolation in religion and nursed a bitter anger which spilled over into plans and schemes. Her courtiers were known as the 'Louvre group'; Sir Henry Jermyn was her close confidant and a Protestant, as were Hatton and Percy, but part of her retinue was composed of English Catholics. Gossip said, without foundation, that Jermyn was the queen's lover. Opposed to the Louvre group was Sir Edward Hyde, whom Charles I had appointed as councillor to his son but whom Henrietta-Maria despised. Hyde was clever, astute and a devoted Anglican. Charles knew the value of Hyde but Henrietta-Maria resented his influence over her son. He was leader of the royal council and at the core of the old royalists who worked for Charles. Hyde thought the schemes of the Louvre group ill-considered and often dangerous and was horrified by the queen's efforts to draw her children into the Catholic church, which would alienate the English elite.

Charles had been changed, first by his father's death but more acutely by his experience in Scotland. He returned from Worcester quieter and sterner, less willing to heed his mother. Charles was a strong and healthy man who enjoyed swimming, sailing, dancing and music. He had his French grandfather's libido and fondness for women and, since he was trapped in the strange career of an exiled king, with diplomacy to pursue but no budget and no country to run, enjoyed himself as he could and began to earn a reputation as a pleasure-seeker. Internally, he was becoming cynical, suspecting that people only attended to him when his political future seemed bright and believing that, in essence, humans were insincere. He was a cautious politician, slow to commit himself and inclined, like his father, when he could not construct a definite policy, to tell different things to different men and his real strategy to no one. Throughout his exile, he retained the men his father had chosen, of whom Hyde, Ormond and Nicholas were the inner circle.

Prince Rupert also reappeared from his privateering adventures, coming ashore at Nantes; but, instead of providing desperately needed funds, he told Charles that he was out of pocket and that the king owed him money for his expeditions. Rupert and his friends were hardened by war and privateering; they were young and homeless, passionate and quarrelsome, given to duels. Known as the 'Swordsmen', they provided a third faction to challenge Charles's personal council and the queen's Louvre group.

Hyde believed that Charles would only be restored through the actions of English royalists but Henrietta-Maria wanted to pursue any plan that offered a swift outcome. Hyde saw the Louvre group as a threat; Joseph Bampfield, a Thurloe spy, was in favour in the queen's circle and even after warnings was received in the palace, while spontaneous plots embraced by the Louvre weakened Hyde's careful management. Charles knew that his minister was right and became distanced from his mother but their relationship was wounded. He was regularly approached by royalist conspirators about whom he had to form judgements; how much support did they have, how organised were they? His council had accepted the Sealed Knot as their principal supporters. This group had formed in November 1653, since when Lord Belasyse and his five co-conspirators had been cautiously at work, each secretly building up a separate network of men ready for action.

Inevitably, enemies of the Protectorate might become allies of Charles, so his future depended on Cromwell's foreign policy. Already, the Netherlands treaty meant he was unable to visit his sister Mary in Holland, while Cromwell's agreements with Sweden, Denmark and Portugal closed any possibility of aid from those states. With limited funds, he kept diplomats in Vienna and the Spanish Netherlands in the hopes of Habsburg support, but in the summer of 1654 Cromwell's diplomacy forced Charles himself to move. The courting of England by France and Spain had not reached consummation but Mazarin needed English military support. Cromwell kept complaining about the Stuart presence in France; he accepted that Henrietta-Maria had returned to her family but the Stuart heirs in Paris were a threat. To please the Protector, Mazarin urged Charles to leave, offering to pay the £2,750 arrears of Charles's pension if he did so swiftly and to continue paying after he was gone.

Charles was willing to accept this offer but where could he go? The German princes solved the problem. Late in 1653, the Emperor had offered Charles £23,000 and the Elector of Brandenburg pledged 200,000 rix-dollars – the equivalent of £45,000.[3] With funds available, Charles left Paris in July to meet his sister Mary of Orange at Spa in the Spanish Netherlands, and from there they went together to Aachen, where they enjoyed sightseeing and dancing parties. When he reached Cologne, Charles decided to settle, and he stayed there until 1656. Despite misgivings, he had left his youngest brother, Henry, with his mother, but soon afterwards the teenage prince wrote to say that Henrietta-Maria was trying to convert him to Catholicism and put him into an abbey, dreaming that he would become a cardinal. Alarmed, Charles sent Ormond back to Paris to fetch the boy. There was a nasty scene with the queen and when Henry fell to his knees to receive a parting blessing, she refused it and stormed out. Ormond and the young duke hastened out of France to Cologne, where Charles and Henry spent the winter together. James, Duke of York stayed on in French military service, despite the demands of Cromwell.

By the late summer of 1654, Cromwell's foreign relations had strengthened and elections were underway. In Ireland and Scotland, there were few authorised electors and officials could manage the outcome. In Scotland, Monck was busy with the summer campaign against Middleton, so garrison commanders and junior officers managed the process. Few Scots could vote and few showed interest: five shires reported 'not one fit to be a parliament man', and in Aberdeenshire no one was eligible to vote. Instead of thirty, only twenty-one members went down to London although Monck, feeling this inadequate, softened the conditions and held at least one by-election.[4] Fleetwood and his officers thought Ireland unprepared, viewed elections as a threat and wanted the seats allocated by government, but the writs were issued from London and elections went ahead. Although the army managed the elections, the Old Protestants held onto their influence and were in a majority among the new members.[5]

In England, there were genuinely contested elections. The government had stipulated that only 'well-affected men' could stand but, even if some filtering was done in the constituencies, it did not keep out opponents of the Cromwellian regime. The franchise had been widened, there was no reliable register of electors and policing of candidates was not thorough. As a result, the 1654 parliament contained republicans such as Bradshaw, Scot and Haselrig, several royalists and a great many Presbyterians. Religious radicals, however, failed to get in. Sir Henry Vane had not stood for election but had withdrawn to his ancestral estate in Co. Durham, where his godly and virtuous wife was managing the property and raising their fifteen children with great efficiency. Here, Sir Henry reflected on the issues and conflicts of his age, working on several texts which were published in the following years.

Cromwell's government had inched forward with its reform agenda during the year and hoped that parliament would confirm its ordinances, endorse the new constitution, vote new taxes and turn to the many issues which needed addressing within the three nations. The Lord Protector was to be sorely disappointed. Despite being given a long speech on what was expected of them, the MPs had their own ideas and it soon became clear that, in their minds, the Instrument of Government had by no means settled the constitution.

The parliament opened with pomp. The Protector travelled to Westminster Abbey for the opening service by coach with his son Henry and Major General Lambert, escorted by a military cavalcade, with the principal law officers and government officials.[6] Cromwell then met the MPs in the Painted Chamber within the Palace of Westminster. He occupied a gilded chair on a dais with a canopy over it while the members sat on benches below. Cromwell was portentous; they met, he said, 'on the greatest occasion that … England ever saw'. His message was simple: the purpose of the parliament was healing and settling. After all the changes, after the effort to oppose 'usurpation and tyranny', God had shown them his providences and doubtless he would put healing in their minds.[7] There had been great challenges: magistracy and the ranks of men, so well established in England, had been threatened by the Levelling tendency. Liberty, both of conscience and of people, was a glorious ideal but not an excuse to overturn magistracy. The notion of the Fifth Monarchy had also deceived people. We all wait and hope 'that Jesus will set up his reign in our hearts', Cromwell said, but that did not entitle the wilder element to rule or to overturn liberty, property and the law. Such uncontrolled behaviour gave openings to the Jesuits and the enemies of government in Scotland and in Ireland.

Cromwell briefed the members on foreign relations. England had been at war with Portugal, France and Holland, the latter campaign being especially expensive, but agreements had been reached with Sweden and Denmark regarding access to the Baltic, and the Protectorate was negotiating with France. He was worried about finance, as all the confiscated lands of the crown and church had been sold, so increasing trade was essential. Current taxation levels weighed heavily on the people and government would reduce the assessment by £30,000 a month for the next three months. 'You have great works upon your hands,' Cromwell told them. 'You have Ireland to look unto.' It was not yet planted, he admitted, but preparations were under way. So, sounding a positive note, the Lord Protector admonished the MPs to go to their chamber, elect a speaker and set about their tasks.

The Lord Protector gave his MPs no directions for legislation. Historians have criticised Cromwellian failures to manage parliament, something the Tudors were adept at and a crucial failure of the Stuarts, but parliament had become far more confident and assertive during the seventeenth century and there was no established method for the executive to get its business through the legislature. Certainly, for Cromwell the first Protectorate parliament was an exasperating failure. Rather than accepting the new constitution and framing useful laws, the MPs began to challenge the Instrument of Government. It contained clauses on religious liberty which Haselrig tried to undermine. Then MPs sought to give parliament the choice of council members and army officers. Meanwhile, Harrison was organising a petition in the army to 'extirpate the present tyranny'; Cromwell had him arrested but the Protector was stung. Within a week, he called the MPs back into the Painted Chamber and emphasised the position: they had been called under the Instrument and were not to alter it.

This time, his speech was more personal. Cromwell was upset by the accusations against him and alarmed about the instability of government. As so often before, he talked about his relationship with God, but also about his background and social position.[8] He refuted the charges of his own ambition. 'I called not myself to this place,' he told them. 'I was by birth a gentleman, living neither in any considerable height, nor yet in obscurity.' He defended his role in the upsets of parliaments. Regarding the Rump, he said that the nation 'loathed their sittings' and that 'there was high cause for their dissolving' – namely, their arbitrary power and unjust confiscations of property. Cromwell said he had called the Nominated Assembly to settle the nation, hoping to lay down his own power, but the result of that 'we may sadly remember'. He claimed to have had no foreknowledge of their resignation, when power had returned to him once more.[9] He spoke of this as a strange and unexpected burden when really it was the consequence of decisions taken by the army over several years. Cromwell knew how much people resented that but he emphasised the need for stable government and the army's efforts to provide it. The City of London seemed satisfied, he said, and stable government was essential for the legal system. Cromwell emphasised that the Instrument of Government had now settled the basic structure of power – it was established in a single person and parliament, who would control the militia. Liberty of conscience would be permitted, but the magistrate had the right to set limits, 'according to his conscience'. Every year £200,000 would be raised in tax to cover the basic costs of government, including 'supporting the Governor-in-Chief'.[10]

> Oh! We have quarrelled for, and we contested for the liberty of England. Wherein, forsooth? For the liberty of the people? I appeal to the Lord, that the desires and endeavours, and the things themselves will speak for themselves, that the liberty of England, the liberty of the people, the avoiding of tyrannous impositions, either upon men as men, or Christians as Christians, is made so safe by this Act of Settlement, that it will speak sufficiently for itself.[11]

The Instrument was not to be challenged and Cromwell demanded that MPs sign a recognition accepting these terms. To enforce that, guards blocked the doors and patrolled the passages leading to parliament's chamber until the MPs signed. Some did so immediately, others within a few days. They promised to be true and faithful to the Lord Protector and the Commonwealth of England, Scotland and Ireland, according to the indenture under which they had been called, and not to alter the government, 'as it is settled in one single person and a Parliament'.[12] Within a month, all but 100 MPs had signed the recognition and taken their seats. The republicans would not sign and left parliament; Haselrig, Scot, Bradshaw and their associates remained absent.

However, dissension continued. Many people, who longed only for reduced taxes and a return to normal life, saw Cromwell as their best option; but the structures of England's government had been riven, and crafting a balanced constitution was not enough to re-establish systems or calm the disturbance. Parliament, even without the republicans, wanted a hand in framing the constitution. While those in power argued, the forms of government were slipping back to earlier patterns, in law courts, in ritual and ceremony, in foreign relations and – against the vehement wishes of republicans – in a single person holding power. Parliament followed its established procedures – with readings, amendments and committees – but tension continued between parliament and the ruler. Cromwell had identified four fundamentals: government by a single person and parliament; that parliament should not make itself perpetual; that there should be liberty of conscience in religion; and that the militia should be controlled by the single person, and by the parliament when sitting. All of these could be questioned. For example, liberty of conscience was limited, as Catholics and Anglicans could not use their forms of service and the sects were being circumscribed. The single person and parliament might control the armed forces, but between parliaments it would be Lord General Cromwell alone. Republicans loathed the concept of a single powerful head of state, but landowners and merchants wanted steady government and they recognised Cromwell's skills. Some thought him able, some considered him a tyrant.

The real enemies of the Protectorate were outside parliament and increasingly active. John Lilburne had been imprisoned in Jersey where he could not claim habeas corpus but John Wildman was busy in England and Edward Sexby was in contact with the royalists. Lilburne wrote, 'I had rather live under a regulated and well-bounded king ... than under any government with Tyrannie.'[13] The Levellers thought a mixed monarchy preferable to rule by the army, despite the new constitution. The army had political power and many officers had generous grants of land, so efforts to overthrow them increased. The Levellers still had influence within army ranks and hostile pamphlets began to circulate in all three nations. Thurloe's spies incriminated Colonel Robert Overton, who was distributing them in Scotland, so Cromwell ordered Monck to arrest him. Vice Admiral Lawson, acting commander of the Navy in the English Channel and a Baptist, was sympathetic to the Levellers and encouraged petitions over pay among the men. They contained republican sentiments but a swift settlement of wages defused the situation.

For Fleetwood in Dublin, 1654 was a difficult and vexatious year. He was already struggling to transplant the Irish and allocate land to both Adventurers and demobilised troops; now MPs posed another threat. He feared that parliament would legislate for Ireland again and complicate his position further. Officials were hurrying to award land but the first survey, done swiftly by Benjamin Worsley, was too inaccurate. A second survey was based on local records, but in

December William Petty was given a contract for a third one. Petty was physician general to the army in Ireland; both he and Worsley were in the circle of Samuel Hartlib, where scientific ideas were developing and among whom interest in Ireland was keen. Here was an undeveloped country on which social engineering could be tried. Petty was a considerable scientist, had trained as a doctor, but also had mathematical skills. A friend of Robert Boyle, he was impatient with Worsley's work and, confident of his own abilities, proposed a better method to government. Petty's 'Down Survey' was begun in February 1655; he trained about a thousand men who not only had to master his survey method but had to be 'fit for leaping hedges and ditches'.[14] The land settlement naturally roused passions, and eight surveyors were killed in one month alone during the autumn of 1655. At the survey headquarters in Dublin, forty clerks kept the records brought from across the island. It was an enormous task.

Fleetwood had other worries. London had ordered him to remove Ludlow's commission but that stirred resentment in the army, whereas London was suspicious of Fleetwood's inability to stamp out disaffection. On the other hand, he was the Protector's son-in-law and a senior commander; London officials knew they must handle him carefully. Managing the army was one problem, settling Ireland a far greater task. Irish combatants were still being sent to the Caribbean and it was decided to send three score Irish women 'that are vagrants, idlers and wanderers' to the West Indies if they 'do not betake themselves to some legal way or means for their livelihood and subsistence', but that meant more shipping.[15] London kept interfering in land transfers. The Committee for Articles was over there, as was the Lord Protector; Fleetwood was alarmed by the way in which they both found in favour of Irish Catholics. Landowners petitioned Cromwell personally and he often accepted their pleas, while army officers supported the committee over matters of honour. That might reduce the land needed for the settlement. London said Fleetwood could modify transplantation orders to make the best job of it he could, but confiscations were being blocked elsewhere.[16]

When Confederate officers for Leinster were allowed to retain their estates, Fleetwood wrote to Thurloe and stressed how dangerous these Catholic grandees were. For once, he was successful.[17] Gradually however, Fleetwood modified his attempt to remove the whole Catholic population. Writing to Cromwell in November, he talked of 'transplanting the Irish proprietors and such as have been in arms in Connacht effectually', suggesting he was now concentrating on large landowners.[18] But he was attempting to remove the Irish from the cities; the townsmen of Galway were ordered out but struggled hard to retain their property.[19] The Protestants, however, were reprieved, even if they had fought for the king. In September, like the Munstermen, they were ordered to pay fines but exempted from transplantation, which had become a policy exclusively for Catholics, some of whom converted hoping to retain their land. The deadline for transplanting had been delayed by a year to 1 March 1655.

Cromwell was inconsistent about the Irish. He had frequently spoken in savage terms about the Irish rebels and, by extension, all Catholics. He talked enthusiastically to parliament about planting and anglicising Ireland. Yet when the Irish gentry petitioned him, he was often lenient, and he insisted on the articles of surrender. The threat of Ireland seemed especially potent in his mind, and during his campaign there he had been uncharacteristically ruthless. Over the settlement he acted swiftly and the transplantation order was sweeping. In government, he was often merciful and seemed touched by the plight of Irish landowners. Yet to Cromwell Ireland always remained a threat, and he made sure that one of his family was always in command there.

In 1654, however, his principal problem was parliament. The members were so engrossed with the constitution that although several bills got as far as a second reading, no legislation was passed – not even money bills. Instead, they proposed cutting the assessment further and complained about the Protector's control of the armed forces and his ability to overturn parliaments. In December, as tensions over the Instrument increased, a man named Garland, supported by Henry Cromwell and Anthony Ashley Cooper, proposed that Cromwell should take the title of king. That would give Cromwell the legitimacy and legal authority that he still lacked as Lord Protector and might solve problems in the courts. The soldiers in parliament were adamantly against the proposal and it was withdrawn. Cromwell became increasingly exasperated but under the Instrument parliament must sit for five months. In the early days of 1655, it was rumoured these would be lunar months, which shortened the term by almost two weeks. Thurloe warned Cromwell that his enemies were stirring up the soldiers, which alarmed the Protector. His greatest fear was further instability.

The members wanted to weaken the powers of the Protector and council in favour of parliament. Then they wanted to define heresy and limit religious toleration. When parliament tried to reduce the army and rely on the militia, matters came to a head. If the funding committee got its way, 27,000 soldiers would have to be disbanded, funding for the Navy would be minimal and soldiers' pay would be reduced. Parliament wanted to supplement the army with the county militias, but they were controlled not by Cromwell but by the county gentry, many of whom sat in parliament. If no militia could be raised 'but by common consent of the people assembled in parliament',[20] Cromwell's military power would be reduced and any overseas military adventures might become impossible.

Control of the military had precipitated war between Charles I and the Long Parliament. The king believed that command of the armed forces was the inalienable prerogative of the monarch. He was commander-in-chief of the army and when the lord lieutenants of counties raised militias, they did so at command of the king. It was one of the core issues on which Charles had refused to compromise and which ultimately had led to his death. Now a single person ruled once more, who was already commander-in-chief of the army. Who was to have control – the Protector or parliament? The issue was urgent as the last assessment bill was about to expire, leaving no provision for paying the army. Parliament made a grant but it did not get through its third reading.

Whitelocke warned Cromwell not to close parliament precipitously, but on 22 January, the earliest possible date counting in lunar months, Cromwell called the MPs together, spoke to them with bitter reproaches and told them it was not 'for the profit of these nations, nor for common and public good, for you to continue here any longer', and dissolved his parliament.[21] Considering he had taken up arms to defend the institution, parliaments were being closed with alarming frequency under his rule. He was discovering, as Charles I had before him, that however extensive his powers, he could not force parliament's compliance even if he winnowed the members or only picked the most acceptable. Cromwell was back with Charles's problems: inadequate revenue, religious divergence and a challenging parliament. The difference was that Cromwell was Lord General of the finest forces in Europe.

In Ireland, administrative confusion was deepening what was already a national tragedy. If a full and severe policy of transplantation was enforced, the social fabric of the country would be rent into tiny pieces as families, villages and the Irish culture were broken up. Any moderation of the policy had been slight. Early in 1655, Vincent Gookin published a pamphlet entitled *The Great Case of Transplantation in Ireland discussed*, in which he argued against a general movement of the Irish people. Gookin's pamphlet was part Christian and part practical. He said that a national blood guilt was wrong and that punishment should be confined to the guilty, most of whom were dead or had left the country. He warned that government policy would drive the Irish into becoming tories, because 'for the poor Commons, the Sun never shined (or rather not shined) upon a Nation so completely miserable'. Of English policy, he wrote that 'the fair virtue of justice (overdon) degenerates into the stinking weed of tyranny'.[22]

Gookin's practical arguments could not be ignored. The soldiers now had land but no money or livestock, so without the animals and husbandry skills of the Irish there would be little produce or tax. The Irish knew the land, the climate and the crops; the women were skilled at making wool or linen cloth. As for religion, if the Irish were ignorant that was the fault of government, which had not provided a decent ministry or striven to implement the Reformation as it had been taught in England. Gookin dismissed fears that the Irish would infect the English with their culture; the Irish no longer held most of the land nor official positions; in future, English culture would dominate and commerce be carried on in English. Gookin argued vehemently against making the Irish desperate by extreme transplantation. If they refused to move to Connaught, what would government do? 'When will this wild war be finished?' he asked, suggesting it might be hard to bring quiet to the country. 'The unsettling of a nation is an easy work, the settling is not.' That was a lesson which the Cromwellians were learning in England.

Fleetwood was very annoyed by this publication, 'which doth very falsely and unworthily asperse those that did and now do serve here'.[23] In March, a petition was published, signed by military men, comparing the Irish to the Midianites and demanding a full transplantation.[24] In May, Colonel Richard Lawrence published his riposte, *The Interest of England in the Irish Transplantation.*[25] Lawrence's brother was president of the council and this pamphlet was effectively the government's view. He warned that papers like Gookin's might instigate rebellion against 'Authority' by the people. Lawrence did not believe it 'safe to admit into any English plantation, above the fifth part to be Irish papists … for the Irish are naturally a timerous [*sic*], suspicious, watchful people, and on the other hand, the English are confidant, credulous, careless people'. In any case, it was only proprietors and men in arms who were to transplant. If their dependents wanted to go too, that was up to them.

Lawrence strongly defended government actions but tacitly admitted that a general transplantation was no longer envisaged. Not more than one-twentieth of the Irish nation was to move to Connaught. By the time that Lawrence's pamphlet was out, the date for transplanting had already passed but still the Irish resisted moving. Small numbers of tories had murdered soldiers, government officers and even the Irishmen who worked for them. Fleetwood was severe with those thought to be harbouring rebels: those remaining in one area of Cork were ordered to assemble into villages under a headman. Women and vagabonds were to be rounded up and sent to the Caribbean. Corn belonging to those who failed to transplant was seized and sold.

In London, however, disquiet was growing about the Dublin government. Cromwell approved of Gookin, who had held official positions. The Protector was alert to problems with transplantation and worried about disloyalty in the Irish army. Henry Cromwell had already reported on the state of government in Dublin, and influential men in London, including Thurloe, who was close to Cromwell, thought that Henry should replace Fleetwood. Both were members of the Protector's family, so a decision was delayed.

While the Irish situation remained disturbed and unhappy, Monck was getting a firmer grip on Scotland. Yet just as those two countries were being fully subjugated, rebellion broke out in England once more.

14

Power Struggles within
and Without

Now he was head of state, Cromwell had to balance the demands
of powerful groups, among whom the London merchants were still
important; they increased commerce and might provide more loans.
After power struggles within the Common Council, the new merchants
were dominant, with their American interests and widespread trade
routes. Under the Commonwealth they had considerable influence and
the Protector had them in mind when he launched his ill-fated Western
Design. However, his primary motive for attacking a Spanish colony
seems to have been religious rather than commercial.

Cromwell revered Queen Elizabeth, looked to her policies for
guidance and was inspired by Elizabethan struggles against Catholic
Spain. The Lord Protector was enraged by Spanish repression of
Protestants and, like Elizabeth, wanted to weaken their hegemony
in the Caribbean. Cromwell was negotiating with both France and
Spain but underlying his efforts lay a simple strategic concern: could
England rival Spain for control of the seas? The Dutch had been
bested, but northern European trade was expanding and Cromwell
knew its importance, not only around Europe's shores but across the
Atlantic. British naval captains had recently attacked French fleets in
the Mediterranean and in America had led New England colonists in
an attack on New Amsterdam (later New York). But Spain remained
the dominant power in the Americas and was the old Catholic enemy.

Once Cromwell decided to launch an expedition to the West Indies,
arguments in council made no impression on him. 'We consider
this attempt because we think God has not brought us hither where
we are, but to consider the work that we may do in the world as
well as at home,' he told councillors; they would keep up their

military reputation, weaken the Antichrist and promote English trade. Hispaniola was the best target as it was central to Spain's trade routes. Cromwell deluded himself that he could attack Spain in America while remaining on decent terms with that nation in Europe. Lambert argued strongly against him in council, on military and cost grounds, asserting that England did not have spare settlers for Hispaniola – but it was all in vain. Cromwell was adamant and said the expedition would pay for itself.[1]

So, in December 1654, while parliament was still sitting, Penn and Venables sailed from Portsmouth for the Caribbean. They had unclear instructions, which exacerbated the friction between them, their supplies were inadequate and their troops, drawn from several units, lacked cohesion. Unusually for a military project of Cromwell's, the expedition failed in its objective, although an unplanned capture later proved valuable.

While the fleet was crossing the Atlantic and parliament was infuriating the Protector, trouble was brewing among the disaffected. Thurloe, using spies and opening the post, knew that royalists were planning a rising without having a full picture of what the government faced. The closure of parliament in January caused further irritation and Thurloe suspected some of the MPs were plotting with the main conspirators, who consisted of Levellers and impatient royalists. In fact, these two groups were in touch but not co-ordinated. Public opinion in general is hard to quantify; the Venetian ambassador, who was there, and Clarendon, who was not, thought that the people were sullenly antagonistic. The ambassador wrote that on the closure 'the constituencies will be offended by the treatment of their representatives', and the frequent dissolutions might 'overthrow suddenly the present order, as it is not believed that it can subsist always upon such violent procedure. But so long as the Protector and the power of the army remain united and the troops are content, he will retain his authority and he will hazard everything before he abandons it.'[2]

To government, the religious radicals were also a threat as they roused both troops and public to disaffection, so several leaders remained in prison. Despite being overworked, Cromwell would spend hours in dispute with these men. Quaker resistance to authority made the Society of Friends a danger and George Fox, founder of the Quakers, was arrested several times for blasphemy and causing a disturbance, but he remained uncompromising. The Fifth Monarchists were more brazen, talking of taking up arms against a government which was 'anti-Christian and Babylonish'. They objected to parliaments, which derived power from the people whereas 'all power belongs to Christ'. Cromwell interviewed Harrison and suggested he and his colleagues retire quietly to the country, but they gave no assurances of good behaviour and were kept in custody. Rogers, who had been in prison for twenty-seven weeks, had a long interview with Cromwell and demanded a 'fair hearing in a legal court', also pleading for Feake who had already been jailed for over a year; Cromwell nonetheless kept them detained, fearing their persuasive tongues or that, in a court, they would be executed under the treason ordinance.

Against this picture of animosity to Cromwell, the attitude of urban educated people seems hopeful about the Protectorate. John Milton had been appointed Latin Secretary in 1649 and brought in Andrew Marvell, who also tutored Cromwell's ward. In his poem marking the first anniversary of the Protectorate, Marvell remarks on Cromwell's 'greater vigour' and his capacity for work, and praises 'Angelic Cromwell who outwings the wind'. The poem lauds Cromwell for creating a stable powerful polity, but Marvell was also friendly with Robert Overton and had expressed both republican sentiments and concerns about liberty elsewhere.[3] Anthony Ashley Cooper, a rising star from the Protestant gentry whose concerns about liberty were growing, left the council that January and did not return. The political

Andrew Marvell.

nation was undecided; over the next three years many would turn against the Cromwellians while others hastened to join.

Cromwell and Thurloe knew that royalist plotting continued, but their information was patchy and the Sealed Knot remained a secret from them. Charles and Hyde had given the Knot preference, but by 1654 a more impatient group was urging the king to action. According to Clarendon, their schemes were 'founded upon a supposition of the division and faction within the army' – they even tried to contact Fairfax. Overton had plotted to lead several thousand men from Scotland to England to overthrow the Protectorate and he certainly was in contact with Wildman's group, but Overton had been imprisoned, and Grey of Groby and Wildman picked up; only Sexby escaped. There were also officials who were sympathetic to the royalists, such as the customs men at Dover and other ports, and probably also prison officers judging by the amount of escapes.

Both Hyde and the Sealed Knot had advised Charles against precipitous action but he was young and impatient himself. With evidence of widespread dissatisfaction, he leaned more and more to the action party. They had exaggerated their position and had neither army nor Presbyterian support for action. Nonetheless, they began importing arms and set a date for a rising: 6 February. Thurloe was thoroughly alarmed. He had information on meetings but how widespread was the network of plotters? To prevent a mass rising, the government brought troops back from Ireland and some were withdrawn from Scotland to defend northern England. The Tower garrison was increased to 1,200 men, regiments were brought into London and made ready, while artillery was noticed in Whitehall. The capital was well-defended. Cromwell warned London's Common Council and set up a new commission to control the City militia, composed of army officers with the mayor and aldermen. Since parliament had dissolved, there was no argument about this arrangement.

Two members of the Sealed Knot were briefly arrested and the hiatus gave the action party sway over Charles. They were building up arms – a gun dealer from Virginia used his colonial connections and trans-Atlantic trade as a cover, bringing in weapons among crates of wine – but in January Thurloe swooped. The arms conspirators were arrested; investigations, examinations and further arrests followed. Cromwell was against torture and corporal punishment but his subordinates seem less squeamish and potential penalties were high, so there were some full confessions. When several key leaders were arrested, the plotters decided on short delays – initially until 13 February. Charles, now committed to action, had sent Rochester to take command while he moved to Middleburg near the coast, ready to cross the Channel. Appointing Rochester was a mixed decision. He was a close friend of Charles, whose perilous escape after Worcester he had shared, and he had military experience and links to 'neutral' Presbyterians, but he was famously louche and bibulous, although it was said he never drank while near the enemy. Daniel O'Neill, a subtle negotiator with a gift for slipping around England surreptitiously, came over to persuade the Sealed Knot to join the rising; he was unsuccessful but was still bent on action.

13 February came and went without the royalists making a move. Cromwell knew this meant little. In London, horses were confiscated and public meetings which might disguise mobilisation were banned – horse racing in particular. Special orders were given to the ports but royalist collusion undermined those. On 19 February, Rochester and Wagstaffe landed at Margate, making their way undetected to London. Here they discovered bad news, the arrests of leaders and the high levels of military preparedness by the regime. The royalists, however, had gone too far to turn back and fixed on 8 March as the new date to rise. They had divided England into six regions but as the Sealed Knot dominated East Anglia, there was little chance of action there. When the day came, many royalists hung back, waiting to see if others would come out, not wanting to hazard their fortunes once more unless a strong groundswell gave them a chance of success. As a result, the rising was an affair of few men and no real fighting. The Cromwellians overestimated Leveller activity, which they feared, and could not judge the strength of royalist feeling. Cromwell, who ultimately was a soldier, chose a military response to the rising and as a result, the government greatly increased the antagonism against itself.

On 8 March, only the north-east and the West Country saw any fighting. One hundred and fifty men gathered on Marston Moor with Rochester at their head, but at some unknown alarm they panicked and dispersed before others came to join them. Many were subsequently arrested and most of their arms were abandoned. Rochester, however, got away. Only Colonel John Penruddock and his Wiltshire associates made a real attempt. Penruddock was a serious country gentleman who understood the risk, put his affairs in order and, hoping for God's blessing, rode out to take Salisbury. The Protectorate judges were holding assize there, a potent symbol of the regime's control. The royalist horsemen duly gathered on Sunday night, rode into Salisbury before daybreak on Monday, and by first light they controlled the city. Rochester sent Wagstaffe to lead the Wiltshire rising and by releasing prisoners they had 400 men, but instead of waiting for reinforcements Wagstaffe led them west to collect more supporters. Cromwellian forces were already coming out from Bristol, Exeter and Taunton, while Cromwell had sent Desborough to take command as Major General of the West. Men began to leave the royalist troop but it held together until 14 March, when Captain Unton Croke intercepted the royalists at South Molton on the edge of Exmoor. There was street fighting until Penruddock accepted Croke's offer of quarter. Wagstaffe slipped away and the Wiltshire leaders were taken prisoner.

Penruddock's Rising posed little serious threat. It had been blighted by Thurloe's excellent intelligence, the weakness of the royalists' communications and their lack of allies – the great aristocrats were unwilling to risk further penalties. Penruddock and his associates were given jury trials, found guilty and sixteen, including the colonel, were executed; others were sent to Barbados as penal labour. But in the north, judges ruled that Cromwell's treason ordinance was unconstitutional, offering a foretaste of problems which would bedevil the Protectorate. Instead, the northern prisoners were fined for riot and released. The council dismissed two of these judges but the basis of government was being questioned. Meanwhile, Rochester, Wagstaffe and O'Neill had slipped across the Channel. The rising seemed to prove Hyde right: it would be better for Charles not to woo potential supporters but wait until they came to him when he proved their best option.

Considering how slight the attempt had been, the long-term reaction of government was severe. Cromwell and Thurloe were relying on information from spies, some of which was grossly exaggerated or invented; informers like Manning made a good living by spicing up what they knew. On the basis of these reports, the government believed that other risings were planned and that there would be further assassination attempts on Cromwell. Searches and arrests were made around Covent Garden, then leading royalists were arrested in Oxfordshire. Throughout the summer, arrests continued until several hundred men were in prison, including the leaders of the Sealed Knot.

A militarisation of local government began. When news of the Salisbury rising reached Cromwell, he had immediately sent his brother-in-law John Desborough to take command, who stayed on after the action ended, in command of the West Country militias.

This pattern was copied throughout England. Owing to budget cuts, the army was being disbanded, leaving 21,000 soldiers in Britain, but, with threats simmering, Cromwell considered this inadequate and raised militias in each county under a captain. The counties were organised into twelve districts, each commanded by a major general. Only known supporters of government were recruited. The major generals were key Cromwellian officers and had considerable powers, primarily regarding security although this was soon extended to enforcing godly reformation. The combination of local military rule and strict Puritanism alienated people; for the royalist gentry it was catastrophic.

The Irish nation had been made culpable for the actions of the few and forced to pay heavily; now, by a similar logic, all those who had supported the king at any time over the previous fifteen years were culpable for Penruddock's Rising. All royalists were made liable to some combination of banishment, imprisonment, confiscation and heavy taxation. There were three categories of royalists, as there had been eight categories of Irish: actively subversive, convinced royalists, and guilty during the war. Any person so described with wealth over £100 was liable to punishment and decimation tax. Royalists who had taken part in the action would be imprisoned, or banished and lose their estates; convinced but inactive royalists would be imprisoned or banished but retain their property. Those who were 'guilty during the war' were to pay decimation tax, one-tenth of their income or 6 per cent of the value of their property annually. They had to give bonds for good behaviour and could not leave home without permission. Royalists were expelled from London; records were kept of their movements and also those of travellers from abroad. These draconian measures prevented conspiracy but they intensified the opposition of royalists: those who were lukewarm began to ally with the actively subversive. Despite this fierce clampdown, messages continued to get through to Cologne.

The government also hit out at the royalists' religion: the ejected Anglican clergy were not to live in the houses of the gentry, preach, teach or use the *Book of Common Prayer* on pain of imprisonment. Without parliament, there was no legal basis for these orders but the government had been skating on thin legal ice since the dissolution. Cromwell also revived an Act of the Long Parliament preventing 'delinquents', or erstwhile royalists, from serving on urban corporations.

The instructions to the major generals were refined by Lambert in October and tightened the Puritans' grip on the people. The officers were to 'encourage' and promote godliness, while discouraging 'all prophaneness and ungodliness'.[4] Working with local magistrates, the major generals must strictly enforce the laws against drunkenness, profanity and swearing, prevent cockfighting, bearbaiting and horseracing, and as for the idle, either see they worked or imprison them. Equally, they were to assist the deserving poor. It was also their job to prevent the ejected clergy from ministering to people.

As Puritans and senior officers of the army, the ten major generals were enthusiastic about their task. At last, the effort to reform the nation was not just legislation or aspiration but would be personally directed and enforced. Yet the system was not especially effective. Whalley, very usefully, tried to regulate markets on behalf of small farmers and to resist the high level of enclosure in parts of his district, but he needed legislation and the second Protectorate parliament quashed it. The generally low attainment of 'godly reformation' was due partly to the mute resistance of the nation but also to inaction by central government. Cases of swearing, drunkenness and fornication came to magistrates but convictions did not increase under the major generals. They did manage to close pubs and they harassed revellers but they made no lasting change in public behaviour. However, central government received their enthusiastic reports and thought the campaign was going well. Cromwell told the London corporation that the country had grown 'stronger in virtue'.[5]

Meanwhile, the fleet had arrived in the Caribbean, and on 14 April the attack on Hispaniola was launched. Troops landed near the city of San Domingo, the object of their attack, but the tropical climate, difficult terrain, dysentery and the lack of suitable weaponry weakened the men's morale. They retreated and refused to renew the attempt. The leaders abandoned the attempt as impossible and turned their attention to Jamaica. Landing in Kingston harbour, Penn could fire from his ships, allowing the English forces to take three small forts. Jamaica had a small Spanish population and weaker defences than Hispaniola, and the governor soon surrendered. English supplies were running low, so Penn sailed for England in June and Venables soon followed, leaving another officer in charge.

The failure of the Western Design was a great blow to Cromwell. Penn and Venables were committed to the Tower for desertion, but ultimately the Lord Protector was responsible for sending the expedition. He seems not to have understood what a tropical war would require. Now he wrestled with his conscience, wondering why God had humbled them by the defeat at San Domingo; it had to be the result of 'our sins, as well as others'.[6] He did not see that it was the result of bad planning or that Jamaica would prove a fertile and strategic possession.

Nor did Cromwell's hope of a limited war prove realistic. The attack on Hispaniola confirmed that England was becoming the enemy of Spain, but allying with France took time as Cromwell reacted against French attacks on Protestants and argued over terms. The Dutch had been beaten and the trade agreement with Sweden was being finalised. 'The Commonwealth of England, Scotland and Ireland etc.' was re-emerging as a European power, a position it had lost under James and Charles. It was true, as Owen had preached in 1646, that 'now we are awakened from our effeminacy'.

The Protector was using military strength to carve out a European position but within the Protectorate he had not established stable government. The council was worried that Ireland had still not been planted; the country was unsettled and Irish commerce was slow to revive. Neither Scotland nor Ireland could contribute to the national exchequer: in both the courts were still choked with military cases, enemy combatants were still being transported from both countries, and in neither had the Puritan regime established civil government or ministry on its own terms. However, the troops had at last gained control of most of Scotland and were gradually being disbanded in Ireland, so in 1655 power in both countries was transferred from the military to civilians. In Edinburgh and Dublin, councils were set up under presidents chosen by the Protector, subordinate to the English council. For Ireland, Cromwell chose his younger son Henry to lead the council and command the forces there. Fleetwood was not demoted but just gently removed; Cromwell wrote a charming letter to him, with 'my dear love to thee; and to my dear Biddy', inviting him to return to England 'if you have a mind to come over with your dear wife' – it was deeply embarrassing for him to recall his son-in-law.[7] Henry arrived in summer 1655 and established himself in Dublin, with a princely retinue.

For Scotland, the choice of president fell on Roger Boyle, Viscount Broghill, an odd selection since he was an Old Protestant from Munster, where all his business and political interests lay. That was probably the issue: Cromwell had a high opinion of Broghill's abilities but wanted him out of Ireland, where he was too powerful. With Broghill in Edinburgh, Henry Cromwell would have a free hand in Dublin and could shape the Irish government as he wished. Broghill only agreed to go to Scotland for one year and arrived in September 1655, while

Henry Cromwell stepped ashore in Dublin Bay on 9 July. Charles and Bridget Fleetwood left Ireland in September but he retained his title as Lord Deputy, which made Henry's early rule more difficult.

Fleetwood had managed some transplantation of Catholics, while Protestants had achieved their aims of clemency and promotion. The Catholics had hoped that the 1654 parliament would offer them concessions, but when it was dissolved early in 1655 it had not even considered Irish affairs. Catholic agent Talbot was in London and Fleetwood worried that he might influence the Protector to issue ordinances about Ireland, but Thurloe reassured him that Cromwell had 'declined the legislative power' and would conform to the Instrument by not doing so. Fleetwood was relieved, although the Protector did in fact bend those rules over the next two years. All the same, by the time that Henry Cromwell arrived in Dublin, Catholic landowners were unlikely to benefit from further legislation.[8]

Fleetwood had given up his attempt at a full transplantation of the Catholic population. Pamphlet arguments had some influence but the policy was too difficult to enforce. When all Catholics were ordered to remove from Dublin they did not go, while attempts to empty five counties in south-east Ireland were unsuccessful because Protestant landowners resisted, wanting to retain their servants, tenants and labourers. Historians have linked the softening of transplantation policy to the arrival of Henry Cromwell but the story is more nuanced. Fleetwood's policy was partial, with different policies for different areas and modified when it suited conditions. By 1655, the process had slowed. The reality was that it was comparatively easy for government to legally confiscate and award land on paper, but much harder to physically shift people, so ownership changed but many people could not be induced to transplant. Some proprietors decided to claim what they could in Connaught and went there but many hung on to tiny portions of what they once had owned.

The city of Galway was designated of strategic importance, and under the surrender articles owners might be obliged to leave but be offered the value of their property elsewhere. After lengthy negotiations under Henry Cromwell, by late 1655 this removal had been achieved but no Protestant settlers were found to occupy the city. 'Galway sitteth in the dust and no eye pittieth her,' wrote a Protestant settler, 'her merchants were princes and great among the nations, but now the city that was full of people is solitary and very desolate.'[9] Many of the merchants took their capital and left Ireland, looking for better conditions elsewhere. Henry Cromwell attempted to people

Galway by awarding property to the corporation of Gloucester but repopulating the city took time and Catholics slipped back.

All the same, Henry Cromwell's period of office was markedly different to that of Fleetwood. Ludlow was dismissed, which he resisted, claiming to have his commission from the Rump; but having given in and sailed for England, he was arrested on arrival. The favour which Fleetwood had shown to Baptists and Quakers ceased; instead, Major General Henry Cromwell courted the Old Protestants whom he considered religiously sound and politically responsible, trusting them to hold together the social fabric. The long reign of the Anglo-Irish over Ireland had begun. Re-established on their estates, they hoped for Protestant tenants and, finding few, attracted them with long and generous leases which caused trouble later.

Oliver Cromwell was determined to get the Irish courts working properly, education improved and a well-informed ministry preaching the Gospel, so Henry did his best. However, money was tight. The extensive Munster plantations under Elizabeth had given Cork a well-established Protestant elite which Dublin could call on. Henry chose John Cook, the chief justice of Munster, to revive the courts and Dr Edward Worth led the revival in the church. In contrast, the Ulster plantations under James had produced a Presbyterian population who were more of a challenge than support to government. Cromwell's aim was to entirely reform Irish society, and despite swerves in administration Ireland was indeed being reshaped. Catholics, of both Norman and Gaelic origin, lost power, while Protestants increased their landholding and controlled institutions which were invigorated or entirely altered. Before the war, the Church of Ireland had been more Calvinist than its sister church in England; it had small congregations but owned the churches with their land. What it lacked was funding, but the Cromwellians hoped to improve that and win over the Irish by preaching and teaching. As in England, bishops and the Book of Common Prayer were outlawed, but a national ministry was reinvigorated under Dr Worth, a Trinity man and Dean of Cork. Baptists were discouraged and Quakers were suppressed. Under Henry Cromwell, local government was revived so that gradually the army's role was reduced and civilians took charge of city and borough corporations.

The Ulster Scots, although Protestant, did not fit government plans. They were numerous and maintained their links with Lowland Scotland where resistance to English rule remained strong. For the Protectorate they remained a threat. Henry tried to conciliate them by arranging government salaries for their ministers but he received little support in return – the Ulster Presbyterians were not easily won over. Towards Irish Catholics generally Henry Cromwell's rule was mixed. The Stuarts had marginalised them politically, but the Cromwellian land settlement had forcibly dispossessed most of them. In 1641 Catholics had owned roughly 60 per cent of Irish land but under the Cromwellian settlement that fell to 20 per cent, and they were expelled from the principal cities and from office. Despite this, some retained their positions. The Marquis of Antrim was once more influential in Ulster. As leader of the McDonnells and Argyll's old adversary, Randal had played a dynamic role during the 1640s and frequently changed his alliances. He had since ingratiated himself with parliament and had regained much of his estate, along with a government pension. After the death of his first wife, Katherine, he married Rose O'Neill from the great Ulster dynasty and spent much of the 1650s on his estate at Glenarm. He was still popular in County Antrim and government hoped he might help to stabilise Ulster. He was proving himself a remarkable survivor.

Government needed men of influence and Henry Cromwell, like Broghill in Scotland, tried to build up the civilian institutions while reducing the influence of the army. Unfortunately, the Protector's own council in London was still dominated by officers. Henry received little support from his father but he corresponded regularly with Thurloe, who was supportive and kept him informed. Fleetwood, however, was in London and still had both title and influence.

The three nations had been amalgamated into a single state which was run on English Puritan principles, but in Catholic Ireland and in Presbyterian Scotland religious and nationalist resistance was solidifying. With much public opinion still against it, the London government could only win people over by swift improvements in living standards and civil government. Changing the administration of law from Latin into English was not much help for Gaelic speakers. In Scotland, the great clan leaders lost their feudal fiefdoms – the palatinates, regalities and shrievalties were abolished. Instead, JPs were appointed, although finding suitable men was difficult. Justice was modernised and standardised but the new judges were English. In Ireland, Henry Cromwell's job was harder as judges generally refused to move there. Nor had union been legislated for. Cromwell had issued an ordinance for Scotland and a bill was drawn up for Ireland, but, when parliament was dissolved in 1655, neither had been passed. The three nations were ruled from London with one council and parliament but there was no legal underpinning for the arrangement.

When Broghill and his council assembled in Edinburgh in September 1655, their task was daunting enough. Unlike Ireland, where one man was in charge, in Scotland Broghill ran the government while Monck commanded the army. Only two council members were Scots and the young viscount knew little of the country he must rule; but his mother was Scottish and his numerous siblings had married well, giving him useful relatives in Scotland. Broghill was a convinced Calvinist with links to English Presbyterians; like them, Broghill favoured a structured church and limits on radical religion. His family were intellectuals who knew Milton and Hartlib, while Broghill's brother Robert Boyle was a scientist of lasting significance. In theory, his outlook should have won Broghill friends in Scotland and, with his charm and persuasiveness, he did influence some Scottish politicians; but many viewed him with suspicion. Archibald Johnston of Wariston, with his lawyer's mind and passionate religious strictures, saw Broghill as a scheming interloper whose aristocratic family only made him more unpalatable.

Wariston was a man of the kirk and the efforts of Broghill, and of Cromwellian government generally, to win over the hard core of the Scottish church were unsuccessful, although a few concessions helped. Among their rivalries and splits, there were individuals who would

Sir Archibald Johnston of Wariston.

co-operate with government. The Resolutioners agreed to stop praying publicly for Charles and some Protestors worked with the council. Scotland desperately needed stability but the hard-core Wariston faction remained opposed. London policy concentrated on maintaining peace, promoting trade and education, while a vigorous preaching ministry was established. They hoped to free the people of Scotland from kirk domination and awaken them to a personal understanding of the Gospels. To pay for government in Scotland, the excise was introduced and the assessment levied on personal goods as well as real estate – with howls of protest meeting the news.

For Broghill, agreeing church policy was a challenge. With their open practices and vigorous debates, the soldiers had made a religious impact but the kirk still had tight control. Gillespie was put in charge of certifying ministers but when he leaned towards Independency it further infuriated the kirk. To soften their antagonism, Broghill let each presbytery choose their own minister, as they had done before. Reports of papist activity in the north alarmed Edinburgh so much that in March 1656 the council set the death penalty for Catholic priests found in Scotland. All Catholics had their arms confiscated and had to give securities for good behaviour.

Broghill was in his early thirties when he became president of the Scottish council but he repaid the Protector's confidence. In Edinburgh, he built a party to support the government, oversaw the re-establishment of the law courts and created a single treasury. The men he brought into ruling circles were not the kirkmen who had dominated the previous decade but gentry and professionals of milder temperament. The territory and power of the Marquess of Argyll were gradually reduced, while his son Lord Lorne submitted to the Cromwellians. Argyll had run up large debts during the wars and was in London from 1655 to 1657, trying to ingratiate himself with Cromwell and raise money, but he was arrested for debt. Wariston, also burdened with war debt, cordially loathed Broghill and Independent religion but when Argyll got him a job offer from government, rather as Wariston himself had feared, he was tempted into accepting. The Scottish leaders were being emasculated or won over.

Broghill had agreed to go to Scotland for one year. By harvest time in 1656, the Cromwellian regime had money problems and would have to call another parliament. Broghill's influence was about to increase even further.

15

Governing by Instrument

When Cromwell dissolved his first parliament, he signalled that he would conform to the Instrument of Government by not issuing ordinances and by honouring parliament's decision on tax. However, Penruddock's Rising two months later unnerved the government and they instigated the decimation tax without any parliamentary sanction. If they were acting unlawfully, only the courts could challenge them. Over the next year and a half, when Cromwell was reminded of the limits to his powers, he sometimes chafed and conformed, sometimes acted anyway.

There is no doubt that the rule of the major generals and the heavy taxation of anyone classified as royalist, whether active or not, undermined the standing of the government. Parts of the population were keen that godliness should be enforced, but they were a minority and most people bitterly resented the repression of merriment and recreation. In foreign policy, however, the position of the Protectorate was taking firm shape. A treaty with France was signed in October 1655 and two days later Cromwell published a bellicose declaration against Spain. France was fighting Spain in both the Spanish Netherlands and Catalonia, leaving Spain overextended and in need of allies. Charles saw his opportunity. Cologne was near the Spanish territory and Ormond was sent to Brussels to strengthen Stuart diplomacy. Soon, negotiations with Charles were opened and in the spring he was invited for personal talks, which swiftly led to a treaty. If Charles could get possession of an English port, Spain would provide 6,000 soldiers. When restored as king, Charles would return Jamaica, Antigua and Montserrat to Spain and provide twelve warships to help Felipe IV recover Portugal.

Charles now received a Spanish pension and settled in Bruges, where he gathered a royalist army. Most useful to him were the Irish regiments and their officers already serving in France; Inchiquin stayed at Henrietta-Maria's court in Paris but Lord Muskerry brought troops to the Netherlands. James, Duke of York left the French army to join his brother as commander-in-chief of the Stuart forces. Within a year Charles had 2,500 men – three Irish regiments and one each of Scots and English. This embryonic force developed into the Grenadier Guards, one of the oldest regiments in the British Army. Gaining a powerful ally was a great step forward for Charles but, for his reputation in England, it was potentially damaging. He had lived in France, now he was allied to Catholic Spain; Charles knew that if he leaned too far towards that faith he would never be King of England. It might win him friends in Europe and Ireland but it would alienate Britain where Protestantism was so strong; his father had tried to walk that tightrope and failed. In Scotland, Charles had signed the Covenant but now he seemed close to the Catholic powers. How could he remain a steady figurehead for Anglicans, whose church he led and whose clergy had been challenged, marginalised or even imprisoned? Cromwell's Protestantism was altogether different, with toleration enshrined in the Instrument at his wish, giving the sects great latitude. The Protector tried to protect Protestants generally and complained to the French ambassador about their treatment in France but, when urged to be lenient to his own Catholics, Cromwell plaintively laid the blame on parliament and his councillors. Oddly, a pattern was emerging whereby British rulers from Charles I to William III advocated religious toleration while the political elite insisted on tighter restrictions.

The recusancy laws had been repealed in 1650, which benefitted Catholics, but conversely they suffered worse penalties under the sequestration system, lost the right to vote or sit in parliament and, after Penruddock's Rising, fell under decimation tax and an oath of abjuration. Mass was illegal and priests were subject to the death penalty, although in England there is record of only one execution of a priest, who was hanged, drawn and quartered. Executions might be few but the threat continued. Irish Catholics were the most vulnerable but English Catholics also lost heavily.

The policy of both Commonwealth and Protectorate was not religious toleration in the broad sense; members of the Rump used that term pejoratively to mean allowing licence to the radical sects. What the Puritans demanded and spoke of constantly was 'liberty of conscience'; they were concerned about religious freedom for the

Calvinist godly or elect. When they tried to legislate and had to define those terms, they faltered. In a speech of 1656, Cromwell spoke of 'men that believe in Jesus Christ ... men that believe the remission of sins through the blood of Jesus Christ, and free justification by the blood of Christ, and live upon the grace of God: that *those men are certain they are so* – they are members of Jesus Christ, and are to Him as the apple of His eye'.[1] He is referring to predestination, the belief that some are destined to be saved. Under Cromwell, the godly were the elite, although he was reluctant to penalise people for their faith. Yet his anti-Catholic statements are numerous, whether against the Irish or Spanish. In foreign policy he wanted to promote an alliance of European Protestants. The Churches of England and Ireland were a problem for the Puritans; they had strong Calvinist elements – the 39 Articles were retained under Cromwell – but the Puritans outlawed their rituals and knew their members were sworn royalists.[2]

Toleration was not widened by Cromwell but rather, the band of acceptable religious practice was shifted along the spectrum. Liberty was given to true Calvinists and Gospel readers such as Independents, Presbyterians and Baptists, who posed no threat. Outside this band, people might be liable to fines, prosecution or imprisonment. Socinians and Arminians were not tolerated. Sects which had no respect for the state or authority were penalised: the leaders of the Fifth Monarchists, Ranters, Familists and others who seethed with visions and apocalyptic beliefs, were warned and many imprisoned. The Quakers claimed the right to toleration under the terms of the Instrument but were seen as both blasphemous and disruptive. As the Protectorate coalesced, with much of its support coming from landowners, merchants and the professions, demands for action against the sects strengthened.

As he became established as head of state, Cromwell faced many problems familiar to Charles I: funding, religion and the limits of his power. Their personalities could not have been more different, yet Cromwell – like Charles I – taxed without consent of parliament and he outlawed certain religious practices as he strove to shore up his position and maintain state security. He was already careworn, as the burden of government weighed on him, and by 1657, especially after two accidents – one on a horse and one in a coach – he was clearly less robust and there was a tremor in his handwriting.

The constitution had not been settled, but in Britain the tumult in society had subsided, albeit uneasily. There was considerable hardship for some, although the propertied classes who had survived the revolution wanted no further upset. They looked at the ageing general with anxiety. What if Oliver Cromwell should die? His undoubted gifts would be hard to replicate – his authority over the army, his sound practical intelligence, his appetite for mercy and his growing skills with officials and ambassadors. The war had taken its toll on fighting men and Cromwell was in his late fifties, under enormous pressure and showing the strain. The elite who had done well under his rule, who held positions and were received at his court, feared what might follow him. The government was not settled on firm foundations and no successor had been identified. There were challenges in the courts, both to ordinances and to laws; some had run out but others had been enacted by dubious parliaments or processes. For example, Cony refused to pay duty on imported silk, arguing that the taxes were not legally constituted. He and his lawyers were imprisoned and only released when they admitted their offence but the problem remained; if the law had an insecure base, perhaps the state had no firm foundation either.

Instability could be whipped up by the printing press; in 1653, a tough and comprehensive licensing Act had been passed which the Commonwealth had applied fitfully depending on the level of threat. The Protectorate, with more enemies and better management, was more vigorous and repressive against unlicensed publications. Cromwell issued draconian new orders on the press in August 1655. These were enforced and all but two government newspapers closed. The orders could be used against political subversion but were widely employed to promote the godly reformation. Anything blasphemous or obscene was pounced on, and burned.[3]

The government was not just censor but propagandist, publishing its orders but also promoting the aims and the legitimacy of the government. John Milton and Marchamont Nedham both wrote for the Interregnum governments, as did godly ministers – of whom John Owen was the most prominent. Poets, too, commented on affairs but were cautious – Andrew Marvell published *The First Anniversary of the Government of the Lord Protector* anonymously and although he showed poems to his friends in manuscript, most of his work was published for the first time after his death.[4] Criticism of Cromwell, or discussion of whether he should take the crown, was muted. The government also worked hard to weaken any support for Charles in official publications, portraying the Stuarts as Scottish or French, and therefore alien, while Charles was mocked as weak and degenerate.

However, suppressing publication is a double-edged sword; as critics of the government went silent so the Cromwellians had less evidence of public opinion. Fears of assassination, rebellion and invasion remained intense. Should the government fall, not only would its project fail but its leaders might lose their property, their newly acquired positions and estates – even their lives. They were acutely vigilant but their methods of suppression made them more unpopular, especially decimation tax and the treatment of royalists. Loyal Protectorate officials sometimes refused to collect the tax from inoffensive landowners. Meanwhile, the networks between Charles and his supporters remained active. While royalist gentry were taxed and watched, active conspirators were imprisoned. Wildman was in prison from 1655 to 1656 and was probably released because he informed to Thurloe, but he continued to plot Cromwell's assassination. Sexby, more flamboyant and fanciful, made high contacts in Flanders and was sent to Madrid for negotiations with Felipe IV but the ministers there were unimpressed with him.

Despite insecurity and excessively high taxation, commerce was improving after the disruptions of war. Now that there was a customs union with England, Scottish prosperity slowly grew, but to most Scots union was not a trading opportunity but highly taxed colonisation. Gradually, some Scottish officials and landowners were won over and worked for the government, but most of the administration in Edinburgh was staffed by Englishmen or army personnel. The English officials benefitted from government salaries, land grants and commercial opportunities in Scotland: 'The English has all the moneyies,' complained a Scottish gentleman. Despite improving conditions, Scotland still could not pay for its own government or the army stationed there. Broghill reorganised the treasury and new taxes were introduced but that made the new regime even less popular, and failed to solve Scotland's fiscal problem anyway.

Irish trade faced greater obstacles as there was no customs union with Britain and the Navigation Act prevented Irish ships from trading with English colonies. The collapse of Irish commerce had been exacerbated by emigration – not only of the fighting men who were young and vigorous but also the Catholic merchants who took their capital with them. Expelling all the Irish from Limerick and Galway left these important trading cities largely deserted. Economic revival was slow in Ireland, so at first trade restrictions had little effect, though they would cause friction before long. Improving government finance was high among Cromwell's concerns.

It was characteristic of Cromwell that one of his famous policies, the readmission of the Jews, was a mixture of religious aspiration and hard commercial calculation. The Jews had been expelled in 1290, although a few still lived quietly in Britain, fleeing the Inquisition in Spain and Portugal. In 1651, on a diplomatic mission to the Netherlands, Thurloe met the Jewish leader Menasseh ben Israel in Amsterdam and advised him to apply for admission to England. Through their trading routes, the Jews had extensive networks which might provide invaluable intelligence, and Thurloe, who was a master of spies, was attracted by that. Cromwell and the council were keen to access Jewish banking capital and expertise. Besides this, two prophecies were at work. Jewish tradition said their diaspora must be complete before they could return to Israel, and Christian prophecy foretold that the conversion of the Jews to Christianity would be the prelude to the millennium – the coming of Christ's kingdom. For Cromwell, there was nowhere more fitting for this conversion to take place than in England where God's people were in power and expecting fulfilment of these promises.

An invitation was issued and Menasseh Ben Israel came to London, where he lodged in the Strand to be near Whitehall. He dined with the Protector and some understanding was reached, so in October 1655 a formal petition was lodged. It was a sensitive issue and Cromwell was cautious, first calling a small conference and then allowing the public to attend. There was strong feeling both ways: some hoped that accepting the Jews would bring rewards both spiritual and financial, others called the Jews a cursed people with whom Christians should have no contact. However, expert opinion said the Jews had only been expelled by royal edict and there was no legal prohibition. Rather than try to legislate for them, Cromwell gave the Jewish spokesmen verbal assurances that the recusancy laws would not be used against them. Several came over from the Netherlands, a burial ground was bought, and gradually Jewish merchants, bankers and their families settled in London. Charles II later refused to expel them and legislation in 1664 would give them rights.

The Protectorate government still had difficult budget problems. The Instrument allowed for an army of 30,000, but the standing forces were well above that number and in case of war parliament had to be called. The war with Spain and need for revenue forced Cromwell to call another parliament. Like his predecessor, he was reluctant because any parliament called on a regular franchise would be extremely difficult for Cromwell to work with. Charles I had led the Church of England, whereas Cromwell's religious views were those of the minority. Both rulers had taxed without parliamentary consent. Curiously, both rulers claimed God's mandate – Charles as an anointed king whose birthright was to rule, Cromwell as a victorious general on whom God's providence had showered victories. Now, the major generals were provoking a clamour around London and south-east England, as people either demanded a parliament or heard rumours that one was imminent.

For Cromwell, heavily burdened with affairs of state, a more worrying demand came from the army, which suggested he give up his command since he was no longer a full-time general. Cromwell was said to be willing if Fleetwood took over, but the officers wanted Lambert. Or so the Venetian resident reported – he may not be accurate. Certainly Lambert was a strong voice of opposition in the council and had proved himself at the victories of Preston and Dunbar; he was influential.

The Lord Protector, hoping to delay calling parliament, suggested he raise money by executive order and seemed untroubled that it would be illegal, but neither his officials nor the army officers would countenance such moves and Cromwell gave in. A parliament was announced on 26 June 1656, and shortly afterwards writs were sent out. Only men of 'known affection' would be permitted to stand but this instruction was either unclear or ignored – in many constituencies, candidates were not filtered. The writs were, of course, sent to Scotland and Ireland, where Lord Broghill and Henry Cromwell had to manage elections. For both men it was a difficult task, but each had political influence and diplomatic skills. Throughout the two islands, the property-owning classes who were not under sequestration, decimation or arrest were being wooed into support for the regime.

The elections of 1656 tested Broghill's management and proved him largely successful. Thirty MPs were duly elected; sixteen were English and fourteen Scottish, reflecting the number of Englishmen holding positions north of the border. Many of those elected were army officers who also held civilian posts. Samuel Desborough, brother of the major general and an in-law of Cromwell, was a Scottish councillor, commissioner for claims on forfeited estates and held other senior positions – he got a seat. The Scottish members were not aristocrats but influential gentry, the type of men whom the Protectorate had promoted. After the elections, Broghill wrote to Thurloe, 'I hope you will not have one unfit person out of this nation.'[5] He himself was among the MPs for Scotland, had managed the election of Desborough carefully, prevented Argyll from using his patronage, and instead had got the English judge Lockhart elected for the marquess's territory.

More than that, Broghill had influenced the elections in Ireland, even though Henry Cromwell ruled in Dublin Castle and had overseen the Irish elections. Several Scottish councillors were elected to parliament and when they left for London the council often had no quorum, which shows how thin government was in Edinburgh, with a few men taking many jobs.

In England, there was tremendous urgency over the elections. Thurloe told Henry Cromwell, 'The day of election now draws near; and here is the greatest striving to get into Parliament that ever was known.'[6] There were angry cries against 'Major Generals and decimators', as opponents of the government rallied support.

In Ireland, the elections were concerned with other issues. Henry Cromwell had pursued a more conciliatory policy than his brother-in-law Fleetwood, aiming to create stability and security. His father spoke frequently of healing and settling, but in Ireland, where death, emigration and confiscation had all been so high, talk of healing was hardly meaningful. Rather, a new society was being built and Henry identified the Old Protestants as the foundation on which to construct it. The war had brought the final collapse of the Catholic Old English and it was the Old Protestants with larger properties and better connections, rather than the new settlers, who were ascendant. Nineteen out of thirty MPs for Ireland came from this group, with eight English officials and three army officers. Henry winnowed them again and prevented six members from travelling to London – only one military man sat for Ireland at Westminster in 1656.

In England, the writs for an election had unleashed the rumbling opposition to the Protectorate. Several critics rushed into print. First was Sir Henry Vane: *A Healing Question* was published in May 1656. Vane was a Commonwealthsman and an idealist. He was not a democrat and did not support a wide franchise but he promoted an alternative to the Protectorate. Like Cromwell, his concern was healing and settling. As to the aim of his pamphlet: 'THE QUESTION propounded is, What possibility doth yet remain (all things considered) of reconciling and uniting the dissenting judgments of honest men within the three nations, who still pretend to agree in the spirit, justice, and reason of the same good cause, and what is the means to effect this?'[7]

The 'good cause', the cause for which they had fought, was to create a government of godliness and liberty which could not be overthrown. Vane argued that 'the whole party of honest men adhering to this cause' had the right to set up that government. It should be for the good of the whole people, but those who won the war had the right to rule. He complained that recently one group had taken over, whereas all those who had supported the 'good old cause' and won power should exercise it. The late king had demanded that he, not parliament, should control the militia; that was the grounds of the quarrel. Now, it was essential that parliament should control the army. Religious freedom was a right, given to people by the sacrifice of Jesus, and magistrates should not meddle with that. The army may have delivered the people into liberty but they must be subject to proper legal control. Arms must not be used to exploit private gain. Rather, both judicature and military must agree so that all supporters of the cause should come together in healing.

Vane proposed an oligarchical system for government, drawing on the republican ideas of classical times. A council would rule, who would be chosen for life and would fill its own vacancies. Only supporters of the cause would have the right to vote for parliaments or sit on the council. There would be no limit on religious freedom. Vane's vision was of permanent rule by people like himself who had challenged Charles I and won the war. The government disliked this publication and Vane was ordered to post a bond of £5,000 to guarantee good behaviour. When he refused, he was imprisoned in Carisbrooke Castle.

Other writers defined liberty differently. By late July, a paper entitled *England's Remembrancers* was being distributed in London and bundles of it sent out to the regions. It encouraged men to vote and to choose representatives who would re-establish the liberties of Englishmen and the honour of the nation.[8] 'Do not your infringed rights speak? Do not your invaded properties speak? Do not your gasping liberties speak?' it asked. The pamphlet was anonymous but several enemies of the regime were suspected and arrests were made.

It was harvest time and, with all these arguments inflaming the nation, elections were duly held. Unfortunately for the Cromwellians, several Commonwealthsmen, stalwarts of the Rump, were elected. On 17 September, the new members assembled in Westminster Abbey for a service and then moved to the Painted Chamber where Cromwell spoke to them at some length. The core of his speech was a defence of the major generals, who Cromwell insisted were both 'a little thing' and essential for safety. The Lord Protector rambled during his oration but he began forthrightly with security. 'Why, truly, your great Enemy is the Spaniard. He is. He is a natural enemy.' The Long Parliament had tried but failed to make peace with Spain. Cromwell thought France less bound to the Pope and so able to act freely, whereas Spain answered to Rome. Spain was at the root of threats to the country because she had allied with Charles Stuart. Cromwell told them, 'It's true and certain that the Papists, the Priests and Jesuits have a great influence upon the Cavalier Party.'[9]

Then on to his recurring worry – 'Our Nation is overwhelmed with debts!' he told them. As to liberty and prosperity, Cromwell believed they depended on reform, both in the law and in godly behaviour. The major generals, in his view, had kept the peace and discountenanced vice.

'The state is hugely in debt,' he announced again. When the Long Parliament was dissolved, according to Cromwell, there had been debts of £700,000. His own government 'abated' £90,000 of debt during its first year and had been thrifty. He emphasised that they had neither embezzled nor wasted the treasure of the nation. Then he returned to spiritual matters, reminding them of the great providence of God and the hopes for the nation. At last, he sent the members to choose their speaker and set to work.

However, when they reached the parliament house, the new MPs discovered that about one hundred of them were to be excluded. To get in, they needed a certificate from the council. At the door of the House, three colonels and a troop of soldiers examined these entry tickets. The council had been unhappy about the list of men elected and had used this method to winnow them. Naturally, there was an uproar. Not only the excluded members but also those admitted protested vehemently. Unable to alter the situation, those who were allowed to sit began work, but across the country people were enraged that their elected representatives had been prevented from taking their places. The parliament which did sit was composed of the government's friends. Cromwell's first parliament had tried to redesign the Instrument of Government and the second one wanted even greater change, but this House had been carefully shaped and it turned out to have conservative, not radical aims. The men in the chamber were looking for stability and, in their hands, England turned away from revolution and towards the structures of the past.

Charles II, after Adriaen Hannemann.
(© National Portrait Gallery, London)

Portrait of King Charles II of England 1653, Philippe de Champaigne. (Courtesy of the Cleveland Museum of Art)

Henry, Duke of Gloucester, by Adriaen Hanneman. (Courtesy of the National Gallery of Art, Washington)

William II, Prince of Orange, and his bride, Mary Stuart, 1641, by Anthony van Dyck.
(Courtesy of the Rijksmuseum, Amsterdam)

Richard Cromwell by John Hayls, *circa* 1658.
(Courtesy of the Cromwell Museum, Huntingdon)

Sir Edward Hyde, Adriaen Hanneman.
(© National Portrait Gallery, London)

Sir Henry Vane the Younger, studio of Sir Peter Lely.
(© Lord Barnard, Raby Estate)

Sir Arthur Haselrig,
artist unknown.
(© National Portrait
Gallery, London)

General George Monck,
1st Duke of Albermarle,
after Samuel Cooper.
(Courtesy of the
Cromwell Museum,
Huntingdon)

John Owen, attributed
to John Greenhill.
(© National Portrait
Gallery, London)

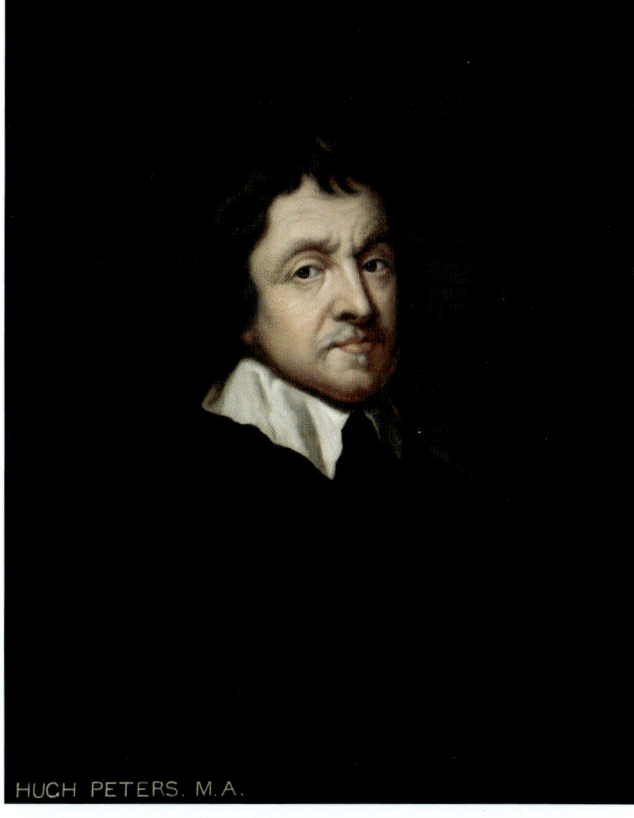

Hugh Peters, by
Gustavus Ellinthorpe
Sintzenich and studio.
(© Mansfield College,
University of Oxford)

HUGH PETERS. M.A.

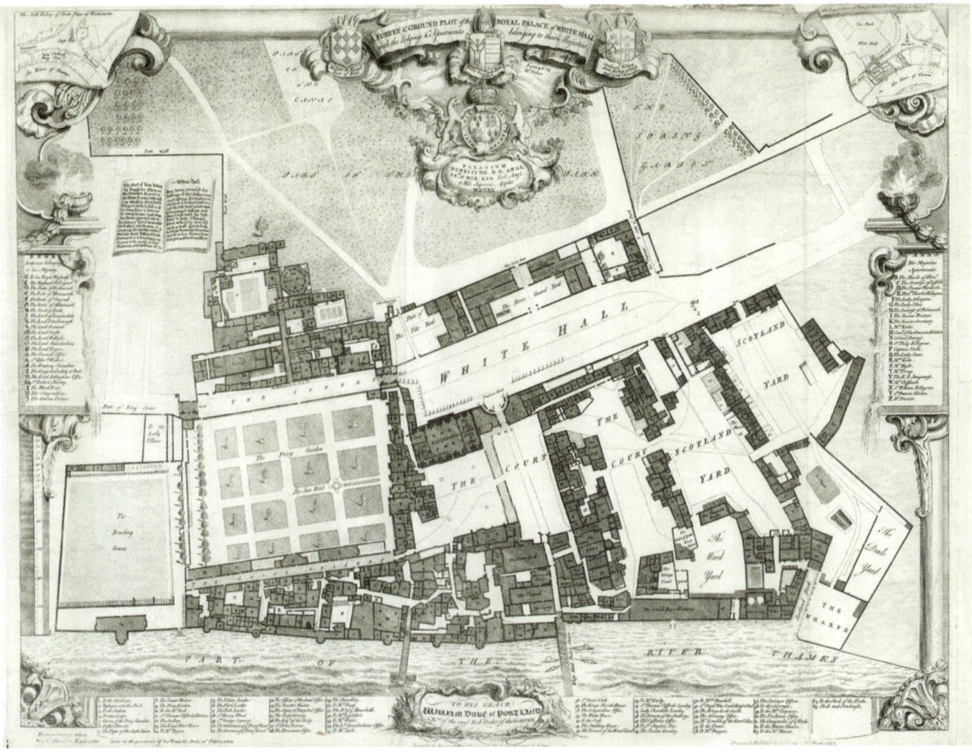

'A Survey & Ground Plot of the Royal Palace of White Hall in 1680',
by John Fisher from an engraving by George Vertue.

Arrival of Charles II, King of England, in Rotterdam, 24 May 1660,
by Lieve Pietersz. Verschuier. (Courtesy of the Rijksmuseum, Amsterdam)

16

Cromwell's Last Parliament

The second Protectorate parliament began, as Cromwell had hoped, by passing government measures, but it soon reverted to the constitution, which the Cromwellians believed was settled. Wrangling over its form had consumed the political elite throughout the 1640s, and since the execution of the king there had been three distinct forms of government: Commonwealth, Barebones and now the Protectorate. However, now that trade was improving and confiscations ending, a solid property-owning class had stabilised, determined on a permanent settlement with decisive government and curbs on radical religion. Their paramount concern was the succession: the fact that no one had been named was all the more alarming because of Cromwell's increasing infirmity and the attempts on his life. Moreover, the recurrent problems in the courts over the validity of legislation demanded a permanent solution.

The succession must have been on Cromwell's mind. Male primogeniture had been the rule for centuries but until now Cromwell had not promoted his eldest son, Richard, who was a country gentleman with negligible military experience. Instead, his younger son Henry had ridden in the coach with his father to his investiture and now commanded in Ireland. Richard was a slim, blond young man, well-liked but not assertive, who was often castigated by his father for profligacy, being too fond of hunting and too little concerned with religion. Once married, he lived with his wife Dorothy on his in-laws' estate in Hampshire. He did win a seat in the 1654 parliament and was appointed as head of the Trade Committee the following year but it was Thurloe who set the agenda there. Still, Richard was becoming more visible in London and had a residence within Whitehall Palace.[1]

Oliver's second parliament began energetically. When the new house assembled, MPs annulled the royal title of Charles Stuart, passed a treason Act, approved the war with Spain and talked about further taxes for the military. Statements of government debt were laid before the House to emphasise the urgency, but a Spanish treasure fleet had been taken off Cadiz and great prizes were hoped for. If chests of gold did come ashore, they did not reach London – only about £250,000 was paid to the government, about half of what was expected. Parliament, unsure how long it would sit, took up many issues but finished few. Taxes, law reform and a myriad of practical issues demanded their attention, but the issue of the constitution seethed. Since those first days when the Long Parliament challenged Charles I, it had been in contention.

During the summer, various publications had tried to influence the election, but in the autumn a more serious work probed the real differences between monarchy and republic. The revolutionaries had proved that cutting off the king's head was not enough: power structures had to alter, but how deep did change have to go? James Harrington's *Commonwealth of Oceana* said that power lay in property ownership. A state where the ruler owned all land, for example the Turkish Sultan, resulted in absolute monarchy. Where it was distributed between ruler and aristocracy, mixed monarchy was appropriate. A wider distribution of land would suit a republic. Harrington argued that the dissolution of the monasteries had shifted power but left a mismatch between ownership and authority. To prevent power swinging back to the aristocracy, he wanted primogeniture discontinued and property distributed among all the children of a family. However, he believed that property ownership should remain linked to military service as in feudal times – the state would be defended by a citizen militia, with the richest making up the cavalry.

Harrington's thesis was pertinent, as the Interregnum governments had made substantial land transfers. The largest awards – in acres, value and effect – were of course in Ireland, where both Gaelic social systems and Catholic dominance had been effectively demolished. In Scotland, changes of land ownership were modest but the powers attached to land had been weakened and feudal forms overturned. In England, the royalists had lost land or were punitively taxed, while the army officers and merchants had emerged well from the various land transfers. So, Harrington's book was timely but it rattled the government, which was sensitive about the issue. The council was about to suppress *Oceana* but it is said that Cromwell's daughter

Elizabeth Claypole got hold of a copy and spoke in favour of it, so Oliver – who thought it dangerous and fanciful – allowed publication to go ahead.

In Cromwell's view, the country was constantly on the brink of strife and only he, acting as Lord Protector, prevented that. Arguments and publications disturbed the uneasy peace and he was not squeamish about suppressing dissent in whatever form. His actions might have seemed justified if the Instrument had produced good government but there were still problems. The exclusion of elected MPs like Bradshaw, Hazelrig, Vane and their colleagues caused resentment, but other influential voices arose in the Commons and by Christmas new leaders had emerged. Lord Broghill was one, as leader of the Irish Protestants and a man of ability. Whitelocke, lawyer and colleague of Cromwell, had returned to parliament, Sir Charles Wolseley was a young but significant councillor and Lord Chief Justice John Glyn was influential. Older men, like Lenthall and Fiennes, retained respect from the war period but, as parliament struggled to improve the Protectorate, younger men were finding a political voice, and their careers would stretch into the Restoration period.

The big issues of this parliament were the succession and the balance of power. The military budget was still a problem and law reform rankled. Religious freedom underlay the revolution but setting limits was contentious. The influence of the army was implicit in every issue. Cromwell praised the major generals for enhancing godly reformation but civilians were fiercely antagonistic to them and when the militia bill was introduced, matters came to a head. If the decimation tax and the major generals became permanent, the Protectorate would surely be a military government rather than a parliamentary one. Members were reminded of just how often the army had determined events. Another assassination attempt that January, in which Sindercombe, acting for Sexby, attempted to set fire to Whitehall, only roused their fears another notch. The future must be secured – and not by the army.

In December 1656, the issue of religious freedom came into the House, not as abstract arguments but in the person of the Quaker James Nayler. Once more, a single problem opened up larger and difficult issues – this time the limits of toleration and the judicial powers of the House. Nayler was a Quaker who had already been imprisoned. He had been a quartermaster under Lambert and was well-regarded in the army, but after joining the Quakers he became influential in the sect and especially admired by women, who saw a Jesus figure in him. On release from prison in Exeter, he rode into

Bristol in a procession much like that of Jesus into Jerusalem, with his followers singing hosannas. He was promptly arrested and sent to London to be tried. His case was brought up in parliament on 31 October; a committee examined him and decided that he had indeed behaved as if he was Christ. This caused furious reactions from many Puritans, enraged by Nayler's blasphemies. Unable to decide how to proceed, parliament called the offender into the Commons for questioning. Nayler admitted acting on a revelation from God instructing him 'to summon this nation', but only to announce that Christ was coming, not to impersonate him.

Nothing seemed to goad Puritan MPs more than scratching their religious sensibilities; any challenge might enrage them. They spent nine days in debate and passed a sentence of savage cruelty on the young Quaker. By forgoing the death sentence, they felt they had been lenient but they fell over each other to heap tortures on Nayler. Whitelocke said it should be left to the courts but there was a debate about whether the Blasphemy Act still stood; the draconian one of 1648 had been annulled and parliament thought the 1650 replacement too lenient. Unwilling to pass a new bill which Cromwell might veto, the parliament assumed judicial powers itself. This was controversial since previously only the House of Lords had that role. However, Lord Chief Justice Glyn backed this interpretation of their powers and the House passed sentence.

James Nayler was to be set in the pillory in Westminster, whipped from Westminster to the Old Exchange, put in the pillory there for two hours, then his tongue was to be bored with a hot iron and his forehead branded. After that, he was to be sent to Bristol and whipped again. Finally, he was to be imprisoned in Bridewell in solitary confinement and put to hard labour. Nayler said he hoped to have the spiritual strength to withstand this. The first part of the sentence was so severe that the second part had to be delayed. Naylor bore his torments bravely but the large crowd stood and watched silently, bare-headed. Archbishop Laud's courts had passed cruel sentences but the punishment of Nayler surpassed them.

Cromwell knew the limits of his powers under the Instrument and did not try to prevent the sentence being carried out, but he did question the legal basis of it, writing to parliament to emphasise his abhorrence of Nayler's activities but asking the House to confirm the grounds on which it acted. After extensive debate, the House failed to reply because they had claimed powers which the Instrument had not awarded them. If a conflict arose between the Protector and parliament, there was no one to arbitrate – but they did not want to admit that in writing. Cromwell later referred to Nayler as a case where parliament acted unchecked. As to funding the state, the Militia Bill was thrown out, which ended the rule of the major generals; without tax they could not hire their militias. Parliament did, however, vote £400,000 to prosecute the Spanish war, which was Cromwell's project and one they wanted to support.

The defects in the constitution were becoming obvious. Not only was the state insecure but the law was not functioning properly. There had been five distinct periods of lawmaking since the war broke out: the Long Parliament, the Rump, Cromwell and his officers by decree, Barebones and lastly the Protectorate, under which both Cromwell's decrees and ordinances, as well as his parliaments' legislation, had been enacted. As a result, judges and magistrates were unsure which laws to uphold. Charles I had been accused of ruling outside the law, whereas the revolution had built up a body of orders, ordinances, decrees and legislation of uncertain status. There were challenges in the courts, sometimes parliament was unsure and merchants argued that taxes were unlawful. In this uncertainty, judges were often unwilling to convict.

Among the elite and in parliament, there was talk of reviving the 'ancient constitution', in which the various institutions and estates had well-established roles. If Cromwell became king – and this had been mooted several times before – the courts could act on behalf of the crown, with continuity from the previous era. It should be possible to use the old forms of government without recreating the whole system and MPs got to work on yet another constitutional blueprint, inserting new features into old forms. Broghill acted as a focus, gathering people at his London house where it was said lights burned late into the night. On 23 February, Sir Christopher Packe introduced a remonstrance into the House.

It proposed that Cromwell become king and name his successor and that parliament should have two chambers, the second nominated by the Protector and acting like a senate, which could block legislation the Protector disliked. The Council of State would be renamed the Privy Council as before, nominated by the Protector but approved by existing council members and parliament. Senior official appointments would need approval by both houses. The sums to support the armed forces and civil government were to be fixed – although Cromwell later got the amount raised to a guaranteed taxation of £1,900,000 a year. As to religion, there was to be a written confession of faith to which clergy must conform and the laity must at least accept the Trinity and the Bible as the received word of God. 'Papists and prelatists' – Catholics and Anglicans – could not practise their religion.

This remonstrance had features of the monarchical system – the Protector could choose the upper house and nominate his councillors – but it gave parliament the powers which Pym had looked for, namely the right to approve councillors and officials. The old forms were to come back – upper house and privy council – but now parliament had some say in executive power. Importantly, this proposal was for civilian government; MPs would control council appointments, not the army, and after Cromwell the head of state would be a civilian.

The officers saw clearly enough what was envisaged and they disliked it. Parliament had already disempowered the major generals; now they were wresting control from those men who had won the war and led the revolution. The London-based officers joined the major generals and a delegation of 100 officers went to visit the Lord Protector, with Lambert prominent among them. Cromwell greeted his officers with petulance. Their chief complaint was the title of king but they disliked the whole initiative. We have a good idea of what was said at the meeting because two letters have survived which recount the main argument.[2]

Cromwell reminded them that he had been offered the kingship before and by the officers themselves. He was no lover of the title and had twice refused it. He ran through the changes which had occurred since the king's death and complained that he had been obliged to adopt the army's policies; they had made him dissolve the Rump against his own judgement and to call the Nominated or Barebones parliament, chosen by the officers but without the skills to rule. It was army officers who drew up the Instrument of Government, which had been enacted swiftly, despite its imperfections. The Instrument clearly needed revisions but he, Cromwell, could not rewrite it. He claimed the officers had 'made a drudge' of him. They had demanded a second parliament, which he did not want. They thought they could get their own people in but they had not. 'It is time to come to a settlement, and lay aside arbitrary proceedings, so unacceptable to the nation,' he said. The parliament needed a balancing power – that is, a second chamber – for he warned them that 'the case of James Nayler might happen to be your case'.[3] The officers were silenced by this speech and some were swayed by it into supporting parts of the remonstrance. Parliament, however, had decided that no cherry-picking should take place – the whole scheme must be accepted in its entirety, or fall. Above all were the urgent demands that Cromwell name his successor.

Parliament debated and modified the remonstrance, then renamed it the Humble Petition and Advice. A committee was set up and a date set to meet the Protector. Cromwell chose 31 March and at 11 a.m. they assembled in the Banqueting House in Whitehall – a venue strongly associated with the Stuarts. Cromwell came with some of his council and many officers – Edward Montagu, now General-at-Sea, carried the sword of state but Lambert stayed away. The Speaker explained and promoted this latest version of the document and, of course, Cromwell said he needed time to reflect and consult God.

It is hard to gauge public opinion because people spoke with caution. Nedham had written articles preparing people for a restoration of monarchy but there was a danger that, for many people, monarchy would mean the Stuarts. Some army officers came around to the idea of Cromwell as king but important men were opposed, even those close to him. The more radical in religion, the more opposed they were to kingship; letters and petitions reached Cromwell from the sects, warning that kingship would be blasphemous and profane since providence had destroyed the institution. Opposition was strong among the Puritans, who believed that all forms of government were temporary and of this world, while the eternal things were of another order. Wariston was furious. Blaming Broghill, he addressed God in his diary: 'Thou sees the instrument, Lord Brochil, of carrying it on is the instrument of our ruyne; he thinks to be very great by his so doing and so hoopes to undoe us. Lord, free us of him if it be Thy will.'[4] Many of Cromwell's supporters thought that monarchy suited England: it was familiar and accepted, so restoring the known forms would bring settlement. It would certainly resolve the problems with the law, which would once more act for the crown.

Cromwell did not ponder long. On 4 April, he told the committee that his conscience prevented him from accepting. The promoters of the scheme were dejected but the major generals and their friends exulted. However, the scheme was not dead and debate continued. Three days later, the committee approached Cromwell again and he seemed to haver. A series of meetings followed which took up most of April. Cromwell made several speeches but he was ill in the middle of the month. On the 21st he spoke at length, again reciting the stages of the revolution. Barebones he referred to as 'a story of my own weakness and folly'.[5] He reminded MPs how much they still had to do to perfect the godly reformation. He wanted them to confirm the acts and ordinances which had been made over recent years, as so many property titles rested on those orders. In Ireland, that was especially important. 'We did the Commonwealth service!' he told MPs. 'And we have in that made great settlements; that we have! We have settled almost the whole affairs of Ireland, the rights and interests of the soldiers there, and of the planters and adventurers.' He was listing his government's achievements, as well as demanding they were underpinned by law.[6] It was true that unless parliament legislated, substantial land grants could be challenged. In all three nations, judges and courts had been appointed by the current elite, but if the Cromwellians lost their hold on power, land titles might be less secure. Parliament took this advice and by the end of April many of the Acts and ordinances were passed *en bloc* and without debate, including the union with Scotland.[7] A union with Ireland was not passed, causing intense disappointment to the Irish elite as it had promised free trade, legal reform, proportionate taxation and guaranteed representation at Westminster.[8]

Cromwell thought the Humble Petition and Advice was preferable to the Instrument but he still wanted changes. Parliament produced an amended version; surely now he would agree. Instead, there was a long delay. No one knew what was in Cromwell's mind, not the ambassadors, not his sons nor his extended family, not even Thurloe. Around Whitehall there was anxiety and speculation. The Protector called a meeting, then cancelled it. Meanwhile, the diehard officers prevailed on John Owen to write a petition against kingship, which was presented to parliament. When Cromwell called a meeting for 8 May, MPs were hopeful. But when they arrived at the Banqueting House, they had a stunning disappointment. Cromwell told them, 'I cannot undertake the government with the title of king.'[9] They had stipulated no cherry picking – the scheme was a whole package – but now they had to compromise. After much wrangling, the title of king was removed, the title of Protector was retained and on 25 May the Humble Petition and Advice was accepted by Cromwell at last.

Yet again, they had spent half the year revising the constitution, when there was much else to be done. On 26 June, Cromwell was reinstated under the new regime and this time with considerable pomp. The coronation chair was moved to Westminster Hall and the Protector wore a robe of purple and ermine, a sword of justice and carried a golden sceptre. Significantly, Cromwell was escorted by his Life Guard and the Yeoman of the Guard, whereas previously his own army with its officers had been his close attendants. The rule of the army had been pushed aside in favour of civilian government – the gentry, lawyers and merchants in parliament had gained the upper hand.

While the great debates were taking their course, the Fifth Monarchists were planning insurrection and Sexby was plotting assassination. The Fifth Monarchists gathered in arms but they were few in number and easily arrested; Sexby was a different form of threat. Working with an accomplice, he produced a pamphlet entitled *Killing No Murder*, published under an assumed name. It argued that since Cromwell was a tyrant, it was no crime to kill him. Most of the print run was seized; Sexby was caught and put in the Tower where he died early the following year of unknown causes.

Having rewritten the constitution and provided for a second chamber, parliament adjourned until January 1658. Cromwell had not yet named a successor but he needed time to assemble his second chamber. Once they were in place, the miserable business of excluding elected members would be unnecessary because, like the House of Lords, the second chamber was hand-picked by the Protector. The council was reorganised because it now needed parliament's approval and members had to take an oath. Lambert refused to take it, so Cromwell made him surrender all his commissions. Nothing could more clearly show the shift of power. Lambert had been a councillor, a major general, colonel of two regiments, Admiralty commissioner and Lord Warden of the Cinque Ports. Now all these posts were gone. Cromwell gave him a generous pension but Lambert was not yet forty and had lost a portfolio of senior appointments. He retired to his property in Wimbledon to garden and pursue artistic interests.

Overseas, England was making gains. Under the treaty with France, English soldiers fought with the French at Boulogne. By the end of 1657 Mardyke, on the coast of the Spanish Netherlands west of Dunkirk, had been taken and handed over to the English. It was difficult and expensive to garrison but it was a strategic acquisition. Blake destroyed the Spanish treasure fleet at Tenerife but died shortly afterwards. The Protectorate might not have created the Protestant union so longed for by Cromwell, but the new treaties had expanded England's trade and military reach.

It was therefore a dismal year for Charles. Royalist hopes were at a low ebb and once more he was short of money. The 2nd Duke of Buckingham, who had shared Charles's childhood and defeat at Worcester, was now estranged from both Charles and his ministers. Taking his title and charm with him, Buckingham got a pass to return to England where he set out to win the hand of Mary Fairfax. The girl was nineteen and the only child of the ex-general, who had been awarded much of Buckingham's confiscated estate. Mary already had a suitor and Buckingham was a rake, but he had a great title, wit and intelligence, polished manners and some of his father's handsome looks. Mary threw over the Earl of Chesterfield and accepted Buckingham's marriage offer. A girl who had been tutored by Andrew Marvell might have been more careful, and her father might have doubted whether Buckingham was a suitable husband, but in September 1657 the two were wed.

An alliance between Buckingham and Fairfax was a potential threat to the Cromwellian regime. Fairfax still commanded great respect in the army, was allied to the Presbyterians and was known to be in touch with royalist agents. Between them, he and Fairfax had wealth and multiple connections, while Buckingham had grown up like a brother to Charles Stuart. Fearing his potential, the government had Buckingham arrested. His detention was changed to house arrest the following spring but when he broke it he was put in the Tower. Fairfax was incandescent with rage at this treatment of his son-in-law and came to London himself, where he quarrelled with Cromwell on the issue.

Other old comrades were meeting to exercise their various grievances against the Protectorate. Ludlow was back in England, so when Harrison was released from prison into house arrest, Ludlow

Edmund Ludlow.

went to call on him – but their views were at odds. Asked for an explanation of the Rump's closure, Harrison said he was certain the parliament 'had not a heart to do any more good for the Lord and his people' and quoted the Book of Daniel: 'That the saints shall take the kingdom and possess it.' Ludlow found this unsatisfactory. They agreed to meet again with other colleagues to thrash it out but no opportunity arose.[10]

When Cromwell was offered the crown, all Ludlow's suspicions were confirmed. 'The usurper having governed as he thought long enough by virtue of the Instrument of Government, which tho drawn up by himself and his creatures, was now thought to lay too great a restraint upon his ambitious spirit; and resolving to rest satisfied with nothing less than the succession of his family to the Crown, he attempted to make himself King.' He had to call a parliament, of course, and was able to get his people in for Scotland and Ireland, 'but knowing the people of England not to be of so mercenary a spirit; and that as they were better instructed in the principles of civil liberty, so they were not wanting in courage to assert it, he used his utmost endeavours to disable and incapacitate such men from being chosen, whom he thought most likely to obstruct his designs'.[11]

Ludlow's harsh views on Cromwell's motives were shared by other republicans who also loathed the Humble Petition and Advice – but they were no longer in power. A new elite was coalescing around the Lord Protector, who was seen as the best hope for 'healing and settling' – Cromwell's repeated aim – and they approved the modernising and professionalism which they saw emerging. Army and navy officers were chosen by merit not aristocratic rank, while the civil service included men of great ability like Thurloe. Should the Protectorate fall, the Cromwellians had much to lose, especially in property.

In Scotland, the settlement of land had slowed down and was referred to Whitehall. Awards were held up when some owners were reprieved under their terms of surrender, as in Ireland. Before awards could be met, outstanding debts on the land had to be settled and some owners were fined rather than suffering confiscation; in both cases the money could not be found. In the end, and fearing the issue might cause renewed rebellion, Whitehall decided on partial fines and largely left the gentry undisturbed. Even great magnates like Argyll, whose vast estates were not confiscated, ended up under arrest for debt in London.[12] In England, the hope of the common soldiers that they would get property and increased rights was not realised but the Irish land grants were different. The soldiers had debentures but, unlike in England, their land was allocated. In both countries, however, the men often sold debentures to their officers, usually at a discounted rate. Once established on land, the army leaders emerged among the Anglo-Irish gentry of the later Stuart period but carrying the stigma of 'Cromwellian' in the minds of the Catholic population.

The redistribution of land underwrites the story of the civil war period in Britain. Under the Tudors, feudal structures had weakened but the state had centralised, requiring more management, better skills and greater funding. The middle ranks of society, composed of educated and generally urban families, began to fill those roles. With capital assets and greater confidence, they expected more political representation. With three kingdoms, the Stuarts had greater opportunities than the Tudors but more complex problems and an assertive professional class – it was among this group that grudges built up which led to revolution. The crisis in government had been precipitated by Charles I's inadequacies but the problem was wider than him; medieval structures had not altered enough under the Tudors to meet the changes in population, commerce and education. Property ownership underlay the whole system. Enclosure and changes in tenancies were altering rural life, which had motivated some men to enlist (although many joined up for the pay). During the Interregnum, a change in land ownership almost on the scale of Henry VIII's monastic awards enriched merchants, lawyers and army officers as well as some careful landowners.

In Ireland, a new elite emerged, who were almost wholly English in origin. Government in Ireland was so dominated by the problems of land confiscation that the efforts of the Cromwellian rulers to modernise the country are often overlooked. Once Henry Cromwell took over from Fleetwood, civil government progressed but Henry lacked the funds to provide the ministry and religious education which his father dreamed of. The government tried to provide preachers and religious books in Irish, with limited success. Outside Dublin, the initiative petered out. Cromwellians had aspirations to improve life in Ireland but what Irish Catholics perceived was cruelty. A Cork poet wrote:

> Transport, transplant is what I understand of English
> Shoot him, kill him, strip him, tear him
> A Tory, hack him, hang him, rebel
> A rogue, a thief, a priest, a papist.[13]

However, as the land settlement was implemented, Puritan rule took shape. Attempts at conversion had some success: several thousand Catholics became Protestant. The number of Catholic priests who were killed was in the hundreds, and perhaps 1,000 fled. Some remained in prison or in island prison camps. But as soon as Henry Cromwell's more moderate policies were observed, Catholic priests began to trickle back. The London government was panicked by reports of this, and before it adjourned passed another Act against Catholics designed to combat 'the increase of popish recusants within the Commonwealth'.[14] All Catholics in the three nations had to visit the assize judges to swear an oath of abjuration, by which they renounced the Pope's supremacy and denied the principal articles of the Catholic faith. If they refused, they were to be jailed and, if convicted, they could lose two-thirds of their land. A man who married a recusant would be judged as one himself, which was hard on those soldiers who had married local girls. Parliament re-introduced compulsory church attendance. The oath of abjuration undermined attempts at healing and settling, and caused chaos in Ireland where labourers were reported as running away from government works, fearful that such strongholds were being constructed to subdue them. Some said the oath was worse than being sent to Connaught. Henry Cromwell thought it ill-judged and dropped it – he thought it sufficient that Catholics be required to renounce all foreign powers and to attend the national church.[15]

Troopers marrying Irish girls was the opposite of what the Puritan government planned. They had remade Ireland, as if it was a blank sheet of paper on which they had drawn a new society. Their power to move people and reshape populations, their efforts at measuring, mapping and valuing land, had excited men with scientific minds and Ireland was the ideal experiment. Science and Puritanism were strange bedfellows – in some ways they were at odds but in others closely linked. Francis Bacon, the Elizabethan intellectual, based his knowledge on careful observation and measurement. Developments in sailing and navigation, then in military technology during the European wars, had galvanised mathematics and engineering. The swift development of scientific enquiry attracted men of talent. Thomas Hobbes studied mathematics while in Europe before he wrote *Leviathan*. Robert Boyle had a laboratory in London and published his theory of gases in 1662. William Petty knew both these men, and while surveying in Ireland he began to develop more ambitious ideas.

Empirical science was quite different from the heady theology of the Puritans but they complemented each other. The Puritans were vigorous entrepreneurs and improvers who believed passionately that the devil made work for idle hands to do. For them, mankind was perfectible; they believed that the Reformation and their own godly revolution might overcome the fall of Adam so that mankind could achieve a godly life under the rule of Jesus. There is little evidence that Petty shared these theological views, but having finished his survey and with a grant of Irish land, his mind moved on. If society could be studied, measured and analysed, it could be redesigned. In the 1670s, he published *Political Arithmetic*, which contained statistics about Ireland, and in 1691 *The Political Anatomy of Ireland* gave a more detailed analysis with prescriptions. One of his ideas was that English Protestant women would be brought to Ireland to marry Irish Catholic men and set up clean, orderly Protestant homes. The idea of reshaping populations was already current. Under the Tudors and the Protectorate, vagrants might be sent to the Caribbean. After Jamaica was conquered, Henry Cromwell proposed to Thurloe that young men be sent there, and suggested 1,000 young Irish women could help to populate the island. 'Although we must use force in taking them up, yet it being so much for their own good and likely to be of soe great advantage for the publique,' he wrote, he was confident that the required numbers could be provided, as long as there was clothing and ships for them.[16] There is no record of whether this plan was carried out.

In terms of remaking society, the Puritan revolutionaries were ambitious. At first it seemed they were thwarted by lack of energetic officials and money, but gradually it became clear that society could usefully be measured and valued but not so easily redesigned. It was too complex an organism, composed of humans with habits and patterns, traditions and opinions, all with a life of their own. By a mixture of influence, propaganda and force the Puritans tried to create the efficient but godly society they so desperately craved. It was their tragedy that hearts and minds proved so hard to win over.

For the Gaelic west, the Puritan revolution was cataclysmic. With military backing, the Commonwealth and Protectorate achieved what no royal government had managed: centralisation of three nations into one state. For over a century, monarchs had struggled to reduce the power of the Gaelic west and assert their own rule. They had been only partially successful. For example, Clan Donald had retained land and power on both sides of the North Channel and Alasdair MacColla with his MacDonnell troops fought on both sides, using traditional methods, to devastating effect. MacColla's death in 1647 foreshadowed the end of that vibrant society. Tudor and Stuart rulers had weakened the Gaelic clans and septs but the Puritan Revolution crushed them. In Ireland the Gaelic Irish lost their land and economic power; in Scotland clan cohesion was more carefully dismantled. Only in culture did Gaeldom retain its vigour, but it was a culture which the ruling elite largely despised. Catholicism too was suppressed. The Lords of the Pale lost not only a political role but their land and across the three nations, and Catholics lost the right to vote and sit in parliament.

The control of the centralised state was almost complete, but curiously there were anomalies. Under cover of war, a bitter conflict had been fought between the Campbells and MacDonalds across the North Channel which, for one season, had altered the course of the greater war. Yet since the Puritan triumph the Marquis of Argyll – Protestant and the agent of government – had lost territory and power, and was now languishing in prison for debt. The Marquis of Antrim, however, who was Catholic and of Gaelic stock, had been reinstated to land and influence in Ulster. Antrim was a survivor but he was in a tiny minority. Across the three kingdoms, the direction of all three nations had shifted as the Puritans set the British state on a new course. The winners were Protestant entrepreneurs, meritocrats with scientific links and commercial ambitions, whose energy defined the political agenda.

Oliver Cromwell was their chosen head of state and a new constitution had been established to cement him in power. In January 1658 parliament reassembled. The ascendancy of the Cromwellian elite was now assured – or so they thought.

17

The Last Days of the Protectorate

Challenged about his ambitions, Cromwell protested several times that he had not aimed to become head of state but had been thrust into that position by others. Yet, even before the king's death he had been criticised for his urge to power and Whitelocke recorded two conversations in which Cromwell seemed to ponder kingship for himself. His elevation to Lord Protector in 1653 roused fury, but by the time he was reinstalled in 1657 his vigour was noticeably weakening and attention fell on his sons.

The fate of his children had been determined by the shape of their father's career. When the first of his children was born Cromwell was a minor country gentleman, but once he joined the parliamentary army he lived among soldiers, which is where his elder daughters found husbands. Bridget, the oldest surviving child, had twice married her father's officers while Elizabeth, or Bettie, Oliver's favourite, had married for love aged sixteen, to a young soldier called John Claypole. Oliver was away at the war at the time but he was fond of all his children and Bettie was not chastised for her choice. The marriage of his sons was different. Oliver went to considerable trouble to arrange Richard's union to Dorothy Mayor and seemed to expect the couple to live a gentry life among her family. Richard was popular with his Hampshire neighbours but, unfortunately, was regularly in debt – about which his father admonished him. Henry's career was unlike Richard's: he was a successful soldier and married the daughter of Francis Russell MP, who had also been in the parliamentary army.

So far, Oliver's children had allied themselves with families much like their own, both in social status and political outlook. The two youngest children had a very different experience because of the gap in ages – after Bettie, eight years elapsed before Mary was born. By the time that Mary and Frances were growing up, their father was head of state and the family was living in Whitehall Palace. The two younger girls revelled in their increased status and both married noblemen, one of her own choosing and one of her father's. When Cromwell was offered the crown, that status might become royal and the girls could then make matches with princes in Europe. At one time, a possible political settlement was discussed in which Frances, the youngest, would marry Charles Stuart. Lord Broghill bravely raised the subject with the Protector who, rather than flying into a rage, said only that the young man would never forgive his father's death. He added that Charles was 'damnably debauched'.[1]

This was also Cromwell's objection to Robert Rich, son of the Earl of Warwick and grandson of parliament's general, who courted Frances. The Protector asked for a large dowry, which delayed the courtship, but actually he thought Rich too given over to pastimes of which he disapproved. Cromwell had been dissolute in his youth but bitterly regretted it later. There was also gossip that Frances might make a dynastic marriage in France, but that was not pursued and she married young Rich in Whitehall in November 1657, with a magnificent wedding feast. Forty-eight violins and fifty trumpets played, and there was 'mixt dancing' until five o'clock in the morning. Only three months later, Robert Rich died of consumption and left Frances a widow. Four years later she remarried to Sir Francis Russell, Henry's brother-in-law. Frances's wedding ceremony showed how far the Protectoral court had shifted since the days when her father had ridden into Whitehall at the head of the army and the king was brought in as a captive. There were royalists among the guests while the music and dancing upset many of the Puritans; Mary's wedding, which occurred a few months after her sister's, was even more shocking.

Mary's marriage, like Richard's, was arranged by her father and in many ways the choice of husband seems strange. Thomas Belasyse, Viscount Fauconberg came from a substantial gentry family in Yorkshire and although Thomas had been in the parliamentary army his family were royalists, many of them were Catholics and his uncle was at the core of the Sealed Knot. Fauconberg was a widower and childless. Dr White, chaplain to the Protector, warned Cromwell that the young man would not produce children, which proved correct: Mary had none. 'I think he will never make your Highness a grandfather,' White joked. 'There are certain effects in Lord Fauconberg that will always prevent him making you a grandfather, let him do what he can.'

The bridegroom learned of this conversation, lost his temper and went for White with his cane.[2] But Cromwell was keen on the match, gave a generous dowry of £15,000 and seems to have wanted the young man in his family and political life.

Cromwell subsequently used Fauconberg's diplomatic skills, but the main motive may be that Cromwell liked Fauconberg personally.[3] Many times in his career, Cromwell took a clear personal liking to a man from an alien group – royalist, Quaker, Catholic – and the liking outweighed any other consideration. The wedding was a private one, held at Hampton Court and, at Fauconberg's insistence, the *Book of Common Prayer* was used. The entertainment included a masque, a form last seen in the days of Charles I. Andrew Marvell, then employed with Milton as language secretary to the council, wrote two pastorals for it and some say that Cromwell himself performed a non-singing part as Jove.

So the Protectoral court, with its gentlemen of the bedchamber, its ushers, grooms and pages, its Lord Chamberlain and Master of Ceremonies, had taken on much of the pomp of the Stuart court. John Evelyn said that Whitehall in 1656 was 'glorious and well-furnished'; Pepys remarked on the security in Whitehall and the ceremony used in the presence chamber. All the same, Cromwell had grown up in modest circumstances and had spent much of his life with the army. He was not a sophisticated man. His idea of fun was boyish; for example, having a drum beaten during dinner when his footguards could come and snatch the food. At Frances's wedding he threw sack-posset, a sweet wine, over the women's dresses and put sweetmeat on the seats – laughing as they inadvertently sat on them.[4] The account comes from a royalist's papers and some historians dismiss it – those with a dispassionate opinion of Oliver Cromwell are few.

In order to keep closely in touch with their concerns and moods, the Protector held weekly dinners for army officers. He also enjoyed convivial times with his civilian friends – Thurloe, Sir Charles Wolseley, Lord Broghill, William Pierrepont and Bulstrode Whitelocke were in the inner circle. The gentlemen smoked tobacco pipes and made verses together, at Oliver's instigation.[5] To run his household he employed only trusted colleagues, many of whom were relatives. It was from these circles – the part military, part civilian group which composed the 'Cromwellians' – that he chose many of his 'senators', or members of the new second chamber, when parliament reconvened. After a strenuous career, he was enjoying the luxuries of his new role – but the contentious business of government still rested heavily on his shoulders.

He was being pressed over the succession. Having turned down the kingship, there was no necessity for the hereditary principle but if his heir was not his eldest son, who was it to be? Henry had ability but it would be difficult to appoint his younger son over the older, and Henry had his father's temper. Lambert, deputy to Cromwell in both the army and council, had side-lined himself, while Fleetwood lacked the skills. Richard had been living quietly in Hampshire but now he was more often in London and had been given increasingly important appointments – he was chairman of the new committee for trade and chancellor of the University of Oxford – as well as several parliamentary committees. In November 1657, he was living at St James's Palace and in December was added to the council. He was an affable young man, lacking his father's dynamism but equally free of the Protector's temper and mood swings. If he did not stand out as an official, nor did he fail in the positions he occupied.

Richard and Henry were among those named for the second chamber when parliament reconvened on 20 January 1658; Henry was still in Ireland. Sixty-three members had been chosen by the Lord Protector, although one-third did not take their seats. The Humble Petition and Advice had been agreed by parliament, so there was every expectation that at last the constitution had been settled. Cromwell still had many anxieties about the instability of the state, but at the opening he said he would speak only briefly, as 'I have some infirmities upon me'.[6] Nor did Fiennes, who held the Great Seal, give the members a brief for their session but only an exhortation to avoid contention.[7]

A few days later, Cromwell spoke to them again. Perhaps he felt better; he certainly wanted to warn them against the Catholic powers – the Habsburgs and the Pope. He said that the 'well-being, yea the being of these nations is now at stake and if God bless this meeting our tranquillity and peace may be lengthened'. He feared the divisions in society, the possibility of further civil war and the determination of every sect, whether religious or civil, to get power into their hands. He urged people to be content, for 'misrule is better than no rule'. Without the army to keep control all those threats might merge, yet still army arrears were unpaid. He warned that if the army quit Ireland, the island would fall into the hands of the 'Popish and Spanish interest'. Protesting that 'I sought not this place', he emphasised that he had taken an oath to serve the Commonwealth and he would carry it out, looking to establish liberty of conscience 'for honest people', maintain a 'godly ministry' and see all men preserved in their just rights.[8]

Cromwell's fear of further unrest and divisions was clear and repetitive – he was realising that the revolution which had been easy to provoke was hard to end. Unfortunately for him, not only was there a Spanish army coalescing around Charles in the Netherlands and various angry groups keen to undermine the Protectorate at home, but also the republicans were back in parliament and eager to attack the new arrangements. Their hopes had resided in the Commonwealth of 1649, when parliament had total power, and they spoke warmly of free elections, meaning no interference from the army. They were not concerned with widening the franchise but with the rights of elected MPs. Coming back to parliament under the Protectorate, they promoted the power of the elected chamber and refused to recognise the appointed one. Haselrig, Scot, Weaver and Ashley-Cooper led the opposition, and with the excluded members now taking their seats, the government could no longer command a majority. The Commons argued about whether the Other House should exist and what its name should be and, following Harrington's logic, whether collectively it commanded enough land to give it legitimacy.

Then they got up a petition. Their main complaint was the veto which the Protector and the second chamber now possessed – a power which replicated the very tyranny they had fought against under Charles I. They demanded that the elected chamber should have supreme authority. The petition remained vague about control of the army and the limits to be set on religion but it made its appeal not only to politicians but to many army members, which may be why Cromwell acted with frantic haste.

He consulted no one. The Thames was frozen and he could not use his barge, so he raced out from Whitehall and called a hackney. At Westminster, he sent for the judges sitting in Westminster Hall before dispatching Black Rod to summon the Commons into the Lords. His presence caused a great stir: Fleetwood and Fiennes tried arguing with him but when Cromwell was roused, he spoke sharply and acted decisively – he told Fleetwood he was a 'milksop'.[9] Haselrig advised the members not to obey, but they trooped into the Lords docilely. The Lord Protector angrily harangued his parliament, as he had before. He had taken up his role reluctantly, he told them, he had thought the Humble Petition and Advice had been agreed. It defined his role and the oath of office he must take, which he had honoured, but they had not honoured theirs. He accused the elected members of disquieting the nation, which would only play 'the King of Scots, his game'. It would all end once more in blood and confusion. With that, he dissolved the parliament – 'and let God be judge between you and me'.[10] The second session had lasted just two weeks.

His enemies were pleased. The new constitution had not been fully enacted, the Cromwellians had passed no more statutes and the actions of the Lord Protector showed he was at his wits' end. The royalists were hopeful but they knew Cromwell's resilience and sure instincts. It was the lawyers who were most distressed as, once again, there was no settled basis for government.

Cromwell called in the London army officers: they drank wine together and he told them to speak freely. There was clearly widespread discontent. The junior officers were if anything more dissatisfied than the senior ones, especially because of the curbs on religion. Cromwell tried to talk them round but the most intransigent he cashiered. This was ominous, for some of the ousted captains came from Cromwell's original regiments. Their general, who had championed religious freedom but had jailed preachers, was now instigating a House of Lords on the old style and had summarily sacked men for questioning that. Both the army and the Independent churches saw that some tide had irrevocably turned.

Rumours whirled but still Cromwell's position was unassailable. He had the unequivocal support of General Monck, who commanded in Scotland and held that country with a firm grip. Throughout the spring, addresses of loyalty were made by the army in all three kingdoms. Cromwell spoke in the City of London, warning of the 'contrivances of Charles Stuart' and his foreign army. The City too signed a loyal declaration and called up their militia of 7,000 men.[11] The Anabaptists and the Fifth Monarchists, however, were enraged.

The enemy without – the army growing in Flanders – was a galvanising force which made the Puritans pull together; intelligence showed just how large a threat it now was. Over the winter of 1657–58, Spanish ministers offered funds for the first stage of a landing in England if Charles provided an open port, so his ministers tried to arouse the English royalists. Presbyterians were shifting away from the Cromwellians towards the royalist cause, which reawakened worries over Fairfax; parliament's great general was fuming and no longer a friend of government. Royalist activity increased once more. To rouse and co-ordinate his supporters, Charles sent Ormond to England early in 1658. It was a dangerous mission but the marquis spent nine days constantly moving his lodgings and stayed ahead of Thurloe's spies. He judged the royalist position weak but thought they might take Yarmouth for the landing. Then he hurriedly crossed to Dieppe just as Thurloe's men discovered where he was. The royalist plan was to hire Dutch shipping to collect Charles's troops from Ostend, but in February the Protectorate sent naval vessels to blockade the port. The Spanish had been too slow to act, the blockade was effective and the expedition to Yarmouth was deferred to the following winter.

The Cromwellians tightened security. Royalists were ordered to leave London and several were arrested. Militias were put on alert. By April, Thurloe was confident that the most active cavaliers had been imprisoned, but when a special High Court of Justice was convened to deal with them, many judges refused to sit, saying regular jury courts should be used. A new group of royalists planned a rising in London for 15 May, aiming to control the City, but once again Thurloe was forewarned and the army came out in force, searched the London inns and lodging houses, making many arrests. The High Court heard these cases; six men were found guilty, of whom three were hanged, drawn and quartered. This punishment was seldom used under Cromwell but the Protectorate government was being worn down by the constant plots and attempted risings; gory executions were a deterrent.

That summer Cromwell's alliance with France paid off. As commander at sea, Montagu led a co-ordinated attack with the French against the Spanish Netherlands. When Dunkirk fell, Louis XIV rode into the city for a service of thanksgiving before personally handing the keys over to Lockhart, the English ambassador. He viewed English support as essential but it galled the French soldiers to see the prize given away. Now, with possession of Mardyke and Dunkirk, the Protectorate controlled the Channel from both sides; even so, garrisoning the two Flanders ports was costly and the local populations were Catholic. The neighbouring Dutch were worried – they had fought off Spain, but now the French and English were moving closer. Trade rivalries between England and the Netherlands were intense, both in the Channel and in the Baltic, which the trade treaties only partially resolved.

By the summer of 1658, although the Protectorate government had achieved many of its overseas aims, its main problem was still money – Cromwell and Thurloe worried incessantly about paying military bills. When Cromwell suddenly closed parliament before taxation was granted, the budget problems looked unresolvable. The deficit was £138,690 and the national debt £2.2 million.[12] There was talk of calling another parliament and the council even mulled over raising money by forced loan. Would they repeat the actions of Charles I, which they had furiously decried? They did not, but even considering it was significant.

As summer came on, Cromwell moved out to Hampton Court. Once a week, his council convened there but it was his family life which preoccupied the Protector. His favourite daughter was seriously ill and in pain; Bettie Claypole moved to Hampton Court with her family – her symptoms suggest cancer in the abdomen. Her husband John Claypole was master of the Protector's horse and part of his household. As his daughter's condition worsened, Cromwell would sit at her bedside through the night. The young woman's condition affected business: Andrew Marvell was left to give a public reception for the Dutch ambassador, which was tactfully refused. Cromwell did go up to London to see the Dutchman but he was distracted. Bettie died on 6 August and Cromwell was so overcome that he was unable to attend her funeral four days later. She was buried at night in Westminster Abbey; hers was the only Cromwellian interment not removed from Henry VII's chapel in later years. Oliver never recovered from his daughter's death; he was already infirm and this blow seemed to strike to the core of him. He was well enough to ride in the park but George Fox saw him there and said 'he looked like a dead man'.

Cromwell's ministers put increasing pressure on him over the future. It was said that the Protector had left a letter in Whitehall naming his successor, but when it was sent for a search of the palace produced nothing. Some speculated that the name was that of Fleetwood or Lambert, but Cromwell did not say. Some thought he had chosen his second son, Henry, over his eldest, Richard. No one knew. On 17 August, he had severe pain in his back and bowels. It was decided to move him to Whitehall, but once there he was overcome by a series of fits. He was a tough man and recovered enough to have dinner with Whitelocke and to see Fairfax. The latter was furious about Buckingham's rearrest and, having come to see the Protector to protest, 'expostulated the case so it put him in a great passion, turning abruptly from him in the gallery at Whitehall, cocking his hat and throwing his cloak under his arm, as he used to do when he was angry'.[13] The two old comrades never met again.

The fits returned and Oliver was rendered barely conscious. Even when he might have done so, Thurloe would not press Cromwell on the succession but confessed it was not Charles Stuart he feared, but 'our own divisions'. Fauconberg let Henry Cromwell know that he would support a claim should Henry make one. In London, the officers held a prayer meeting as they searched for direction. On 30 August, the hot weather broke in a storm. Cromwell rallied, but now that he was near the end, his mind was on God and the Lord's Covenant with the elect; on this rested his hopes of pardon and salvation. Several councillors gathered at the Protector's bedside and later said he had confirmed that he wanted his son Richard to succeed him, but the General could not speak – he may have nodded. 3 September was the anniversary of his great battles, Dunbar and Worcester. Somehow Oliver Cromwell contrived to die at about three o'clock on the afternoon of that day. He was fifty-nine years old.

The death of a head of state is often a precarious moment, and the government of which Oliver Cromwell had been head was not safely established. His last parliament had been dissolved in acrimony, there were doubts over the succession and the temper of the army was volatile, so it is surprising that the elevation of Richard Cromwell as the second Lord Protector went as smoothly as it did. Thurloe, who had been so close to Oliver, was grief-stricken but decisions could not wait and, on the evening of his death, the Privy Council visited Richard to confirm that his father had appointed him to take over.

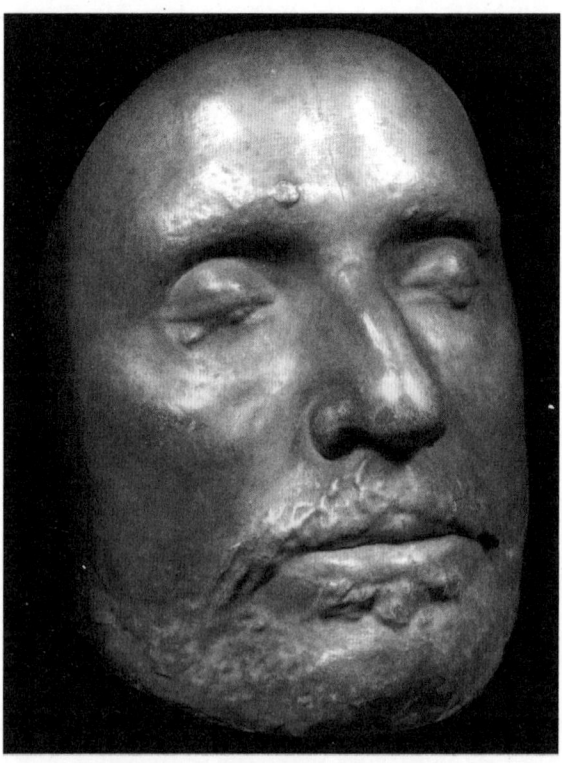

Oliver Cromwell's death mask.

The Lord Protector's body was to be buried in the Henry VII chapel in Westminster Abbey, using the ceremonies customary for a monarch. Oliver was embalmed but he was found to have a suppurating spleen which, despite a lead coffin inside a wooden one, made such a stench that the actual burial was done swiftly, the date unrecorded. For monarchs, an empty coffin and an effigy had been used for lying-in-state, and so they were for Cromwell. His effigy was life-size and had a wax face taken from a death mask but with glass eyes. It lay on a bed of state in Somerset House where the public were allowed to visit. Four state rooms were draped in black velvet with arms and heraldic devices, where guards kept watch with great solemnity. After some days, however, the display changed. The effigy was stood up and its eyelids opened to reveal the glass eyes. A crown, which had been on a chair beside it, was put on its head despite Oliver's stringent efforts to avoid being a king. Finally, on 23 November, there was a funeral procession. The coffin was put on a magnificent catafalque, with the effigy in an open chariot, surrounded by officials, servants and the grandees of the Protectorate, with soldiers formed up in troops or lining the streets. The whole procession wound its way through the streets of London, which took seven hours, so when they arrived at Westminster Abbey it was dark and no one had provided candles. No ceremony was attempted: the trumpets were blown, the catafalque and effigy parked in the abbey and the mourners dispersed. Such was the ceremonial funeral of the first Lord Protector.[14]

Richard's accession was proclaimed by the council 'together with the Lord Mayor, Aldermen and citizens of London, the officers of the army and members of the principal gentlemen', who did 'with one full voice and consent of tongue and heart, publish and declare the said noble and illustrious Lord Richard, to be rightful Protector of this Commonwealth of England, Scotland and Ireland, and the dominions and territories thereunto belonging ... to whom we do acknowledge all fidelity and constant obedience according to law, and the said Humble Petition and Advice'.[15]

Letters were immediately dispatched to the sister capitals of Edinburgh and Dublin, as well as the regional cities. All seemed to go well. As in 1653, the government was reassured that everything had passed off peacefully. Thurloe used Oliver's 1653 metaphor when he wrote to Henry Cromwell: 'There is not a dog that wags his tongue, so great a calm are we in.'[16] Thurloe expressed his profound grief – he and Oliver had been close. There was no stir in the English cities, although in Oxford the students pelted the sheriff with carrots and turnips; perhaps they were just boisterous students, but royalist Oxford showed some animosity.

In Edinburgh, General Monck had the situation well in hand. The sturdy soldier served the government unswervingly and tolerated no protest or vacillation. If he could stamp out crime in the Scottish Highlands, Monck could handle the announcement in Edinburgh of a new chief executive. Over the preceding few years Monck had purged troublemakers from the army, and when the news of Oliver's death arrived he banned meetings of officers. In fact, they signed letters of loyalty without fuss. By keeping a close watch on royalists and religious radicals, Monck maintained order. In Dublin, Henry Cromwell proclaimed his brother's accession without trouble and hoped to go to London to support Richard in person but was dissuaded. In October, his brother promoted Henry from Lord Deputy to Lord Lieutenant. Henry called in the officers, who professed their 'cheerful obedience and faithfulness' to the new chief magistrate, and Henry wrote to Thurloe that 'their temper seems to me at this time better than what I could have expected'.[17]

From The Hague, the English resident George Downing, whose career was to leave a lasting print on the British state, wrote to Thurloe:

> Right Honourable, By the post yesterday, I gave you an account of my having received yours, with the most sadning news of his late hyghnesse's death; as also, that it hath pleased God so wonderfully to guid things, as that my lord Richard is with that unanimity proclaymed; a most surprizing astonishing mercy, such as I assure you doth most wonderfully amaze all that heare of it, who expected nothing but confusion in England, after his late hyghnesse's death, and thereby a wide doore opened for Ch. Stuart. The Lord carry you on with the same unity, in pursuance of the good old cause...

He had printed the proclamation and informed the Dutch government.[18] Downing too was a firm servant of government, whichever one it might be.

So far, the change of Protector had gone smoothly. General Monck wrote Richard a useful letter, advising him to call the clergy together and put a stop to the 'blasphemies' of the 'wilder sects'. He thought regiments could be amalgamated and insolent spirits discharged. Richard had fewer obligations than his father; if he cultivated men of influence in the regions he could widen support. He should add steady men to the Other House and be careful about calling a parliament.[19] It was good advice, but Richard faced the same restless spirits who had vexed his father: the army officers who were determined to control government on their terms and the republicans who wanted a single elected chamber which they hoped to dominate. Oliver's great strength had been his command of the army, which he had so successfully led, whereas Richard had little military experience. He was likeable and not without skills, willing to attempt the impossible task which his father had left him. If Charles I and Oliver Cromwell could not settle how the realm should be governed, perhaps a mild spirit like Richard Cromwell, with Thurloe at his shoulder, had a chance. Royalists mocked him as 'Tumbledown Dick', making play of several accidents – with horses or when the stairs in the Banqueting House collapsed during Oliver's speech and Richard was injured. The nickname also signalled the young man's impending fall.

In his later years, Oliver had increasingly relied on his civilian councillors, some of a younger generation, and it was these men to whom Richard turned for support and advice: Thurloe, of course, as his chief councillor and secretary, plus Broghill and Whitelocke. He retained his father's half-civilian, half-army council. Oliver had kept his relatives close and often in command, with Fleetwood at the head of the army, closely allied to Desborough who was Richard's uncle but disliked the young man. Trouble began fairly quickly when junior officers pressed for Fleetwood to have greater autonomy over the army. Richard insisted with calm dignity that Fleetwood's command was subject only to his own as head of state. By December, the weekly meetings of officers in London were becoming more of a worry, with demands that officers who had been cashiered by Oliver be reinstated. The reverberant phrase 'the Good Old Cause' was in print or on the officers' lips. The main problem, as always, was that army pay was in arrears, and to raise tax Richard would have to call a parliament. That would bring the civilian enemies of the Protectorate back into play.

Broghill was in Ireland when Oliver Cromwell died. Henry had begged him to stay in London and see the constitution settled but Broghill was disillusioned. Although Ireland was part of the Protectorate, old and new restrictions on Irish exports continued because English producers feared Irish competition, especially in wool, and could influence policy. Nor had Ireland been permitted to raise its own militia under the Protectorate. The Old Protestants had worked hard for the Cromwellian settlement but had not seen Ireland rewarded. Their fathers had settled in Ireland, the sons had fought for the Protestant interest and wanted to develop the country but London was disobliging. Broghill had gone home in some bitterness but in December, when a parliament was called, he helped Henry Cromwell manage the Irish elections. Of the MPs elected, only three were from the army; the rest were loyal to Henry or were Old Protestants, some under Broghill's sway and others in Vincent Gookin's circle. The two groups squabbled.

Monck managed the Scottish selections, with support from Broghill who had kept up a useful correspondence with the Edinburgh Resolutioners. Some MPs chosen by Monck had never been anywhere near Scotland but he got them in anyway. However, Monck's control was not absolute and despite his efforts Argyll got a seat along with several Scots. Wariston, having been seduced into working for Oliver, was now a member of the Other House, so the Covenanters had a voice in London once more.

Parliament assembled on 27 January 1659. Richard gave a speech, which was written by Thurloe but well delivered. Parliament recognised Richard as Lord Protector but was still disputing the Humble Petition and Advice. The right of the Irish and Scottish members to sit was challenged on the grounds that no valid Act of Union existed for either country. The Protectorate had spawned an elite composed of lawyers and gentry who made a strong bloc in parliament and included Broghill's group. But the anti-Cromwellians were now hopeful – the influential Commonwealthsmen, some crypto-royalists and the army officers in the Commons. The aims of the last three groups differed but their object of attack was the same: the Cromwellian Protectorate which they abhorred. However, if the Cromwellians could stabilise the regime, if the army officers would support Richard or if the enemies of the Protectorate turned on each other, all might be well. Richard, Thurloe, Broghill and their friends had to win more support. In fact, the Protectorate could not survive even this first meeting of parliament.

Initially, the army commanders probably hoped to control Richard, especially since he was their junior relative, but the army at large had views of its own and pressure was coming to bear on Charles Fleetwood via his officers. Fleetwood had the use of Wallingford House in Whitehall, which became the meeting place for those officers who opposed Richard's succession. Initially, they demanded an end to Richard's command of the army and revisions to the Humble Petition and Advice. Boldy, the young Protector went to Wallingford House to see his brother-in-law, faced Fleetwood and told him that he would only part with the generalship of the army and his own life together. Like Charles I, Richard knew that the head of state must control the military.

The army and the Commonwealthsmen might form an alliance or turn on each other, but first they intended to curb the power of Richard, 'the young gentleman'. Unexpectedly, Richard did not give way easily. The Commonwealthsmen did not have a majority in parliament and could not control events; it was the army which brought Richard down. Pamphlets started appearing promoting the 'Good Old Cause'. By late March, the army was trying to ally with the republicans but their main strategy was to heap pressure on Richard. In parliament, Vane and Haselrig talked and filibustered, making themselves deeply unpopular. Pamphlets in Vane's style appeared, contemptuous of Richard Cromwell and demanding wider religious freedoms, as well as 'readmission of the Long Parliament'. Republicans wanted to reverse the creation of the Protectorate and reinstate the Commonwealth but, inadvertently, the spool rolled back further than that.

The army was already divided: Monck commanded the forces in Scotland and Henry Cromwell those in Ireland, both of which they pledged to Protector Richard, although whether they could deliver those troops in Richard's defence was doubtful. The army in England was technically under Richard's command but his hold was theoretical and weak. It was Major General Fleetwood who led the land forces and he hoped to press his officers' demands with the backing of the troops but, although the men looked to him more than to Richard Cromwell, Fleetwood also failed to control his men completely. With its religious hopes and powerful emotions, the army was a difficult animal to manage. Fleetwood persuaded Richard to call a General Council of the Army which brought together about 500 officers on 2 April. A petition was written, complaining about arrears of pay, the derision shown to the 'Good Old Cause', and demanding that 'the wicked' be plucked from their positions. Richard received it and gave it to the Commons, who ignored the document.

A triangular struggle ensued between the Protectorate leaders, parliament and the army officers. The Commons voted to curtail army meetings and Richard issued such an order, which Fleetwood obeyed; but the officers in turn wanted parliament dissolved. The tensions among the power centres in London were coming to a head. The City militia, so often a focus for power struggles, was now wrestled over. Parliament wanted to have joint control over it with the Protector, which the Lord Mayor supported, but the militia itself declared for the army. Both armed forces feared losing their leaders and falling back under the control of the nobility. If that happened, how long before the Stuarts returned?

The showdown came when Fleetwood ordered a general rendezvous of all the regiments about London on 22 April at St James's. Richard gave a counter order for the troops to assemble at Whitehall but the junior officers obeyed Fleetwood and took their men to St James's. That evening, Desborough came to see his nephew and demanded that Richard dissolve parliament. Without the support of the army, Richard had little choice and the following day he complied. Despite the efforts of MPs to block the dissolution by refusing to go to the House of Lords, Black Rod broke his emblem of office at the door of the Commons, signifying that the sitting was over. Montagu believed that Richard should have prorogued, not dissolved his parliament, which 'had much of the interest of the Nation in it'. He thought that was where the fundamental error was made.[20]

Fleetwood and his colleagues saw they could command Richard, and briefly the Wallingford House group asserted control. The council of officers proclaimed Fleetwood as commander-in-chief but once Lambert was reinstated and other officers were brought in, the dynamic changed. Throughout the army, there was restlessness and discontent. The troops remembered those heady days when their glorious victories promised better government, rule by the people of God and proper pay. Instead, the Protectorate had reinstated aristocratic rule and curtailed religious freedom. Now, Leveller talk became current again. The army saw a Commonwealth as their just right. When pamphlets and republican propaganda linked the 'Good Old Cause' to the 'Good Old Parliament', junior officers began demanding that the Rump be reinstated. Many English people still burned with indignation at Oliver's closure of the parliament – now calls for its restoration mounted, leaving the military men with few alternatives. Sir Henry Vane held two meetings at his house, bringing together Commonwealthsmen with sympathetic officers to create an alliance. John Owen, the minister whom Oliver had so valued and promoted, extracted a list of the surviving members of the Rump from Ludlow and took it to Wallingford House. Into the cacophony, the Fifth Monarchists raised their voices against the Rump and reminded the faithful to look for the approaching King of Saints.

Richard was still nominally head of state but his position was impossible. It was not he but the council of officers who took the initiative and sent for the Rumpers to reconvene. Richard called on Monck, on his brother and on Montagu for armed support to maintain his rule but none of them could get their men to challenge the main army under Fleetwood.

On 6 May, forty-two members of the Rump convened in the House of Commons. Pride's Purge had reduced the Long Parliament and since then a decade had elapsed, so the eligible members were few. Speaker Lenthall was persuaded to join and others gradually trickled in. As the chamber filled up over the ensuing days, the army sent in a new petition. They hoped to reinstate the Commonwealth, influence the parliament and provide for Richard, who was, after all, the son of their old commander. The Rumpers agreed to take over his debts and confirmed he should have an income for life. On 25 May, Richard, who had ruled for nine months, signed a submission to the Rump and stood down. The young man was afraid of his creditors and for some time he moved secretively around London to avoid them as the government, short of money and with other problems, did not honour its promises. Eventually, it put his debts on the government books, and in May 1660 Richard left England. He would spend the next two decades in France and Geneva.

With the overthrow of the Protectorate, the union also collapsed, so no MPs were called for Scotland and Ireland. Instead, the Commonwealth as it had existed in 1653 was reconstituted and, as it had then, parliament created an executive – first a Committee of Safety to manage the immediate crisis and then a Council of State to run the government. With such small numbers, many MPs had several positions.

The Protectorate was over, the Commonwealth had been re-established and the remaining members of the Rump were now ostensibly in charge. The revolution had rolled itself back to 1653 but it no longer had its mighty general to knock heads together and give it authority. Fleetwood and Lambert, Vane and Haselrig – these men would have to steer the ship of state.

18

The Army Splits

Between the resignation of Richard Cromwell and the restoration of a Stuart king there was a period of only one year, but during that time there were four parliaments, two Committees of Safety and three Councils of State in England. Government changed twice in Scotland and Ireland. Trying to discern who was ruling England became increasingly difficult and government there began to break down, until the only army commander with genuine stature took a stand and demanded a parliament untrammelled by military intervention. Once the army was no longer able to call, purge and dismiss parliaments, the revolution was effectively over. The collapse of the revolutionaries' hold on England was swift and chaotic, as factions formed and broke up, governing bodies were created and shut down, and the fortunes of its leaders rose and fell. Ultimately, the Puritans were in a minority and lost power. The increasing disorder among the rulers sealed their fate; those who had accepted the Protectorate because it created some stability and order, despite its high tax and restrictive culture, lost all faith in the Puritans once they fractured, split and fought with each other. The calls for the 'Good Old Cause' became demands for the 'Good Old Parliament' and, with gathering momentum, for the known and tested forms of government – which led inevitably to the return of the young king.

Scotland and Ireland certainly mattered in this process and steps were taken by London to maintain government on their terms but they lacked officials and attention. Those with local power took control in Edinburgh and Dublin. But in neither country did the original insurgents make a showing – they had been too thoroughly conquered. Nor did Scotland and Ireland influence the outcome in England.

On the whole, Scotland longed for the reinstatement of the Stuarts but worried about their church. In Ireland, Protestants feared losing their land while Irish Catholics hoped for some restoration of their property and status. Both countries lost their representation at Westminster early in the process; it had been heavily controlled and in many cases was nominal but it had affected politics at Westminster and had started to bind the three nations together politically. The disintegration of that nascent union meant that by the end of 1659 – that year of chaos – the two outlier countries had a skeleton of their future: elites had come forward and were in positions of authority, putting themselves in as strong a bargaining position as possible for the era to come. By the time that Puritan rule finally collapsed, Scotland had a tiny measure of self-determination while the Old Protestants had taken control in Ireland. The losses of the Confederate Catholics in Ireland were inestimable and the Covenanters were no longer a coherent group in Scotland, so the men who had initiated revolution in both countries had fallen heavily as a result of their efforts. In England the outcome was mixed but it was the regicides who lost their lives. Oliver Cromwell had been right about that – young Charles Stuart would never forgive the murder of his father.

When Desborough came to visit Richard Cromwell that night in April 1659 and demanded that his nephew close the parliament, he was once more asserting the power of the army, and when Richard resigned not long afterwards, Charles Fleetwood and John Desborough with their colleagues were only doing what the army had done before, in 1648 and 1653, when they reshaped parliament to suit their aims; but this time there was no General Cromwell to assert authority over the resulting instability. During the meetings at Wallingford House, as the army leaders gathered and schemed, we hear nothing of Bridget Fleetwood. Between them, she and her husband Charles had nine or ten children, many of whom were still young. So Wallingford House was a family home but, for Bridget, who had grown up among soldiers as they met under urgent circumstances, planned and debated, it was not unusual to have politically engaged soldiers coming and going through her front door. This time they were plotting the end of her brother's parliament, and although there was sometimes talk of keeping Richard on as a figurehead, the army officers planned to usurp his rule.

Desborough had married Oliver's sister, so the coup was a family affair. Charles Fleetwood was assertive in the spring of 1659, or perhaps was urged forwards by his colleagues; Oliver had called him a milksop and, as commander-in-chief, Fleetwood had none of his father-in-law's abilities. Oliver had promoted his own family throughout his career but during the Protectorate he had side-lined some senior officers for political reasons – Lambert, Ludlow and Harrison for example – so Charles Fleetwood had become supreme commander almost by default. He had none of the qualities necessary for a political leader, and when the monarchy was restored it did not bother to punish him. By then he was in two minds about approaching the king himself.

Vane and Haselrig were back in parliament but were now squabbling with each other. Haselrig had military experience, and was decisive and assertive. Sir Henry Vane was a far more subtle man, clever with diplomatic skills, complex with deeply held Puritan ideals, yet proud and ambitious. These two were among a handful of men who attempted unsuccessfully to fill the vacuum of leadership left when Oliver Cromwell died. A commanding leader was essential. Would the three nations accept yet another change of government? Who had ultimate control of the armed forces? These were vital questions. So were the terms on which the parliament sat. Would there be new elections? On what franchise? Would the constituencies be remodelled? Who would decide? In 1653, parliament had been making these choices when Cromwell and the army intervened. That simmering rivalry had not been resolved.

The Rump parliament acted decisively, taking the armed forces under its own command, which made Speaker Lenthall the nominal head of the military. Fleetwood was to be commander-in-chief for England and Scotland. As to its own duration, parliament would dissolve no later than 7 May 1660. To be certain of their loyalty, parliament reorganised the army. Monck asked that his own officers be left in place but this was disregarded and considerable changes were made. In England, about 160 officers were dismissed: Cromwellians whom parliament was unsure of. Officers whom Oliver had cashiered were reinstated, with Lambert replacing Fauconberg. The junior officers and men had views of their own and some murmured about agitators, remembering the days in Putney when they had real influence. There was discontent because either pay was not forthcoming or they were paid in debentures. Nonetheless, with purges and grumbling, in England parliament managed the transition.

A parliamentary committee met weekly to discuss the future shape of government. With republicans back in the House, Vane, Haselrig and their associates asserted their views: parliament was supreme, and there should be no single person in power nor an unelected senate.

The senior army officers, however, were keen on an upper house which provided a check on the elected members and in which they hoped to sit, guiding the direction of the nations, while the junior officers were suspicious of a second chamber. The end of the Protectorate nullified its legislation, leaving a vacuum. In Scotland, Monck acknowledged the rule of the Rump over Scotland but the legal basis of government was unclear and the council in Edinburgh was suspended, as were the appointments of judges. Only Monck's firm control of the country kept Scotland stable; JPs continued to sit and soldiers were able to manage petty crime.

It was possible to travel from London to Dublin in two days but generally it took a week for letters to reach Henry Cromwell. When he heard of his brother's resignation, he put out feelers to Monck but received an ambivalent response, and by then it was too late to go to Richard's aid. In June, Henry wrote to the Speaker. 'Knowing in general,' he said, 'how busy the common enemy [Royalists] was in all the three nations', and that they would try to rouse 'a more dangerous, numerous, and exasperated people, the Irish natives and Papists', he had ordered the army to hold firm and was confident of their loyalty to the reconstituted parliament. With his brother and his father's memory in mind, Henry felt he could not serve the Rump himself.[1] He prepared to leave Ireland, while parliament sent five commissioners including Ludlow, who once more was to lead the Irish army.

More urgently for the Irish Protestants, the land settlement was now in jeopardy. It had been set up since the Rump was dissolved and now that parliament had reconvened, orders passed in the interim were no longer considered valid.[2] Nor was the settlement complete; many men were still making claims or protesting against decisions. The Irish officers sent delegates to London, with a petition demanding action on land-ownership and religious teaching. Parliament responded and gave a bill on Irish land two readings but it was not passed. Irish Protestants remained anxiously in limbo.[3]

The question of security was still vital to the London government. When the Protectorate fell, Thurloe lost his job and Thomas Scot was hired as spymaster but Thurloe refused to hand over his ciphers, calling Scot a 'noisy windbag'. When royalist activity began to stir in the summer of 1659, Scot's network of informers warned of a rising but seemingly lacked intelligence from Cheshire, where a significant attempt was gathering strength. In other parts of the country royalists hung back waiting to see if the king might land, but in Cheshire Sir George Booth, a local magnate and Presbyterian, made his preparations unmolested. The English Presbyterians were becoming more active and engaged. It was this group which had been removed from parliament in 1648 but they had not been penalised and were often spoken of as neuters. They might accept a restored monarchy but not without conditions, their key aim being a Presbyterian national church. They harked back to negotiations with Charles I on the Isle of Wight in 1648 as a basis for terms with his son.

On 31 July, Booth made his move at Warrington. Gathering about 500 men, he was admitted to Chester. For about two weeks, he controlled Cheshire and part of Lancashire while government troops arrived from Ireland and Lambert marched north with 5,000 men to eject him. Booth had previously fought for parliament and his manifesto was not overtly royalist but he called the current situation oligarchical tyranny and demanded a free parliament. However, he had no support from other parts of the country. The militia put down stirrings in the Midlands and Lambert met Booth, with their respective forces, near Nantwich. There was hardly a battle, a skirmish of sorts, after which Booth was arrested and put in the Tower, where he remained for six months.

From across the water, Charles and his advisers watched, but acted with caution. If now was their moment, they must be careful not to squander it. There had been profound disappointment when neither Oliver's death nor his son's dismissal had brought on the collapse of the Puritan regime or a spontaneous royalist revival; but Charles had been cautious throughout, sometimes unsure just what was happening in England, but mainly careful in case any premature move led to deaths and losses which would further weaken his cause. Now, when his enemies were floundering, his chief tactic was seduction. Letters were sent to men who were known to be sympathetic, or not wholly adverse to a restored Stuart monarchy, and who were in a position to make it happen.

Edward Montagu was perhaps the chief of these because he was known to be open to overtures and was Admiral of the Fleet. His father owned Hinchinbrook House, previously the seat of Oliver's uncle, near where the Lord Protector grew up. Edward was a generation younger, had fought for parliament and was a 'stout and sober young man', according to Clarendon. He was a friend of Cromwell, who made him a general at sea and then admiral. He served Cromwell loyally and after Oliver's death he supported Richard, but the subsequent confusion and return of the Rump had alienated him. A royal message was delivered to him in the summer when he was stationed with the fleet off Copenhagen, watching over England's interests in the Sound. Montagu responded positively and sailed for England, but by the time he reached the coast Sir George Booth had been defeated. Montagu made excuses, namely that he lacked provisions and that autumn had already come – he had arrived in September. Parliament waited on information from Copenhagen before proceeding against him, so Montagu laid down his command and retired to the country.

The collapse of Booth's rising, with 'the King's hopes so totally destroyed', as Clarendon recorded, allowed parliament to concentrate on domestic issues, but everywhere they faced grave problems.[4] The most pressing was pay for the army, while in parliament arguments had broken out about the constitution. England had developed its forms of government gradually over the centuries; when several key institutions were removed, the remainder malfunctioned and those with power – the army and the republican MPs – were incapable of agreeing a new system. Lambert was away on campaign, which pushed up army costs and increased the grievances of his men. From Derby, they wrote a petition demanding godly reforms, a senate and that officers should have more power over the army.[5] This document had also been sent to Monck in Scotland but he refused to sign it. When Lambert arrived back in London, Fleetwood and his officers debated this document and then sent it to Haselrig. In 1647, army petitions had caused a crisis, so Fleetwood might have expected trouble. Sure enough, Haselrig reacted badly and created a drama, rushing to the house, locking the doors and reading out the dangerous Derby petition. He wanted Lambert arrested but parliament calmed him down and ordered Fleetwood to prevent further petitioning.

Unfortunately, parliament had also upset the City of London by trying to interfere in their governance. The Corporation reminded MPs of the old and well-established rules for their elections and emphasised the large sums which parliament owed them. The debt was becoming critical – the troops had to be paid but parliament was running out of ways to raise money. When men were unpaid they took free quarters with civilians, which caused intense aggression. People had already been policed by the army, had been raided by soldiers to stop them celebrating Christmas, had been turned out of pubs or had seen their maypoles broken by troops – having them march into your house to share your lunch turned a tense situation poisonous. The soldiers disliked it too; it had to be avoided.

Trying to extract tax, selling delinquents' lands or borrowing were the government's expedients but these only raised a fraction of the money needed. Before two weeks passed, another petition arrived, this time from the army around London and delivered by Desborough. As lack of money and army demands built up, debates over the form of government intensified and relationships became fraught. Members were becoming panicky; when the army started sending in demands that generally meant it was going to make a move. Thinking they might be ejected, the House passed two bills which would make government all but impossible should that happen and, invigorated by a message of support from Monck, they acted quickly against the army, revoking the commissions of nine officers including Lambert and taking overall control from Fleetwood. Haselrig called in his own regiments to defend the House, but Lambert was back in London and called in troops from around the capital, most of whom answered his summons.

On 13 October, two rings of soldiers surrounded the Palace of Westminster, the inner one under Haselrig defending it from dissolution, the outer one under Lambert determined to take control. In the confrontation, Lambert won. Many of the defenders joined his troops and Haselrig ordered the remainder of his troops to go home. Speaker Lenthall, trying to get into parliament, reminded the men that he was their true commander but the troops said they had not seen him on the battlefield and Lambert ordered him home as well.[6] Haselrig's troops left and Lambert's marched in. Once more, the Rump was dissolved and the parliament house locked.

Under pressure of this collapse, the republican leaders split. Haselrig refused to negotiate with the army and withdrew, but Vane was more pliable. Fleetwood was again confirmed as head of the army but Lambert was emerging as leader and rumours circulated of his negotiations with Vane. The army created a new Committee of Safety and for two weeks there were two executive bodies claiming to rule, as the existing Council of State still sat. Inevitably the army officers gained control, but after discussions Vane and Whitelocke, with others, joined them. On 25 October, the Council of State held its last meeting. The Rump and its executive were gone; the army was back in control.

A blizzard of pamphleteering broke out and in the London coffeehouses informed citizens buzzed with ideas and opinions. In New Palace Yard, Miles' Coffee House became a focus of debate; every evening the newly established Rota Club discussed the ideas of *Oceana* – men such as Harrington himself, Pepys, Aubrey, Wildman, Wolseley and William Petty were all there.[7] Harrington's ideas of wider property ownership linked to citizens' rights and duties were influential, for English society was struggling its way into a new paradigm – but the birth pangs were intense.

Ludlow had been in Ireland since July, reorganising the army and especially its officers. Leaving John Jones in charge, he sailed for England, but on coming ashore in Anglesey he heard of Lambert's coup against the Rump. He rushed to London, hoping to find a compromise because, as an army commander but also a staunch republican, he viewed the dissolution of the Rump with grave alarm. Like many men, he had his own blueprint of how to organise government, but in London he and his fellow commanders received a devastating communication from the north.

On 17 October, the message of parliament's closure of the Rump reached General Monck in Edinburgh. Unlike much of the revolutionary army, George Monck had been a career soldier since the age of sixteen. He had served under Cromwell with great success; the two men liked and respected each other and indeed had much in common. Monck had brought order to Scotland with a stern hand but had won the respect of many Scots by his efficiency and consistency. 'Honest George Monck,' his men called him. He had remained firm and loyal when the Protectorate was dissolved, despite his association with both the Cromwells, father and son. He disliked the way that parliament had reorganised his officer corps against his express wishes, but as a professional soldier he was steeped in military discipline. 'Obedience is my great principle,' he had written to the Speaker in June, that 'I have alwaise, and ever shall, reverence the Parliament's resolutions in civill things as infallible and sacred.'[8]

Now the army had dissolved parliament once more. Monck was not a politician; he was a tough, shrewd man in his early fifties, who had commanded armies and overseen Scottish government. He held more conservative religious views than Cromwell but, like the Lord Protector, he intended stability, and the only explanation he gave for his next move was that 'fanatics' were taking over the government. Monck liked order and was able to create it. He had watched Cromwell hold the government together against fractious spirits in England and had himself suppressed the seething factions of Scotland. Clearly, now he would have to tackle disorder in England as well. He made his dispositions first, creating a unit of men he trusted and sending them to visit each army base, where men of dubious loyalty were replaced with those whom Monck had picked. This took a month but the stand-off and deliberations in London also took time. Monck did not wait for news to filter south. A week after he heard of the dissolution, he felt strong enough to announce his position, sending three letters to London – one to Fleetwood, one to Lambert and one to Speaker Lenthall – announcing that England would not submit to arbitrary government and that he intended to uphold and defend parliament.[9] These created a sensation and a military response; on 3 November, Lambert was despatched north with forces to meet Monck.

Throughout the extraordinary events which followed, General Monck was slow to state his motives or to position himself too closely among the aims and factions which were clamouring for control of England. As early as August, Monck's brother brought him a letter from Charles, which was said to offer the enormous sum of £100,000 a year for life should he enter the king's service. Monck refused to accept the letter. Hyde believed that Monck 'saw he should quickly be overrun and destroyed by Lambert's greatness', for despite Fleetwood's command it was Lambert who was leading the army's bid for power.[10] Monck had stated that he loathed religious fanatics and his conduct generally was of a conservative Englishman without complex intellectual interests who supported the social order and disliked extremes. He kept his cards close to his chest and it may be that he responded to events as they unfolded, or perhaps his aim was to avoid bloodshed during a handover of power. In either case, his strategy proved masterful.

Monck knew his army. He called all his officers together, including the junior ones, to debate the situation. He also published a gazette called *Mercurius Britanicus*, the name used by Nedham in the parliamentarian cause during the Civil War. So far, Monck's only aim appeared to be to restore parliament. His actions suggest a man calculating each move as circumstances altered. Clearly able and shrewd, Monck appears to some as duplicitous while others view him as a man of determination and honour who prevented a slide into anarchy; the latter view has much evidence behind it. Lambert was indeed dynamic but, of the army leaders left by Cromwell's death, only Monck had the stern purpose and organisational abilities of the first Lord Protector. More importantly, Monck was able to pay his men. He had put sufficient pressure on London to get £20,000 from them towards the army and had been fairly successful at collecting Scottish tax, so he had funds sufficient for several months.

In London, the Committee of Safety was struggling. Apprentices were rioting in support of a free parliament, whereas in Scotland that November, Monck called together representatives of the burghs and shires, allowing them to form a modest self-government while he went south to maintain the rights of parliament and the ancient constitution against tyranny. They were to keep the peace and prevent correspondence with Charles Stuart, to which they agreed. The nobility chose Glencairn, a royalist champion, to represent them but Monck made no objection. He had been in Scotland for most of the 1650s and supported her interests, setting up meetings to forward Scottish grievances and hopes to London. He now undertook to get tax reduced and to see that Scotland was treated equally with England as regards finance.[11]

The Committee of Safety was in a weak and nervous situation. Lambert was at Newcastle by 23 November. Neither side wanted a fight; instead Monck sent delegates to negotiate, but when they moved south to London Monck's men buckled and agreed to army demands. However, the talks had bought time while Monck mustered his forces and set off south, leaving Morgan, his senior and trusted officer, in command of Scotland. On 8 December, Monck was at Coldstream with about 8,000 men, where he recruited more men to fill his regiments, building a corps from which the Coldstream Guards originate.

Lambert was pulling in other northern troops and could command 12,000 men, so if Monck's initiative was to succeed he needed not just numbers but support and a diversion in northern England. In Yorkshire, at his seat of Nun Appleton, was one of the figureheads of the 'Good Old Cause': General Lord Fairfax. He had disliked the conduct of his army over the death of the king and had been enraged by Cromwell's recent imprisonment of his son-in-law the Duke of Buckingham. After intermediaries visited Nun Appleton, Fairfax offered Monck support. His name and his ability to raise men in Yorkshire created a powerful alliance. Monck was given added legitimacy when the dissolved but still legal Council of State appointed him commander-in-chief for England and Scotland. Armed with a valid commission and with Fairfax as ally, Monck prepared to cross the River Tweed and enter England.

In Portsmouth, Governor Whetham agreed to deliver this vital port to parliament and on 3 December Haselrig with colleagues took control. In London, demands for a free parliament were growing as army authority weakened; there were demonstrations at which soldiers fired on the mob, killing several. More ominously for Fleetwood and his colleagues, Vice Admiral Lawson, who now controlled the navy, wrote to the Lord Mayor of London demanding the Rump be reinstated. As a committed republican, Lawson was cautious of Monck, whose moves might lead to a restoration of monarchy. Receiving no response from the City, Lawson took twenty ships and sailed to Gravesend, where he anchored, thereby blocking the Thames and the approach to London.[12]

The coup against the Rump by the army in London had lost them Scotland – Monck was now crossing the border – but the army in Ireland was of a different temper. Ludlow was still in London, involved in the furious debates about the future of government and leaving John Jones in charge. Since then, Jones had been propositioned by Monck but repudiated his overtures. Other Irish Protestants viewed Monck's position differently. Coote and Theophilus Jones had sent a positive message to Monck and hoped to win over Sir Hardress Waller. The next news that Ludlow received was shocking: Jones had lost control and a group of dissentient officers had seized Dublin Castle.

Nowhere had the revolution of the 1650s produced greater change than in Ireland, so it was inevitable that the winners had most to fear from another upheaval, in case their new property should be lost. The land settlement was still unfinished – Petty's survey was still being completed to sort out claims, acreages and titles – but the Catholics had been dispossessed. If there was another change of government, most of all a Stuart restoration, the Protestants feared those land titles might be in jeopardy and the Catholics reinstated. But if they took the initiative and got control, they would be able to dictate terms.

Under Cromwell, Lord Broghill had emerged as leader of the Old Protestants. After the fall of the Protectorate, he had hurried back to Ireland in case of disorder, but finding none and disillusioned with the situation in London, he retired to County Cork and was at Ballymaloe in the summer of 1659, trying to get some order into his Irish property. Through his royalist brothers, he received overtures from Charles and the exiled court but he was slow to commit himself.[13] He tolerated the Rump but when Ludlow returned to power in Ireland and then Lambert and the army took power in England in October, Broghill was roused. Sir Charles Coote had a firm hold on both Connaught and Ulster and was already in touch with Charles. The Old Protestants had a mixed record during the war but had prospered under the Cromwells. Both they and the New Protestant planters were worried about the land settlement and so too were those still serving in the army. Colonel Jones was aware that his army was splitting but he had no control over the wider Protestant community, who ultimately unseated him.

Coote, Waller and several Old Protestants made a simple plan, which was shockingly successful. On 13 December 1659, two officers who were known to the guards entered Dublin Castle and walked about there, before calling on the sentinel to let them out. When the gate was opened, a party of soldiers rushed in, overpowered the guards and took control of the fortress. Horse troops rode through Dublin shouting, 'A parliament, a parliament.'[14] The shouts of the horsemen for a parliament could be interpreted in several ways – a return of the Rump, the readmission of the full Long Parliament or a new parliament altogether. Whatever it signified, it allowed all those who abhorred army rule to coalesce.

John Jones was arrested and Ludlow, who rushed back to Ireland, landed only briefly before hurrying away to avoid being arrested too. Coote got control of the garrisons in Connaught, their fellow Old Protestants struck in Munster and Leinster, and although Ulster took longer to subdue, swift action and considerable support gave this group control of the principal strongholds of Ireland.[15] The Old Protestants soon formed an army council of their own to manage the troops, and by late December Broghill had joined them. He disliked Lambert intensely, deplored military government and had to move swiftly if he was to secure his position. In January, the group sent a message of support to General Monck and announced that an assembly would be held in Dublin in February.

In southern England, the tide was turning against army rule too. The Committee of Safety had decided to call a parliament of its own but this met with public resistance. Lawson declared for the Rump and Lambert was in the north, unable to leave Monck and Fairfax unchallenged. The corporation of London declared for the Rump as well; some of the junior officers were of the same mind and Haselrig gathered enough troops to march on London. Law and order were breaking down in the principal southern cities of Gloucester, Bristol and Exeter. Significantly, on 26 December, the Speaker received a message of support from the garrison in Dunkirk. Lambert decided that protecting London was more important than facing Monck, so he sent Lilburne with his troops to take York and turned south – but his troops were leaving him. When Lilburne reached York, he found Fairfax there with 1,800 men and duly declared for parliament. On 26 December, Fleetwood capitulated and handed over the keys of the parliament house to Speaker Lenthall; he and his officers resigned their commissions to parliament and the Rump reassembled. It looked as though the coup had been reversed, but by now unrest was widespread and the government extremely weak.

On 1 January, Monck crossed the Tweed and began his march south, arriving in London on 3 February 1660. England was seething with discontent because reinstating the Rump was no longer sufficient; everywhere there were demands to readmit all the MPs who had been expelled by the army in 1648. As he marched, Monck demanded the removal of all other troops from London. This order was obeyed, so when Monck arrived he controlled the city. Technically, he was a servant of the Rump. The City of London was on the point of a tax strike and, to prove their supremacy, the Rump ordered Monck to pull down the gates of the City and assert their control. Monck did so, but with a bad grace. The Rump was at least a parliament and not the army, but it was no more popular than it had been in 1653. Determined to control the army, parliament introduced a bill to give overall command to a commission, but Monck was not going to give up his command. He conferred with his officers, his chaplain and other friends, then wrote to parliament insisting that it hold elections to fill all the empty seats. When there was delay, the demand altered: the members purged in 1648 must be readmitted so that the full elected parliament could be reconstituted and legally dissolve itself; then new elections would be held. There was little doubt in anyone's mind what free elections would bring.

Monck went to meet the City Corporation. When news leaked out that he was supporting the City of London and a free parliament, there was an explosion of joy. Suddenly he was a hero. Bonfires were lit, church bells rang and, in the streets, rumps were roasted in lieu of actually sizzling that group themselves. Some people openly toasted the king. The Rump was only a fraction of the original Long Parliament and its unpopularity was clear. Now it was being challenged, there were wild expressions of joy across southern England: in Oxford, Gloucester, Bristol, Exeter and elsewhere. The Rump tried to parley but Monck was soon in touch with the excluded members. Cautiously, he advanced his cause, careful to keep control and not to let the frustrated aims and hardened angers of the last decade break out. Only when the excluded members agreed to proper elections were they permitted to take their seats. The normal rhythm of parliamentary representation was gradually to be resumed.

It was over a decade since Pride's Purge, and the men who were allowed to re-join parliament in February 1660 were neither committed royalists nor Catholics, both of whom had been barred during the war. The men who came back to Westminster in spring 1660 had supported parliament during the Civil War but had been willing to close a deal with Charles I in 1648. They were mostly Presbyterians, wanting a Calvinist national church but with some toleration of separatists. Whenever Monck spoke or wrote at this stage, he made clear that the Commonwealth would continue and purchases of crown or church lands would not be reversed. He insisted that the excluded members must come back as a prelude to elections; but what did the shouts of a 'free parliament' mean? It meant a properly elected representative, not one hand-picked by the army. Once the Long Parliament was back in its chamber, it confirmed Monck as commander-in-chief and since he also headed the new militia commissioners, all the armed forces were now at his disposal. The Long Parliament, now properly reassembled, could legally dissolve and 15 March was named as the end date.

Primarily because it lacked funds, Ireland had already provided itself with a representative assembly which convened on 27 February. Catholics were excluded and the meeting was dominated by Old Protestants, not the new settlers. To allow 'a full confluence of all members', they adjourned until 2 March. Once in session, members of the Convention proclaimed their aims: loyalty to England, an Irish parliament free from control by the one in Westminster, a ministry supported by tithes and no toleration of radical religion. By law, a parliament could only be called by the monarch but Coote was already in touch with the king, offering his service and suggesting that Charles come to Ireland. Broghill, subtle and astute, hung back; he held Calvinist views and had a mixed record of loyalties. Since his political group now controlled the fortresses and corporations of Ireland, Broghill tried to time their overtures to Charles to obtain the maximum concessions. Coote hurried on, so Broghill was obliged to also offer his service to the royal cause, but Charles was not proclaimed king in Dublin until 14 May.

The mood in Scotland was more excited, as Scots awaited the restoration of the Stuart dynasty. The nobles and gentry were pressing to bear arms once more, as they had before Cromwell's conquest. Monck's deputy struggled to restrain their exuberance, but the Scots apparently believed that General Monck would play fair and not let them down. Scotland was aroused but caused no trouble.

It was the English army which caused Monck the most difficulty. He conducted a minor purge but the council of officers was demanding that he maintain the republic and was restive about the terms for the elections. Monck said that those who had fought against parliament would not be able to sit, and warned them that if they forced another dissolution there would be anarchy. If that happened, he declared that he would not take government upon himself. As the only man whose authority might have replaced that of Cromwell, Monck knew his worth. Fleetwood had lost his position, while Lambert was ordered to post a huge sum for good conduct and, when he proved unable, was arrested. Gradually, the civilian government of England was re-emerging. Monck kept control and managed the process in careful stages, still asserting a Commonwealth, supporting a Presbyterian national church but removing the most ardent troublemakers. He even kept Lawson on side.

The Long Parliament dissolved itself on 16 March. The Convention was to assemble in Westminster on 25 April, so there was just over a month to hold elections. Public opinion seems to have accepted that monarchy was on its way back. Once the Long Parliament had dissolved, General Monck accepted the king's letters. He responded positively, sending a verbal message via his kinsman offering to Charles his service and his life, while advising the exiled king to leave Spanish territory. Charles moved back to the United Provinces and settled at his sister's estate at Breda.

Lambert escaped from the Tower and promptly called for a reinstatement of the Protectorate under Richard and a rendezvous at Edgehill, but the response was slight – only four troops of horse turned out – and he was recaptured. He lived for another twenty-three years but was never again a free man.

The elections were keenly contested and, as the army had feared, many royalists were elected. Tellingly, republicans fared badly and very few Rumpers got in. When the Convention met on 25 April 1660, it was a new house indeed; after two decades of carefully selected members, a free parliament returned novices – half had never sat in parliament before. The House of Lords also assembled, where some young lords appeared who had inherited during the revolutionary period; a new generation was coming into parliament.

Four days later, a declaration from Charles was brought into the council. The Declaration of Breda was read in both houses on 1 May and received with great acclaim. It was the House of Lords which moved 'that according to the ancient and fundamental laws of this kingdom, the government is, and ought to be, by King, Lords and Commons'. This motion was passed in the Lords, and later that day the Commons voted in favour.

The revolution was over: the king was coming home.

19

The King Returns

Few people in the three kingdoms had seen Charles Stuart. Those who had either caught a glimpse of him in Scotland in 1650 or saw his army march through north-west England to defeat at Worcester. Londoners may have seen the small boy with his parents, dressed in their fine clothes, but he had left the city when he was eleven. For the citizens of Oxford, King Charles I and his teenage sons had been a constant presence, coming and going from their quarters in Christ Church during the war, but Prince Charles had been sent to Bristol with his own council when he was fifteen and they soon had to flee further west, sailing from Cornwall when the prince was sixteen.

The man who waited in the Netherlands as the revolutionary regime in England crumbled was twenty-nine years old and, for a prince, had undergone an unusual education. Rather than learning statecraft from his father – a ruling monarch – he had learned warfare and negotiation of terms. His mother had been a difficult presence, hurt, angry and full of opinions, but as a princess she had been poorly educated herself.

Prince Charles's councillors, on the other hand, had been well-chosen. James Butler, Marquis of Ormond was a man of steady temperament and principles while Sir Edward Hyde proved an astute politician and diplomat, willing to live poorly or make long, risky journeys to serve the king. Hyde was passionately committed to the Church of England and the traditional English constitution. Charles teased him but relied on him – when the treaty with Spain was agreed in 1656, he wrote to Hyde to 'make as much haste as your gouty feet will give you leave to me'.[1]

It was Hyde's view that Charles would regain his thrones not by external military force but through the support of English royalists.

In the long run he was correct, although in the meantime royalists were strongly suppressed and their small risings ineffectual. They were disarmed, severely taxed and their land confiscated, while the Cromwellian regime had a powerful army and capable spy network. By 1659, however, there was such widespread revulsion against rule by the Puritan army that, as the regime crumbled, a surge of longing for the traditional forms emerged.

It was not that the Stuarts were well loved. Despite his failings, Charles I had won sufficient loyalty to fight a long war, but he had alienated large groups by his autocratic methods, repressive religious practices and illegal taxation. Among the plain people of England, these were not the big issues. Most traditional taxes were levied on land or trade, so had not touched poorer people, whereas now they paid excise. Many working people had supported revolution, hoping for land rights, better pay, no tithes and some civic liberties. Those aims had not been met, whereas the Puritans imposed their religion, suppressed popular pastimes, banned Christmas, closed pubs and theatres, and stopped dancing and maypoles, while unleashing a culture of prayer and preaching. For the three nations taxation was high during the Interregnum, yet the troops were often unpaid while many officers had become grandees with great estates.

The Scots had originally risen in support of their church, and had paid heavily for the Covenanter armies which invaded England, but they never intended to depose the king. The Scots longed passionately for something they could not have – a king who shared their beliefs, a Covenanted king. When they imposed this on Charles II in 1650 they alienated him, and he later said he would rather die than return to Scotland. Nor could the Scots withstand the English Puritan army, which imposed total conquest, so Scotland's losses were great.

The most profound loss, however, was that of the Irish Catholics. In numbers they were still considerable, despite the casualty rate during the war and the expulsions which followed. Historians have concentrated on the 40 per cent loss of Irish land which the Catholics suffered but they were still the large majority of the Irish population and they still retained roughly 20 per cent of the island. Charles II was their only realistic hope. He had a Catholic mother and his father had shown a willingness to treat with Catholics and offer terms – those had in fact not been honoured, but the Stuarts were nonetheless more sympathetic to Catholics than the Puritans. The Convention in Dublin offered the Catholics little but the Convention parliament in London jubilantly invited the king to return and resume the traditional forms of government. So, the Irish Catholics – impoverished, dispossessed and exhausted – nonetheless had a glimmer of hope. For the Irish Protestants, the situation looked positive yet full of uncertainty. The leaders of the coup controlled the army and the principal strongholds in Ireland, and they had allied themselves with Monck, but if the land settlement was reopened, all the Protestants had a great deal to lose.

If the king was to return, on what terms would that happen? Presbyterians, especially in England, had been raising this issue for some time. They wanted the 1648 Newport Treaty to be used as the basis for negotiations and they expected that, with Monck's support, they could dominate the Convention parliament. But first many royalists were elected to the Commons and then Monck gave up filtering admission to the Lords. Young peers, untainted by war, came in first but soon older lords followed.

The process of restoration was managed gradually by Monck and separately by Charles and his councillors, as both groups rode the tide of public opinion. Monck was very keen to protect the land purchases which his soldiers had made; he also supported the aims of the Presbyterians until it became clear that the elections had returned a royalist parliament and that the people, many of whom could not vote, supported that position. Once Monck was in touch with the king he gave Charles sound advice: move out of the Spanish Netherlands and confirm the legality of the Convention parliament, so that when it reinstated him that decision would have legal force. Monck advised that Acts and ordinances made since 1640 should be endorsed, that indemnity should be confirmed because soldiers often feared prosecutions, and to allow freedom of worship pending a more detailed settlement. The Convention in London made suggestions about limiting royal appointments and directing government itself, but these ideas arose in the Lords and the Commons did not support them.

Since the early spring, Charles had been making his own overtures. The process of wooing the most important officials had begun earlier, but as it became clear that his restoration was inevitable a trickle of well-wishers and jobseekers turned into a flood. The young man who had lost weight because he could not afford good meals and had shocked visitors by his poor clothing and lodgings had become a king in waiting, surrounded by adulation and supplicants. His ministers had put out a proclamation in September 1659 offering pardon to all but regicides, the abolition of most taxation and regular free parliaments. As the spring came, Charles wrote to his royalist supporters in England

and Scotland, urging reconciliation on them. Nothing would blast his chances more than a surge of vengeful royalists promising retribution. Early in April, as events in England sped forward, Charles and his councillors drafted a document in which, by offering broad terms to be settled by a future parliament, the king forestalled a long wrangle about terms for himself.

The Declaration of Breda was signed by Charles on 4 April and delivered to parliament on 1 May 1660.

> If the general distraction and confusion which is spread over the whole kingdom doth not awaken all men to a desire and longing that these wounds which have so many years together been kept bleeding may be bound up, all we can say will be to no purpose. However, after this long silence, we have thought it our duty to declare how much we desire to contribute thereunto and that, as we can never give over hope in good time to obtain the possession of that right which God and nature hath made our due, so we do make it our daily suit to the divine providence that He will in compassion to us and our subjects (after so long misery and sufferings) remit us and put us into a quiet and peaceable possession of that our right with as little blood and damage to our people as is possible. Nor do we desire more to enjoy what is ours, than that all our subjects may enjoy what by law is theirs by a full and entire administration of justice throughout the land, and by extending our mercy where it is wanting and deserved.[2]

The Declaration of Breda offered a general pardon to all who pledged loyalty, except those excluded by parliament. On religion, Charles offered liberty to tender consciences so long as the peace of the kingdom was not disturbed. Titles to land were to be settled by parliament. Monck's men were to be taken into royal service on current pay and conditions and once parliament legislated for their arrears, the king would assent. The Declaration handed over all decisions of weight to parliament: regarding pardon, religion, land titles and army pay. It referred to the traditional forms of government but said nothing about the issues in contention in 1648 such as bishops and control of the militia, and it only nodded in passing to the monarch's veto or negative voice. In the end, there were discussions and offers, but Charles II returned to the triple thrones unconditionally. After two decades of war for the constitution, no preconditions were set. How could this be possible? How could politicians in London agree to it?

The fact of the Restoration proved that two decades of constitutional wrangling had exhausted the nation. Blueprints, treaties, formulas for parliament had all been tested to destruction. During the last year of the Interregnum it seemed as though every man and probably most women were proposing their individual blueprint for government; no one could stomach any more. The real outcome of the struggle was to show everyone just how difficult it is to write a constitution and how the traditions which England had developed gradually over centuries, by law, experience and through other contests, had created a system of strength and subtlety. It was not perfect and could be abused, and certainly it would have to adapt to swiftly changing times, but the revolutionary experiment had driven many people back towards it as the best arrangement they had, the bedrock on which the future must be built.

In the event, statecraft allowed Charles to come back without conditions. The king and his three close councillors – Ormond, Nicholas and especially clever Sir Edward Hyde – devised a simple and effective document which covered the key issues. Its timing was perfect. The Declaration of Breda arrived in London just as the Convention parliament was settling to business but when public opinion was running strongly in the king's favour.

In the mood of the spring of 1660, it was sufficient. Regarding the restoration of the Stuart monarchy, public opinion, especially in London, played an enormous part. Monck was to be commander-in-chief, his men would be paid and well cared for while Montagu, the Admiral of the Fleet, had come over to Charles the year before. Who was left to prevent a restoration of the monarchy when lords, commons and the people demanded it? In London, it was clear that the people were ecstatic at the fall of the army, joyous at the prospect of normal life and that Charles meant exactly that: dancing and maypoles, merry old England. In that, at least, he fulfilled their expectations – Charles played the part of 'the merry monarch' energetically and his reputation remains.

The United Provinces, which a few years before had asked him to leave, now invited him as their guest and Charles set out for The Hague. The citizens of Breda provided a yacht and James, Duke of York organised the thirteen ships which carried the royal party as far as Delft, which included Princess Mary and her three-year-old son William with Henry, Duke of Gloucester and Charles's loyal ministers. At Delft they were met by crowds and cannons; a convoy of seventy-three coaches was provided to take Charles and his entourage to The Hague. Though feted by the Dutch, Charles needed all his characteristic charm to mollify the Spanish, who had been his allies but whom he had now left. At The Hague there was a state banquet in his honour, a night of fireworks, salutes by cannon and many speeches. Now he was returning to rule England, which had proved a formidable enemy to the Netherlands during the Interregnum, the States-General showered honours on him. A deputation came from the City of London to whom Charles was generous, telling them he was a Londoner himself, born in St James's Palace. Other deputations came from the Convention and from the Kirk. Even Lord Fairfax arrived and had a private interview with the king.

An English fleet had arrived to fetch him, with Montagu in command. They were anchored off the harbour of Scheveningen. Princess Mary of Orange and her son William were among the party who escorted the king to his ship on 23 May, as Charles and his brothers rode to the harbour between files of Dutch soldiers. The flagship, named the *Naseby* after Cromwell's great battle, was renamed the *Royal Charles*. The king, whose knowledge of ships and navigation was later remarked on by officials, renamed other ships and walked about on the harbourside, clearly excited.

The crowds were enormous: 100,000 people lined the road or clustered on the quays to see off the young king. Montagu was on the flagship to welcome Charles as the royal party were rowed out to the fleet. At 3 p.m., Princess Mary and her son were taken back to the quay and the English fleet weighed anchor. Luckily Samuel Pepys was on the flagship, as he was a relative of Montagu, for whom he was working, so there was a first-rate diarist to record the crossing. Charles recounted the story of his escape from Worcester, a story he retold in later years more often than his courtiers would have liked – it grew in the telling. The young king had not led a courtly life, which showed afterwards in his informality, but those perilous six weeks when he traversed Puritan England remained a thrilling memory to him, the only time he lived among and was dependent on ordinary people.

The fleet was under sail all night, heading for Kent, and the next day the weather was glorious. By the evening of 24 May, the royal party could see the coast of England. On the morning of the 25th, Charles and James ate sturdy seamen's rations for their breakfast before coming ashore at Dover. To greet them was the splendid figure of General George Monck. Charles fell on his knees to thank God for his return, embraced the general, kissed him and called him 'father'. In a sense this was true, since Monck had given him back his inheritance.

The Speaker of the Commons was there, to whom Charles confirmed that he would maintain the law and the Protestant religion. He was presented with a Bible and expressed his love for it. From Dover it was not a long journey to Canterbury, the archdiocesan capital of England.

Charles was greeted everywhere by bonfires, church bells ringing and crowds cheering. His Privy Council held its first meeting at Canterbury and foreign ambassadors gathered to pay their respects, noting that the king spoke several European languages fluently – his disrupted education had been balanced by other skills. The begging for places and lists of worthy royalists grew oppressive but his ministers were in attendance, Monck was at his service and, as he made his way to London, he was escorted by volunteer troops of cavalry.

Not everyone was pleased. John Milton had published two versions of a tract promoting the Commonwealth only weeks before Charles returned, but now the unrepentant republicans were lying low and the regicides were uncertain whether they would be included in the pardon and amnesty. It was no longer their time: power had gone elsewhere. Royalists of course were in a state of bliss – Sir Thomas Urquhart is said to have died laughing with pleasure at this restoration – but there can be little doubt that the plain people of England were joyful. At Rochester, Charles left his coach and rode the 30 miles to London on horseback so that everyone could see him. At Blackheath, Monk's army was drawn up, a declaration of welcome was presented and Charles reviewed five regiments of cavalry who were now in his service.

On his thirtieth birthday, 29 May 1660, escorted by his two brothers, King Charles rode into Southwark and so into the City of London. According to John Evelyn, there were 200,000 horse and foot 'brandishing their swords and shouting with unexpressable joy; the way strewed with flowers, the bells ringing, the streets hung with tapestry, fountains running with wine'. The mayor, aldermen and the guilds processed with their chains of gold and banners; everyone was in their finery, with great ladies at the windows to watch the procession pass. 'I stood in the Strand and beheld it and blessed God,' wrote John Evelyn, 'and all this without one drop of blood.'[3]

It was a magnificent procession, with the horses and dignitaries making their stately way through the city. There were 300 gentlemen in cloth of silver, footmen in purple or sea-green costumes edged with lace, and sheriff's men in red cloaks. The London companies wore golden chains and the aldermen robes of scarlet. The noise was tremendous, with guns and cannon firing, and more bells ringing. Crowds jostled to see the new king, shouting and cheering.

The man the Londoners saw on his fine horse was tall and strong with thick dark hair. There were the first flecks of grey in it but they could not distinguish that as he rode by. He was not handsome – with his long nose and full mouth his features were excessive – but he had fine, intelligent eyes. Young and vigorous, physically quite unlike his parents, he cannot have reminded his subjects of their late king. Unable to follow another profession like his brother, who had made a career as a soldier, Charles had spent his youth planning, waiting or struggling to maintain dignity, even a reasonable standard of living, dependent on the charity of other princes. There was a cynicism hidden behind the charm, a wariness of men and motives, but Charles knew how to behave as a king and he was determined never to go on his travels again.

They reached Whitehall around seven in the evening. As he rode through the palace gates and dismounted, he had the warm wishes of his people, their shouts and acclamations ringing in his ears. Here there were such long speeches of welcome that the king expressed his gratitude and affection graciously but briefly and, after further orations, confessed he was too tired to speak. The service of thanksgiving was accordingly held in the Presence Chamber, not in Westminster Abbey. Charles must certainly have remembered Whitehall Palace, with its warren of structures and styles, as it had been his parents' chief home throughout his childhood. More recently it had been the centre of Oliver Cromwell's court. Beside the gates stood the Banqueting House, from which Charles I had stepped to his execution. Now the son had returned. On the men who murdered his father, Charles II and his government would take vengeance, but for his three kingdoms his stated wish was for reconciliation, a benevolent religious settlement and parliamentary government.

It was a joyous day for the royalists and an incomparable experience for the young king. After two decades of turmoil, he had been restored to his thrones without conditions. To him fell the task of establishing government and resolving the issues which had defeated not only his father, but also Oliver Cromwell and his Puritan colleagues. Charles II was a strong and clever young man – his people hoped and believed that he would meet the challenge.

The Instrument of Government, 16 December 1653[1]

Abridged by Jane Hayter-Hames

The government of the Commonwealth of England, Scotland and Ireland and the dominions thereunto belonging.'

Articles

1. The supreme legislative power is in one person, and the people assembled in parliament, that person styled Lord Protector.

2. The chief magistracy and administration is in the Lord Protector and Council.

3. All writs, commissions, grants etc. now given under the Keepers of the Liberties of England...shall run under the Lord Protector.

4. The Lord Protector commands the military, by consent of parliament, and between parliaments, by consulting his council.

5. The Lord Protector manages foreign policy.

6. Laws are only to be made, altered or repealed by parliament – except see article 30.

7. Parliament will meet on 3 September 1654 and every three years thereafter.

8. Parliament will sit for at least five months.

9. There will be 400 members for England, Wales and the Channel Isles. Scotland and Ireland shall have thirty members each.

10. A list of the constituencies and the number of members for each.

11-13. Directions for holding elections.

14. No-one who fought against parliament since January 1641 can vote or sit in the next four parliaments.

15. No-one involved in the Irish rebellion can ever vote or sit in parliament; nor can any Roman Catholic.

16-18. Qualifications for electors. They must be of known integrity, fearing God, aged twenty-one or over, with £200 worth of real estate.

19-21. Directions given for managing the elections.

22. A minimum of sixty persons are needed for a parliament to be valid.

23. The Lord Protector, with the advice of the council, may call a parliament when necessity requires it or in case of war. It must sit for three months.

24. Bills passed by parliament are to be sent to the Lord Protector. If he does not consent to them within twenty days or explain why, the bills become law.

25. Fifteen members are named for the Protector's council. If they die or are removed, parliament is to pick six people, the council will choose two of them and the Protector will pick one. Members can be suspended for corruption.

26. The Lord Protector and council may add people up to the number of twenty-one members for the council.

27. A constant yearly revenue will be raised to maintain 10,000 horse and dragoons with 20,000 foot in England, Scotland and Ireland, and also for ships guarding the seas. £200,000 will be raised for other government expenses from customs and by other means.

28. The yearly revenue is to be paid into the treasury.

29. If there is a surplus it shall be kept in a bank for the public service and parliament's consent will be required for it to be used.

30. The current costs of war must be raised by consent of parliament. However, until the first parliament is called, the Lord Protector with the consent of the council may raise money and issue laws and ordinances for the peace and welfare of the nation.

31. Confiscated property not yet sold will be vested in the Lord Protector, as well as the income from the property, but it must not be alienated.

32. The office of Lord Protector is elective not hereditary. After the death of the Lord Protector, the council will elect his successor. No child of the late king or member of his family can be elected.

33. Oliver Cromwell is to be Lord Protector.

34. The Chancellor and other high officials shall be chosen by the approbation of parliament and between parliaments by the council, later to be confirmed by parliament.

35. The Christian religion, as contained in the Scriptures, is the public profession of these nations. Provision must be made for the maintenance of 'able and painful teachers,' and until it is, the present maintenance system must continue.

36. People should not be compelled to attend the public profession [of faith] by penalties but they should be taught and persuaded in those beliefs.

37. Those who profess faith in Jesus Christ (though differing from the public doctrine) shall be allowed freedom of practice as long as they do not abuse this liberty – but they may not practise Popery or Prelacy, nor licentiousness calling itself faith.

38. Laws which contradict this liberty are null and void.

39. Acts and ordinances of parliament made for the disposal of confiscated property must remain firm and valid, as well as securities given against public debts.

40. Articles given to the enemy and confirmed by parliament must remain valid; any appeals against sales of delinquents' lands must be heard by the next parliament.

41. Any successive Lord Protector must take an oath to seek the peace and welfare of these nations, and must uphold the law and this Instrument.

42. Each council member must take an oath to be faithful to his trust and in electing a new Lord Protector to proceed impartially and not take rewards or be coerced.

The Humble Petition and Advice, 25 May 1657[1]

Abridged by Jane Hayter-Hames

To His Highness the Lord Protector of the Commonwealth of England, Scotland and Ireland, and the dominions thereto belonging; the Humble Petition and Advice of the Knights, Citizens and Burgesses now assembled in the Parliament of the Commonwealth.'

We thank God for delivering us from the tyranny and bondage, spiritual and civil, 'which the late king and his party designed to bring us under, and pursued the effecting thereof by a long and bloody war'; and we also thank God for preserving your person and making you an instrument for preserving our peace, as has the army; 'so also we will use you and them in settling and securing our liberties, as we are men and Christians'; we fear what will happen when you die and therefore we desire:

1. You name a successor.
2. You call parliaments consisting of two houses once in every three years at the 'furthest' or oftener.
3. That the liberties of parliament be preserved, that you will not break or interrupt parliaments nor exclude those who are freely elected.
4. That the following persons be excluded from being elected or voting:
   Those involved in the rebellion in Ireland
   Roman Catholics

Those who supported the war against parliament since 1 January 1641

All who have been engaged in plots against you, or causing insurrection in England since 16 December 1653

Scots who were in arms against the parliament of England before 1 April 1648, except those who lived peaceably after 1 March 1651

Except that Protestants, of English or Scottish descent, who fought for parliament before 1 March 1649 should not be incapacitated

If people vote who are barred, they should lose one year's value of their real estate and one third of their personal estate.

People elected to parliament must be of good affection, fearing God, aged twenty-one and not disabled by the blasphemy act nor the act passed in the seventeenth year of the late king which disenabled people in Holy Orders, is not married to a Roman Catholic or bringing up their children in the Popish religion, no-one who denies the Scriptures or Sacraments, no profaner of the Lord's Day, no profane swearer or curser, no drunkard or haunter of taverns.

We desire forty-one commissioners to be appointed by Act of parliament who will examine whether members are capable to sit, each parliament to appoint such commissioners and to give evidence for their findings.

The current parliament is to decide the number of MPs and the distribution of seats.

5. Members of the Other House are to conform to this article, be chosen by the Lord Protector and approved by this House. There will be no more than seventy or fewer than forty, nor new members to replace those who die or are removed without the consent of the House. The Other House is not to undertake legal proceedings or bring court cases nor take any legal judgements, which must be taken by the House.

6. Calling and holding parliaments must conform to law and no laws may be altered or made but by parliament.

7. Parliament is willing to settle £1.3m a year – £1m for the Army and Navy, £300,000 for government – none of it to be raised by land tax and not to be altered but by consent of parliament. It may grant other supplies if necessary. No-one should be compelled to give loans or pay tax without the consent of parliament.

8. No-one should be admitted to the Protector's council unless they are of known piety and devoted to the rights of these nations and just Christian liberty in religion. New members need the consent of the council to join and approval by both houses of parliament. They cannot be removed without the consent of parliament. The council shall be a maximum of twenty-one people, with seven as a quorum. After the death of your Highness, the commander-in-chief and officers at land and generals at sea must be appointed with the consent of the council.

   The standing forces will be disposed of by the Chief Magistrate, by consent of parliament when sitting or the council when parliament is not sitting. Your Highness and your successors are to govern by advice of the council.

9. Chief officers of state are to be approved by parliament.

10. Whereas your Highness has encouraged a godly ministry, we desire that those who revile the ministry may be punished by law and where the laws are defective that you will consent to new ones.

11. That the Christian religion as contained in the Old and New Testaments and no other shall be asserted as the public profession of these nations and that a Confession of Faith be asserted, as agreed between you and parliament. If people hold the basic beliefs of Father, Son, Holy Spirit and Scripture as the revealed word of God but they differ in practice from the public profession, endeavours should be made to convince them but not compel them by penalties as long as they do no injury nor disturb the peace, but this liberty does not extend to Popery or Prelacy, nor those who hold forth licentiousness as a form of Christianity. Those who hold the main beliefs but differ in practice may hold positions of trust and employment but those who do not hold the main beliefs cannot receive the public maintenance for the ministry.

12. That all Acts to abolish bishops, deans and cathedral officials and to sell the lands of those offices, or Acts for selling the lands of the late king, queen and prince, also those of delinquents, shall remain firm.

13. Those persons disqualified from being elected or voting under article 4 may not hold public office.

14. This petition does not mean you can dissolve the present parliament.

15. Acts and Ordinances are not made void by this Petition and Advice.

16. Writs out of Chancery and Justices of one Bench, Barons of the Exchequer, JPs and other commissions, patents and grants made and passed under the Great Seal of England, Scotland or Ireland shall stand good in law.
17. Your Highness and your successors are to take an oath to govern these nations according to the law.
18. If you do not consent to all the contents of the Humble Petition and Advice, then none of it shall stand.

We hope that your acceptance of these terms will bring settlement and we will work with you to heal divisions and restore unity to these poor nations.

Presented to the Lord Protector 25 May 1657

'The Lord Protector doth consent'.

Acknowledgements

I am very grateful to Amberley Publishing for taking my books and especially to Connor Stait and Alex Bennett. Research for this book has naturally overlapped with the work I did for *The Fall of Charles I*, so I would like to say thank you once again to everyone who assisted me with that book.

John Plumer has made maps and plans for several of my books, which are always excellent, and I would like to express my appreciation. Many thanks to Stephen Terry who edited this book with great care and attention. If anything has slipped through, it will be my mistake and not his.

I would like to acknowledge the late Professor John A. Murphy of University College Cork for everything he taught me, not only about the dynamic of the seventeenth century in Ireland, but his much wider sense of historical narrative. Irish sung history will be much poorer without him.

Professor Karl Bottigheimer's work on the Cromwellian land settlement in Ireland is essential and he kindly responded to my email queries swiftly and informatively. Professor Michael J. Braddick was equally helpful about finance. Dr Clive Holmes brought the period to life with tremendous enthusiasm.

Dr Christopher Southgate, Professor John Minford and Timothy Wright helped me with books and enthusiastic interest – thank you.

For pictures I am most grateful to Julie Biddlecombe-Brown, curator, and to Lord Barnard at Raby Castle, to Sally Jones at Mansfield College Oxford and to Stuart Orme at the Cromwell Museum. The National Portrait Gallery have been most helpful with their pictures on an academic basis. I would especially like to thank the Rijksmuseum in Amsterdam, the National Gallery of Art in Washington and the Cleveland Museum for making some of their images available without charge.

Lastly but perhaps most importantly, I spend much of my life in libraries and am more grateful than I can say for the service they provide. To the librarians of the Bodleian Library in Oxford, the British Library, Boole Library at University College Cork, Exeter University Library, the London Library and Edinburgh University Library, I must express my warmest appreciation.

Glossary of Religious Terms

Chiliast	Millenarian. A person who believes that after the millennium Christ will reign on earth for one thousand years.
Covenant	Bond or agreement with God. The Scottish Covenanters asserted the sovereignty of their church and insisted on their form of church government.
Elect	Those predestined to be saved.
Erastian	(From Thomas Erastus, Zwinglian theologian) Supremacy of the state in ecclesiastical affairs.
Eschatology	The science of the four last things: death, judgement, heaven and hell.
Gathered church	A group of Christ's followers who gather together regularly to read the Gospels, listen to the preaching of God's word, to confess their sins and worship God.
Godly	Those who live according to God's word, the Elect.
Grace	Divine favour given to individuals, to which they must respond.
Irenicism	Making peace, the reconciliation of churches.
Kirk	Church. The Presbyterian Church of Scotland. From the Greek *kyriakos doma*, 'the Lord's house'.
Millennium	A period of 1,000 years, or in this context the period of 1,000 years during which Christ will reign in person on earth.
Millenarian	A believer in the millennium.
Predestination	The belief that each soul is predestined to either be saved or damned, and that the individual cannot

alter this as it is predestined by God. The opposite belief to that of salvation by merit.

Presbyterian   The form of the Scottish church, run by assemblies of church elders, not bishops. Calvinist, with a belief in the sovereignty of God and the authority of the Scriptures.

Saints   True Christians who rule with Jesus at the Millennium and create his kingdom.

Endnotes

1. The King's Burial and the New Regime

1 *Journal of the House of Commons 1648-1651*, Vol. VI (London: HMSO, 1802), pp. 110-1
2. *Mercurius Elencticus*, in Williams, J. B., *A History of English Journalism to the Foundation of the Gazette* (London: Longmans, Green, 1908), p. 205
3. Fraser, A., *Cromwell, Our Chief of Men* (London: Phoenix, 2002), pp. 364-5
4. Herbert, Sir Thomas, *Memoirs of the last years of the reign of King Charles I* (London: G. & W. Nicol, 1813), pp. 198-207
5. *Commons Journal*, Vol. VI (London: HMSO, 1802), 6 & 7 February 1649, from https://www.british-history.ac.uk
6. Gardiner, S. R., *History of the Commonwealth and Protectorate 1649-1656*, Vol. 1 (London: Longmans, Green & Co., 1903), pp. 3-4; *Commons Journal*, Vol. VI, p. 138, 13 February 1649
7. Later in the year, the Oath of Engagement was made compulsory for all adult males.

2 The Claimant to the Thrones

1. *The Diary of John Evelyn* (Oxford: University Press, 1985), p. 132
2. Stevenson, D., *Revolution and Counter Revolution in Scotland, 1644-51* (Edinburgh: John Donald, 2011), p. 125
3. Ibid., p. 126

3 Security

1. Gardiner, S. R., *Constitutional Documents of the Puritan Revolution* (Oxford: Clarendon Press, 1968), p. 388
2. Scott, J., 'What Were Commonwealth Principles?', *The Historical Journal* (Sept., 2004), pp. 591-613; Kelsey, S., *Inventing a Republic: The Political Culture of the English Commonwealth 1649-1653* (Stanford: University Press, 1997)
3. Peters, H., *God's doing and Man's Duty* (London: Cornmarket Press, 1646) on EEBO

4. L'Estrange, Sir R., *The Dissenter's Sayings: The Second Part* (1681), p. 73, quoted in Capp, B., *The Fifth Monarchy Men* (London: Faber & Faber, 1972), p. 39

5. Thirsk, J., 'The Sales of Royalist Land during the Interregnum', *The Economic History Review*, New Series, Vol. 5, No. 2 (1952), pp. 188-207; Reid, C. R., 'The Seventeenth Century Revolution in English Land Law', *Cleveland State Law Revue* (1995), pp. 221-302

6. McFarlane, A., *The British in the Americas 1480-1815* (London: Longman, 1994), p. 96

7. Zakai, A., 'Orthodoxy in England and New England: Puritans and the Issue of Religious Toleration, 1640-1650', *Proceedings of the American Philosophical Society*, Vol. 135, No. 3 (1991), pp. 411-29

4 Cromwell's Expedition to Ireland

1. Durston, C., 'Let Ireland be Quiet: Opposition in England to the Cromwellian Conquest of Ireland', *History Workshop*, No. 21, 1986, pp. 105-12

2. *The English Soldiers' Standard*, quoted in Gentles, I., *The New Model Army* (Oxford: Blackwell, 1992), p. 330

3. Barber, S., 'Marten, Henry', *Oxford Dictionary of National Biography*, online (2004)

4. Abbott, W. C., *The Writings and Speeches of Oliver Cromwell*, Vol. II (Cambridge, Mass.: Harvard University Press, 1939), p. 30

5. Gentles, I., 'The Sales of Crown Lands during the English Revolution', *The Economic History Review*, Vol. 26, No. 4 (1973), pp. 614-35

6. Gentles, *New Model*, p. 354

7. Abbot, *Writings*, II, p. 102

8. Fraser, A., *Cromwell, Our Chief of Men* (London: Phoenix, 2002), p. 407

9. *The Letters and Speeches of Oliver Cromwell*, Carlyle, T., ed., Vol. I (London: Methuen & Co., 1904), pp. 466-72

10. *Ibid.*, p. 471

11. Burghclere, Lady, *The Life of James First Duke of Ormonde*, Vol. I (London: Murray, 1912), p. 374

12. *Letters and Speeches*, Carlyle, Vol. I, pp. 492-3

13. *Letters and Speeches*, Carlyle, Vol. II (London: Methuen, 1904), pp. 5-23

14. *Ibid.*, p. 23

15. Bodleian, Carte Ms. 26, f. 696

5 The Struggle for Scotland

1. Baillie, R., *Letters and Journals*, Vol. II (Edinburgh: Wm Creech & Wm Gray, 1775), p. 342

2. Baillie, R., *Letters and Journals*, Vol. III, p. 512, in Buchan, J., *Montrose* (London: Thomas Nelson and Sons Ltd, 1928), p. 332

3. Buchan, *Montrose*, p. 341

4. Buchan, *Montrose*, pp. 343-5; Jones, J. R., *Charles II, Royal Politician* (London: Allen and Unwin, 1987), p. 16

5. Gardiner, S. R., *History of the Commonwealth and Protectorate*, Vol. I (London: Longmans, Green & Co., 1903), p. 192

6. Gardiner, *Commonwealth and Protectorate*, Vol. I, p. 200

7. Survey of London: Volume 14, *The Parish of St Margaret*, Westminster (London: County Council, 1931) pp. 46-55; *Journal of the House of Commons*, Vol. VI (London: HMSO, 1802), pp. 371, 343-44

8. Whitelocke, B., *Memorials of the English Affairs*, Vol. III (Oxford: University Press, 1853), p. 197

9. *The Poems of Andrew Marvell*, Smith, N., ed. (Harlow: Pearson/Longman, 2007), pp. 267-279

10. Whitelocke, *Memorials*, Vol. III, p. 211

11. *Upon Appleton House, to my Lord Fairfax*. First published 1681, see *Poems of Marvell*, Smith, N., ed. (Harlow: Pearson, 2007), pp. 210-41

12. Gardiner, *Commonwealth and Protectorate*, Vol. I, p. 235

13. Kenyon, J., Ohlmeyer, J., eds., *The Civil Wars: A Military History of England Scotland and Ireland 1638-1660* (Oxford: University Press, 1998), p. 66

14. Abbott, W. C., *The Writings and Speeches of Oliver Cromwell*, Vol. II (Cambridge, Mass.: Harvard University Press, 1939), p. 303

15. Abbot, *Cromwell*, Vol. II, p. 314

16. *Letters and Speeches of Oliver Cromwell*, Carlyle, T., ed., Vol. II (London: Methuen, 1904), pp. 106-08

17. *Ibid.*, p. 112

6 Completing the Conquest

1. Tory: probably from the Irish *toruidhe* or *toruighe*, meaning 'to pursue' or 'to hunt'.

2. *Journal of the House of Commons*, Vol. VI (London: HMSO, 1802), p. 239, 22 June 1649

3. *Journal of the House of Commons*, Vol. VI, pp. 434-36, 2 July 1650

4. Colonel Jones to Vavasour Powell, 8 Oct. 1652, National Library of Wales, Ms. 11,440D, f. 75.

5. Quoted in Ramsey, R. W., *Henry Ireton* (London: Longmans, Green, 1949), pp. 184-5

6. Ramsey, *Ireton*, p. 181

7. Cunningham, J., *Conquest and Land in Ireland: The Transplantation to Connacht, 1649-1680* (Woodbridge: Boydell Press, 2011), p. 16

8. Cunningham, *Conquest and Land in Ireland*, pp. 19-23, 25

9. Quoted in Woolrych, A., *Britain in Revolution* (Oxford: University Press, 2002), p. 490

10. *Journal of the House of Commons*, Vol. VI, pp. 550, 580

11. Abbot, W. C., *The Writings and Speeches of Oliver Cromwell*, Vol. II (Cambridge, Mass.: Harvard University Press, 1939), p. 395

12. Abbot, *Writings and Speeches*, Vol. II, p. 444

13. Woolrych, *Britain in Revolution*, p. 497

14. Sydenham, T., *His Life and Original Writings* (Berkeley: University of California Press, 1966), p. 21

15. Professor John Minford contributed information on the royalist career of Urquhart.

16. Abbott, *Writings and Speeches*, Vol. II, p. 461

17. *Ibid.*

18. *Ibid.*, p. 463

7 *The Commonwealth Sets Its Course*

1. Evelyn, J., *The Diary of John Evelyn* (Oxford: University Press, 1985), p. 145
2. Brenner, R., 'The Civil War Politics of London's Merchant Community', *Past & Present*, No. 58 (Feb. 1973), pp. 53-107
3. *Mercurius Elencticus*, Issue 6, 4 June 1649
4. Farnell, J. E., 'The Navigation Act of 1651, the First Dutch War, and the London Merchant Community', *The Economic History Review*, New Series, Vol. 16, No. 3 (1964), pp. 439-54
5. Kupperman, K. O., *Providence Island 1630-1641* (Cambridge, 1993); 'Warwick, Robert Rich, 2nd Earl of', and 'Fiennes, Lord Saye and Sele', *Oxford Dictionary of National Biography*, online (2004)
6. See Weber, M., *The Protestant Ethic and the Spirit of Capitalism* (London: George Allen & Unwin Ltd, 1952)
7. *Mercurius Politicus*, 9-16 October 1651
8. Farnell, 'Navigation Act', pp. 442-3; Brenner, 'Civil War Politics', p. 78
9. Brenner, 'Civil War Politics', p. 104
10. Thomas Burton, *Diary*, Rutt, J. T., ed., Vol. I (1828), pp. i-li, 126
11. Tawney, R. H., *Religion and the Rise of Capitalism* (New Brunswick: Transaction, 2008), p. 235
12. Farnell, 'The Navigation Act', p. 445
13. *House of Commons Journal*, Vol. 7 (London: HMSO, 1802), 14 December 1652
14. Whitelocke, B., *Memorials of the English Affairs*, Vol. III (Oxford: University Press, 1853), p. 162
15. Quoted in Gardiner, S. R., *History of the Commonwealth and Protectorate*, Vol. II (London: Longmans, Green & Co, 1903), p. 2
16. Milton, A., *England's Second Reformation* (Cambridge: University Press, 2021), Ch. 9. Thanks to Dr Christopher Southgate for this reference.
17. Whitelocke, *Memorials*, p. 297

8 *The Cost of Government*

1. Gardiner, S. R., *Commonwealth and Protectorate*, Vol. II (London: Longman, Green & Co., 1903), p. 21
2. *Charles I, King and Collector* (London: Royal Academy of Arts, 2018)
3. Millar, O., 'The Inventories and Valuations of the King's Goods 1649-1651', *The Forty-Third Volume of the Walpole Society 1970-1972* (London, 1972), p. xv
4. Rowe, V. A., *Sir Henry Vane the Younger* (London: The Athlone Press, 1970), p. 7; Mayers, R., 'Vane, Sir Henry the Younger', *Oxford Dictionary of National Biography* (2015)
5. Gentles, I., 'The Impact of the Sales of Confiscated Land on English Society during the Revolution, 1647-1660', *Histoire Sociale/Social History*, Vol. xiii (Nov. 1980), pp. 292-4
6. Gentles, 'The Impact of the Sales', p. 296
7. Durston, C., 'Hesilrige [Haselrig], Sir Arthur', *Oxford Dictionary of National Biography* (2006)
8. *Ibid.*
9. Habakkuk, 'Public Finance and the Sale of Confiscated Property during the Interregnum', *The Economic History Review*, New Series, Vol. 15, No. 1

(1962), pp. 70-88; Tatham, G. B., 'The Sale of Episcopal Lands during the Civil Wars and Commonwealth', *The English Historical Review*, Vol. 23, No. 89 (Jan., 1908), pp. 91-108

10. Dunlop, R., *Ireland under the Commonwealth* (Manchester: University Press, 1913), pp. 51-3
11. Dunlop, *Ireland*, p. 80; Bottigheimer, K., *English Money and Irish Land* (Oxford: Clarendon Press, 1971), p. 119
12. *Journal of the House of Commons*, Vol. VI, p. 550; Gardiner, *Commonwealth*, Vol. II, p. 21
13. Spurlock, R. S., *Cromwell and Scotland: Conquest and Religion 1650-1660* (Edinburgh: John Donald, 2007), p. 20
14. Dow, F., *Cromwellian Scotland* (Edinburgh: John Donald, 1979), pp. 23-5
15. Petty, W., *The Political Anatomy of Ireland* (Dublin: 1691), pp. 17-20
16. Lenihan, P., 'War and Population 1649-52', *Irish Economic and Social History*, Vol. 24 (1997), pp. 1-21
17. *Journal of the House of Commons*, Vol. VII (London: HMSO, 1802), 6 Jan, 1652
18. Hutchinson, L., *Memoirs of Colonel Hutchinson*, Firth, C., ed. (London: Routledge, 1906), p. 291
19. Cunningham, J., *Conquest and Lands in Ireland: The Transplantation to Connaught, 1649-1680* (Woodbridge: Boydell Press for the Royal Historical Society, 2011), pp. 15-16
20. Bottigheimer, *English Money*, p. 120; Cunningham, *Conquest and Land*, p. 24
21. 'Humble Petition of the Committee of Adventurers', 6 April 1652, see Bottigheimer, *English Money*, pp. 121-4
22. *HMC Report on the Manuscripts of the Earl of Egmont*, Lomas, S. C., ed., Vol. I, Pt I (London: HMSO, 1905-09), p. 514
23. *Ibid.*, p. 517
24. Bottigheimer, *English Money*, p. 127
25. Farr, D., *John Lambert* (Woodbridge: Boydell, 2003), chapter 6
26. Dunlop, *Ireland*, Vol. I, p. 133-4
27. *Ibid.*, p. 245
28. *Ibid.*, pp. 247-8
29. *Ibid.*, p. 269
30. Gardiner, *Commonwealth*, Vol. IV, p. 82
31. Dunlop, *Ireland*, p. 274
32. *Ibid.*, p. 288
33. *Ibid.*, p. 290
34. *Journal of the House of Commons*, Vol VII, 4 January 1653
35. *Ibid.*, 15 March 1653
36. *Ibid.*, pp. 274-80

9 *The Dissolution of the Rump*

1. B.L. Add. Ms. 3809, quoted in Dow, F., *Cromwellian Scotland* (Edinburgh: John Donald, 1999), p. 36
2. Spurlock, R. S., *Cromwell and Scotland* (Edinburgh: John Donald, 2007), p. 16
3. *Ibid.*, pp. 36, 37 (quoting the Commission of the General Assembly of Scotland, *A Short Exhortation*)

4. *Ibid.*, p. 14
5. Dow, F., *Cromwellian Scotland* (Edinburgh: John Donald Publishers Ltd, 1999), pp. 67-8
6. Capp, B., *England's Culture Wars* (Oxford: University Press, 2012), p. 24
7. *Ibid.*, pp. 143-4
8. Gardiner, S. R., *History of the Commonwealth and Protectorate 1649-1656*, Vol. II (London: Longman, Green & Co., 1903), p. 100
9. Capp. B., *The Fifth Monarchy Men* (London: Faber and Faber, 1972), p. 53,
10. See Gentles, I., *The New Model Army in England, Ireland and Scotland, 1645-1653* (Oxford: Blackwell, 1992), p. 415; 'Lilburne, John', *Oxford Dictionary of National Biography* (2004–9)
11. Gentles, *New Model*, pp. 420-1
12. *Ibid.*, pp. 419-20
13. Whitelocke, B., *Memorials of the English Affairs*, Vol. III (Oxford: University Press, 1853), p. 468
14. Quoted in Gentles, *New Model*, p. 425
15. Abbott, W. C., *Writings and Speeches of Oliver Cromwell*, Vol. II (Cambridge, Mass.: Harvard University Press, 1939), p. 626, taken from *Life of Henry Neville*, p. 35
16. Extracts from Newsbooks in Clarendon Mss., 1 April 1653, in Firth, C. H., 'Cromwell and the Expulsion of the Long Parliament in 1653', *The English Historical Review*, Vol. 8, No. 31 (Jul., 1893), pp. 526-34
17. *Journal of the House of Commons*, Vol. VII (London: HMSO, 1802), p. 273
18. For analysis of the dissolution of the Rump: Worden, B., *The Rump Parliament* (Cambridge: University Press, 1974); Firth, C. H., 'Cromwell and the Expulsion of the Long Parliament in 1653', *The English Historical Review*, 1893, Vol. 8, No. 31, pp. 526-53; Underdown, D., 'Party Management in the Recruiter Elections, 1645-1648', *The English Historical Review*, 1968, Vol. 83, No. 327, pp. 235-64; Worden, B., 'The Bill for a New Representative: The Dissolution of the Long Parliament, April 1653', *The English Historical Review*, 1971, Vol. 86, No. 340, pp. 473-79
19. *Letters and Speeches of Oliver Cromwell*, Carlyle, T., ed., Vol. II (London: Methuen, 1904), p. 288
20. *Ibid.*, p. 286
21. Whitelocke, B., *Memorials of the English Affairs* (London: J. Tonson, 1732), p. 554
22. *Several Proceedings in Parliament*, 21 April 1653; 'News-letter from the Clarke Papers, April 23 1653', *The English Historical Review*, July 1893, pp. 531-2
23. Whitelocke, *Memorials* (1853), Vol. IV, p. 6
24. Ludlow, E., *Memoirs of Edmund Ludlow*, Vol. I, p. 357, quoted in Gardiner, *Commonwealth*, Vol. II, p. 265
25. Abbott, W. C., *Writings and Speeches of Oliver Cromwell*, Vol. IV (Cambridge, Mass.: Harvard University Press, 1937-1947), p. 489
26. Burton, T., *Diary of Thomas Burton*, Rutt, J. T., ed., Vol. III (London: H. Colburn, 1828), p. 112
27. Whitelocke, B., *Memorials* (1853), Vol. IV, p. 6

10 *Rule without Parliament*

1. Abbott, W. C., *Writings and Speeches of Oliver Cromwell*, Vol. III (Cambridge, Mass.: Harvard University Press, 1945), p. 453

2. See Burns, J. H., *Cambridge History of Political Thought 1450-1700* (Cambridge: University Press, 1991); Scott, J., *Algernon Sidney and the English Republic 1623-1677* (Cambridge: University Press, 1988); Judson, M. A., The *Political Thought of Sir Henry Vane the Younger* (Philadelphia: University of Pennsylvania Press, 1969)

3. Gardiner, S. R., *History of the Commonwealth and Protectorate*, Vol. II (London: Longman, Green & Co., 1903), p. 269

4. Abbott, *Writings*, Vol. III, pp. 5-8

5. Ludlow, E., *The Memoirs of Edmund Ludlow*, Firth, C. H. ed., Vol. I (Oxford: Clarendon Press, 1894), p. 537

6. Gentles, I., *The New Model Army* (Oxford: Blackwells, 1992), p. 437

7. Abbott, *Writings*, Vol. III, p. 3

8. Gardiner, *Commonwealth*, Vol. II, pp. 275-6

9. *Ibid.*, p. 278

10. Woolrych, A., *Britain in Revolution* (Oxford: University Press, 2002), p. 540; Abbott, *Writings*, Vol. III, p. 27

11. Abbott, *Writings*, Vol. III, p. 34

12. Petition with Council Order, Ms. E, 697, 18, quoted in Gardiner, *Commonwealth*, Vol. II p. 281

13. Woolrych, *Britain*, pp. 545-7; *Oxford Dictionary of National Biography* (2004-9)

14. Dow, F., *Cromwellian Scotland* (Edinburgh: John Donald, 1979), p. 82

15. Macinnes, A. I., *The British Confederate* (Edinburgh: John Donald, 2011), pp. 274, 304

16. Gardiner, *Commonwealth*, Vol. III, p. 92

17. Dunlop, R., *Ireland under the Commonwealth* (Manchester: University Press, 1913), p. 328

18. *Ibid.*, p. 343

19. Dunlop, *Ireland*, p. 330

20. *Ibid.*, pp. 343-4

21. *Ibid.*, p. 340

22. Cunningham, J., *Conquest and Land in Ireland: The Transplantation to Connacht, 1649-1680* (Woodbridge: Royal Historical Society, 2011), p. 37

23. *Calendar of State Papers Domestic, 1652-53* (London: Longman & Co. and Trübner & Co., 1878), p. 394

24. *Calendar of State Papers Domestic, 1652-53*, p. 333

25. Dunlop, *Ireland*, p. 350

26. See Map 4: Ireland – the Scheme for Settlement

27. Thomason Tracts, E. 1062 [3]

28. Thomason Tracts, E. 1062 [4]

29. Gardiner, S. R., 'The Transplantation to Connaught', *English Historical Review*, October 1899, p. 708

30. The figures for the war debt and Irish land settlement come from various sources and have been reconciled. See Gardiner, *Commonwealth*, Vol. IV, pp. 89, 104; Bottigheimer, *English Money and Irish Land* (Oxford: Clarendon

Press, 1971), pp. 121, 131, 135-6; Dunlop, *Ireland*, pp. 380-3; Petty, *The Political Anatomy of Ireland* (London: Brown and Rogers, 1691), p. 1 facsimile Shannon; Prendergast, J. P., *The Cromwellian Settlement of Ireland* (London: Constable, 1996), p. 199

11 Rule by the Saints

1. *Letters and Speeches of Oliver Cromwell*, Carlyle, T., Lomas, C. S., eds, Vol. II (London: Methuen, 1904), p. 272
2. Fraser, A., *Cromwell, Our Chief of Men* (London: Orion Books, 1973), p. 542
3. *Letters and Speeches*, Carlyle, ed., Speech I, p. 272-301
4. Ibid.
5. Abbot, W. C., *The Writings and Speeches of Oliver Cromwell*, Vol. III (Cambridge, Mass.: Harvard University Press, 1945), p. 67
6. Quoted in Woolrych, A., *Commonwealth to Protectorate* (Oxford: Clarendon Press, 1982), pp. 154-5
7. Capp, B., *The Fifth Monarchy Men* (London: Faber and Faber, 1972), p. 71
8. *Calendar of State Papers Domestic, 1652-53*, 20 June 1653 (London: HMSO, 1878), p. 426
9. For example, pamphlets: 'A plea at large, for John Lilburn gentleman, now a prisoner in Newgate. Penned for his use and benefit, by a faithful and true well-wisher to the fundamental laws, liberties, and freedoms of the antient free people of England; and exposed to publick view, and the censure of the unbyassed and learned men in the laws of England', Aug. 6. 1653; Lieut. Col. John Lilburn's plea in law, against an Act of Parliament of the 30 of January, 1651; Malice detected, in printing certain informations and examinations concerning Lieut. Col. John Lilburn, the morning of his tryal; and which were not at all brought into his indictment, 1653.
10. Newsbook quoted in Woolrych, A., *Commonwealth* (1982) p. 250
11. Woolrych, *Britain* (2004), pp. 545-7
12. Dunlop, R., *Ireland under the Commonwealth* (Manchester: University Press, 1913), pp. 369-70
13. There were three surveys during the Interregnum: the Gross Survey of 1653, the Civil Survey of 1654-56 and the Down Survey of 1656-58.
14. The Council of State, signed by J. Thurloe, 'Further instructions unto Charles Fleetwood esq., Lieutenant-General of the Army in Ireland, Edmund Ludlow Esq., Lieutenant General of Horse, Miles Corbet Esq., and John Jones Esq.' Thomason Tracts E.1062 [4] (London, 1653)
15. Firth, C. & Rait, R. S., *Acts and Ordinances under the Interregnum*, Vol. II (London: HMSO, 1911), p. 751
16. See McCormick, T., *William Petty and the Ambitions of Political Arithmetic* (Oxford: University Press, 2010), p. 88
17. Dunlop, *Ireland*, p. 384
18. *Journal of the House of Commons*, Vol. VII (London: HMSO, 1802), p. 278-80
19. Dunlop, *Ireland*, p. 381; Bottigheimer, K., *English Money and Irish Land* (Oxford: Clarendon Press, 1971), pp. 136-7
20. Dunlop, *Ireland*, pp. 392-4; Co. Cork was reserved for government and was not part of the ten-county scheme.

21. Gardiner, S. R., *History of the Commonwealth and Protectorate*, Vol. II (London: Longman & Green, Co., 1903), pp. 303-5
22. *Ibid.*, p. 315
23. *Ibid.*, p. 321

12 *The Protectorate in England, Scotland and Ireland*
1. Gardiner, S. R., *History of the Commonwealth and Protectorate*, Vol. III (London: Longmans, Green & Co., 1903), pp. 1-2
2. *Ibid.*, p. 7
3. Firth, C. & Rait, R. S., *Acts and Ordinances of the Interregnum* (London: HMSO, 1911), pp. 831-35
4. Terry, C. S., *The Cromwellian Union* (Edinburgh: University Press, 1902), p. lxxiv; Barnard, T., 'Planters and Policies in Cromwellian Ireland', *Past & Present*, No. 61 (Nov., 1973), pp. 31-69
5. Ludlow, E., *The Memoirs of Edmund Ludlow*, Firth, C., ed., Vol. I (Oxford: Clarendon Press, 1894), p. 365
6. Thurloe, J., *Thurloe State Papers*, Vol. II (London: Fletcher Gyles, 1742), pp. 106-07 (Lymerick, 12th month, 25th day 1653), british-history.ac.uk
7. Mayer, J., 'Inedited letters', in *Transactions of the Historical Society of Lancashire and Cheshire*, new ser. (1810), pp. 224-5
8. Gardiner, *Commonwealth and Protectorate*, Vol. III, p. 98
9. *Ibid.*, p. 102
10. Firth, C. H., *Scotland and the Protectorate* (Edinburgh: University Press, 1899), p. 82
11. *Ibid.*, p. 89
12. Gardiner, *Commonwealth and Protectorate*, Vol. III, p. 102
13. Dow, F., *Cromwellian Scotland* (Edinburgh: John Donald, 1999), pp. 121-2
14. Gardiner, *Commonwealth and Protectorate*, Vol. III, p. 107
15. *Ibid.*, p. 123
16. Hutton, R., 'George Monck, Duke of Albemarle', *Oxford Dictionary of National Biography*, online (2004)
17. Dow, *Scotland*, p. 58
18. Barnard, T. C., 'Planters and Policies in Cromwellian Ireland', *Past and Present*, No. 61 (Nov. 1973), pp. 31-69; Cunningham, J., *Conquest and Land in Ireland* (Woodbridge: RHA, 2011), p. 54
19. Barnard, 'Planters', p. 45
20. Little, P., *Lord Broghill and the Cromwellian Union with Ireland and Scotland* (Woodbridge: Boydell, 2004), p. 70
21. *Journal of the House Commons*, Vol. VII (London: HMSO, 1802), 8 September 1653
22. Gaunt, P., 'Henry Cromwell', *Oxford Dictionary of National Biography*, online (2004); Prendergast, J. P., 'Missing Records. No. I. Records of the Kilkenny Confederate Assembly, A.D. 1642-1650', *Transactions of the Kilkenny Archaeological Society*, Vol. 1, No. 3 (1851), pp. 420, 427
23. *Ludlow's Memoirs*, Vol. I, p. 381; *Thurloe State Papers*, Vol. II (London: Fletcher Gyles, 1742), pp. 140-152
24. Henry Cromwell, DNB; *Thurloe State Papers*, Vol. II, 1654, p. 169

25. Act for settling Ireland, Firth & Rait, *Acts and Ordinances of the Interregnum*, pp. 598-603

26. Connolly, S. J., *Divided Kingdom* (Oxford: University Press, 2008), p. 107

27. *Thurloe State Papers*, Vol. II, p. 343

28. Prendergast, J. P., *The Cromwellian Settlement of Ireland* (London: Constable & Co, 1996), pp. 244-49

29. Firth & Rait, *Acts and Ordinances*, Table for 1654 and Vol. II, p. 933

30. *HMC Report on the Egmont Mss.* Vol. I, Pt I, p. 544, viewed online

31. Barnard, 'Planters', p. 37

32. *HMC Report Egmont*, Vol. I, Pt I, p. 546

33. *Ibid.*, p. 556

13 A Familiar Set of Problems

1. Fraser, A., *Cromwell, Our Chief of Men* (London, 2002), p. 597

2. Abbot, W. C., *The Writings and Speeches of Oliver Cromwell*, Vol. III (Cambridge Mass., 1937-1947), p. 165

3. Hutton, R., *Charles II, King of England, Scotland and Ireland* (Oxford: University Press, 1989), pp. 84-5

4. Dow, F., *Cromwellian Scotland* (Edinburgh: John Donald, 1999), p. 150

5. Little, P., *Lord Broghill and the Cromwellian Union with Ireland and Scotland* (Woodbridge, 2004), pp. 76-8

6. *Letters and Speeches of Oliver Cromwell*, Carlyle, T., ed., Vol. II (London, 1904), p. 338

7. Abbott, *Cromwell*, Vol. III, pp. 434-43

8. *Ibid.*, pp. 452-65

9. *Ibid.*, pp. 452-55

10. *Ibid.*, pp. 458-60

11. *Ibid.*, p. 461; liberty was a contested issue. It signified the rule of law and freedom from arbitrary government. For many Englishmen it meant property rights. Some argued for economic and trade freedom. Puritans looked for religious liberty, the freedom to submit to God directly and be an instrument of his providence. For Cromwell in particular, this meant toleration for those practising religion outside a state prescription. Others believed that Cromwell had overturned this liberty by asserting his own will as chief magistrate. See, for example, Davis, J.C., 'Religion and the Struggle for Freedom in the English revolution', *The Historical Journal*, Vol. 35, No. 3, Sept. 1992, pp. 507-30

12. *Ibid.*, p. 465

13. Haley, K. H. D., *The First Earl of Shaftesbury* (Oxford: Clarendon Press 1968), p. 111

14. Prendergast, F., *The Down Survey of Ireland*, https://arrow.dit.ie, p. 48

15. Dunlop, F., *Ireland under the Commonwealth* (Manchester: University Press, 1913), p. 432

16. *Ibid.*, p. 442

17. Cunningham, J., *Conquest and Land in Ireland: The Transplantation to Connacht, 1649-1680* (Woodbridge: Boydell Press 2011), pp. 68-9

18. *Ibid.*, p. 457-59

19. Cunningham, *Conquest*, pp. 57, 71

20. *Journal of the House of Commons*, Vol. VII (London: HMSO, 1802), pp. 420-1
21. Gardiner, *Commonwealth and Protectorate*, III, p. 252; Whitelocke, B., *Memorials of the English Affairs* (London: J. Tonson, 1732), p. 610
22. Gookin, V., The *great case of transplantation in Ireland discussed* (London, 1655)
23. *Thurloe State Papers*, Vol. III (London, 1734), p. 139
24. Gardiner, *Commonwealth*, Vol. IV, p. 100-01
25. Lawrence, R., *The interest of England in the Irish transplantation, stated* (London, 1655)

14 Power Struggles within and Without

1. E. Montagu's notes, *Clarke Papers*, Vol III (London: Longmans, Green & Co., 1899), Appendix B, pp. 207-8
2. https://www.british-history.ac.uk/cal-state-papers/venice/vol30, 7 Feb 1655
3. Marvell, A., *The First Anniversary of the Government under His Highness the Lord Protector*, first published Jan 1655, see Smith, N., ed., *The Poems of Andrew Marvell* (Harlow: Pearson Longman, 2007), pp. 281-98
4. *Calendar of State Papers Domestic, Interregnum* (London: HMSO, 1881), 22 August 1655
5. *Thurloe State Papers*, Birch, T., ed., Vol. IV (London: Fletcher Gyles, 1742), pp. 587-8
6. Abbott, W. C., *The Writings and Speeches of Oliver Cromwell*, Vol. III (Cambridge, Mass.: Harvard University Press, 1945), p. 858
7. *The Letters and Speeches of Oliver Cromwell*, Carlyle, T., ed. (London: Methuen, 1904), pp. 451-2
8. Cunningham, J., *Conquest and Land in Ireland: The Transplantation to Connacht, 1649-1680* (Woodbridge: RHS/Boydell, 2011), p. 72
9. Reuben Easthorp to H. Cromwell, Galway, 17 July 1657, Lansdown Ms. 822, fos 154-6

15 Governing by Instrument

1. *The Letters and Speeches of Oliver Cromwell*, Vol. II, Carlyle, T., ed. (London: Methuen & Co., 1904), p. 536, author's italics
2. Worden, B., 'Toleration and the Cromwellian Protectorate', in Sheils, W. J., *Persecution and Toleration* (Oxford: Blackwell, 1984); Loomie, A., 'Oliver Cromwell's Policy toward the English Catholics: The Appraisal by Diplomats', *The Catholic Historical Review*, Vol. 90, No. 1 (Jan. 2004), pp. 29-44; Kirby, E. W., 'The Cromwellian Establishment', *Church History*, Vol. 10, No. 2 (Jun. 1941), pp. 144-158; Coffey, J., 'Puritanism and Liberty Revisited: The Case for Toleration in the English Revolution', *The Historical Journal*, Vol. 41, No. 4 (Dec. 1998), pp. 961-98; Fraser, A., *Cromwell, Our Chief of Men* (London: Phoenix, 2002)
3. Capp, B., *England's Culture Wars* (Oxford: University Press, 2012), pp. 59-61
4. *The Poems of Andrew Marvell*, Smith, N., ed. (Harlow: Pearson-Longman, 2007), p. xii
5. *Thurloe State Papers*, Birch, T., ed., Vol. V (London, 1742), p. 259

6. *Thurloe State Papers*, Vol. V (London: Fletcher Gyles, 1742), 12 August 1656, https://www.british-history.ac.uk
7. Vane, Sir H., *A healing question propounded and resolved, upon occasion of the late publique call to humiliation, in order to love and union* (London, 1656)
8. *England's remembrancers: or, A word in season to all Englishmen, about their elections of the members for the approaching parliament* (London, 1656)
9. *The Letters and Speeches of Oliver Cromwell*, Carlyle, ed., Vol. II, pp. 508-53

16 *Cromwell's Last Parliament*

1. Andrews, C. M., *British Committees, Commissions, and Councils of Trade and Plantations 1622-1675* (Baltimore: Johns Hopkins Press, 1908), p. 42; Gaunt., P., 'Richard Cromwell', *Dictionary of National Biography*, online (2008)
2. Anthony Morgan to Henry Cromwell in *Lansdowne Ms.*, 821, f. 314; *Diary of Thomas Burton*, Rutt, J. T., ed., Vol. I (London: H Colburn, 1828), p. 382; as detailed in Firth, C. H., *The Last Years of the Protectorate*, Vol. I, 1656-1657 (London: Longman, Green and Co., 1909), p. 135
3. *Burton Diaries*, Vol. I, 7 March 1657, p. 382
4. *Diary of Sir Archibald Johnston of Wariston, 1655-1660*, Ogilvie, J. D., ed., Vol. III (Edinburgh: Scottish History Soc, 3rd ser., Vol. 34, 1940), pp. 61-2
5. Abbott, W. C., *The Writing and Speeches of Oliver Cromwell*, Vol. IV (Cambridge, Mass.: Harvard University Press, 1937-47), p. 489
6. Abbott, *Writings of Oliver Cromwell*, IV, p. 495
7. *Journal of the House of Commons*, Vol. VII (London: HMSO, 1802), p. 525
8. Little, P., *Lord Broghill and the Cromwellian Union with Ireland and Scotland* (Woodbridge: Boydell, 2004), p. 136
9. *The Letters and Speeches of Oliver Cromwell*, Vol. III, Carlyle, T., ed. (London: Methuen, 1904), p. 129
10. Ludlow, E., *Memoirs*, Firth, C. H., ed., Vol. II (Oxford: Clarendon Press, 1894), p. 6
11. *Ibid.*
12. Dow, F., *Cromwellian Scotland* (Edinburgh: John Donald, 1999), p. 184
13. Connolly, S. J., *Divided Kingdom Ireland 1630-1800* (Oxford: University Press, 2008), pp. 117-18
14. Little, P., Smith, D. L., *Parliament and Politics during the Cromwellian Protectorate* (Cambridge: University Press, 2007), p. 208
15. Firth, *Last Years*, Vol. II, p. 147
16. *Thurloe State Papers*, Vol. IV (London: Fletcher Gyles, 1742), pp. 23-4, https://www.british-history.ac.uk/thurloe-papers/vol4

17 *The Last Days of the Protectorate*

1. Burnet, G., *Bishop Burnet's History of his own Time*, Burnet, T., ed., Vol. I (London: Samuel Bagster, 1818), p. 124
2. Noble, Rev. Mark, *Memoirs of the Protectoral House of Cromwell* (Birmingham: 1787), quoted in Fraser, A., *Cromwell, Our Chief of Men* (London: Phoenix, 1993), p. 805

3. Stater, V., *Dictionary of National Biography*, online (2004)
4. Abbott, W. C., *The Writing and Speeches of Oliver Cromwell*, Vol. IV (Cambridge, Mass.: Harvard University Press, 1937-47), p. 662, from Richard Symonds' pocketbook, *Harl. Mss.* no. 991, f. 23
5. Whitelocke, B., *Memorials of the English Affairs*, May 1657 (London: J. Tonson, 1732), p. 656
6. Abbott, *Writings of Oliver Cromwell*, Vol. IV, p. 708
7. Whitelocke, *Memorials*, pp. 666-72
8. Abbott, *Writings of Oliver Cromwell*, Vol. IV, pp. 712-21
9. Letter to John Hobart, 12 Feb. 1658, *English Historical Review*, Vol. VII (1892), p. 108
10. Abbott, *Writings of Oliver Cromwell*, Vol. IV, pp. 728-33
11. Abbott, *Writings of Oliver Cromwell*, Vol. IV, p. 761
12. *Diary of Thomas Burton*, Vol. IV (London: H. Colburn, 1828), 16 April 1659, https://www.british-history.ac.uk/burton-diaries/vol4/pp439-448
13. The account was given by Brian Fairfax, cousin of the general who accompanied him to Whitehall. Quoted in Abbott, *Writings of Oliver Cromwell*, Vol. IV, p. 869
14. Fraser, *Cromwell*, p. 856
15. Whitelocke, *Memorials*, p. 674
16. Quoted in Firth, C. H., *Oliver Cromwell and the Rule of the Puritans in England* (London: Putnam, 1972), p. 444
17. *Thurloe State Papers*, Birch, T., ed., Vol. VII (London: Fletcher Gyles, 1742), p. 381, www.british-history.ac.uk
18. *Ibid.*, 20 Sept. 1658
19. *Ibid.*, 15 Sept. 1658
20. Montagu, E., Earl of Sandwich, *Journal, 1659-1665*, Anderson, R. C., ed. (London: Navy Records, 1929), p. 70

18 The Army Splits

1. *Thurloe State Papers*, Vol. VII, Birch., T., ed. (London: Gyles, 1742), 15 June 1659, pp. 672-98, www.british-history.ac.uk
2. Little, P., *Lord Broghill and the Cromwellian Union with Ireland and Scotland* (Woodbridge: Boydell, 2004), p. 137
3. Clarke, A., *Prelude to Restoration in Ireland* (Cambridge: University Press, 1999), pp. 35-7
4. Clarendon, Sir E. Hyde, Earl of, *The History of the Rebellion and Civil Wars in England*, Vol. VI (Oxford: Clarendon Press, 1888), p. 143
5. Hutton, R., *The Restoration: a political and religious history of England and Wales 1658-1667* (Oxford: University Press, 1993), p. 64
6. Roberts, S. K., 'Lenthall, William', *Oxford Dictionary of National Biography*, online (2004)
7. Aubrey, J., *Aubrey's Brief Lives* (London: Secker and Warburg, 1649), p. 125
8. *Clarke Papers*, Vol. IV, Firth, C. H., ed. (London: Longman Green & Co., 1901), 18 June 1659, pp. 22-23, quoted in Davies, G., *The Restoration of Charles II* (London: Oxford University Press, 1969), p. 110
9. *Ibid.*, p. 85
10. Clarendon, *History of the Rebellion*, Vol. VI, p. 156

11. Dow, *Cromwellian Scotland*, p. 258
12. Penn, G., *Memorials of the professionale life and times of Sir William Penn, Knt. Admiral and General of the Fleet: From 1644 to 1670*, Vol. 2 (London: J. Duncan, 1833), p. 186
13. Little, *Broghill and the Cromwellian Union*, p. 172
14. *Mercurius Politicus*, 29 December 1659
15. Clarke, *Prelude*, Chapter 4; Hutton, *Restoration*, p. 80

19 The King Returns

1. *Clarendon State Papers*, Vol. 51, f. 242
2. *His Majesties gracious letter and declaration sent to the House of Peers by Sir John Greenvill, knight, from Breda, and read in the House the first of May, 1660* (London: Printed by John Macock and Francis Tyton, 1660), p. 3
3. Evelyn, J., *The Diary of John Evelyn* (Oxford: University Press, 1985), p. 183

Appendix 1: The Instrument of Government

1. Gardiner, S. R., *Constitutional Documents of the Puritan Revolution* (London: Oxford University Press, 1968), pp. 405-17

Appendix 2: The Humble Petition and Advice

1. Gardiner, S. R., *Constitutional Documents of the Puritan Revolution* (London: Oxford University Press, 1968), pp. 447-59

Bibliography

Manuscript Sources

Bodleian Library
Carte Mss. 26 f. 696; 29 f. 416; 67 ff. 230, 236, 253, 256-7, 258, 259
Rawlinson Ms. A208, ff. 458-62

British Library
Egerton Ms. 1048 ffs. 123-9
Lansdown Ms. 822, ffs. 154-6; 821, f. 314

Printed Primary Sources

Aubrey, J., *Aubrey's Brief Lives* (London: Secker and Warburg, 1649)
Baillie, R., *Letters and Journals*, Vol. II (Edinburgh: Wm Creech & Wm Gray, 1775)
Bethel, S., *The World's Mistake in Oliver Cromwell* (Exeter: The Rota, 1972)
Calendar of State Papers Domestic (London: Longman & Green, 1875-1886)
Calendar of State Papers Ireland (London: HMSO, 1905-1910)
England's remembrancers: or, A word in season to all Englishmen, about their elections of the members for the approaching parliament (London: 1656)
'Five Letters of Charles II', *Camden Miscellany*, Vol. V (London: 1854)
Gookin, V., *The great case of transplantation in Ireland discussed* (London: 1655)
Haller, W., Davies, G., *Leveller Tracts 1647-1653* (New York: Colombia University Press, 1944)
Henry Marten's Familiar Letters to his Lady of Delight (Oxford: A. Lichfield, 1663)
His Majesties gracious letter and declaration sent to the House of Peers by Sir John Greenvill, knight, from Breda, and read in the House the first of May, 1660 (London: Printed by John Macock and Francis Tyton, 1660)
Lawrence, R., *The interest of England in the Irish transplantation, stated* (London: 1655)
Ludlow, E., *A Voyce from the Watch Tower* (London: Royal Historical Society, 1978)
Mercurius Elencticus, Issue 6, 4 June 1649
Mercurius Politicus, 3-10 Feb 1653, letter of the army; 29 December 1659

Peters, H., *God's doings, and man's duty ... a sermon preached before both Houses of Parliament, the Lord Maior and Aldermen ... April 2 ... 1645* (London: Cornmarket Press, 1971)

Perfect Diurnall, 28 March – 4 April 1653

Several Proceedings in Parliament, 21 April 1653

Sexby, E., *Killing No Murder* (London: Frederick Farrar, 1864)

The Moderate intelligencer: impartially communicating martiall affaires to the kingdome of England (London: 1645-49)

Thomason Tracts: E1062.3&4, E5552.26, E555.3, E555.25, E556.12, E557.5, E559.3

Vane, Sir H., *A healing question propounded and resolved* (London: 1811)

Secondary Sources

Abbott, W. C., *Writings and Speeches of Oliver Cromwell*, 4 Vols (Cambridge, Mass: Harvard University Press, 1937-47)

Andrews, C. M., *British Committees, Commissions and Councils of Trade and Plantations 1622-1675* (Baltimore: The John Hopkins Press, 1908)

Ashley, M., *General Monck* (London: J. Cape, 1977)

Ashley, M. P., *Financial and Commercial Policy under the Cromwellian Protectorate* (Oxford: University Press, 1934)

Barnard, T. C., 'Planters and Policies in Cromwellian Ireland', *Past and Present*, No. 61 (Nov. 1973), pp. 31-69

Barg, M. A., *The English Revolution of the 17th century through Portraits of the leading Figures* (Moscow: Progress, 1990)

Bottigheimer, K., *English Money and Irish Land* (Oxford: Clarendon Press, 1971)

Braddick, M. J., *The Oxford Handbook of the English Revolution* (Oxford: University Press, 2015)

Brenner, R., 'The Civil War Politics of London's Merchant Community', *Past & Present*, No. 58 (Feb. 1973)

Buchan, J., *Montrose* (London: Thomas Nelson and Sons Ltd, 1928)

Burnet, G., *Bishop Burnet's History of his own Time*, Burnet, T., ed., Vol. I (London: Samuel Bagster, 1818)

Burns, J. H., *Cambridge History of Political Thought 1450-1700* (Cambridge: University Press, 1991)

Burghclere, Lady, *The Life of James First Duke of Ormonde*, 2 Vols (London: Murray, 1912)

Calendar of Clarendon State Papers, Vols III & IV (Oxford: University Press, 1876)

Calendar of State Papers Domestic, Interregnum (London: Longman & Co. and Trübner & Co., 1875-86)

Capp, B., *The Fifth Monarchy Men* (London: Faber and Faber, 1972)

Capp, B., *England's Culture Wars* (Oxford: University Press, 2012)

Charles I, King and Collector (London: Royal Academy of Arts, 2018)

Clarendon, Sir E. Hyde, Earl of, *The History of the Rebellion and Civil Wars in England*, Vols IV-VI (Oxford: Clarendon Press, 1888)

Clarke, A., *Prelude to Restoration in Ireland: The End of the Commonwealth 1559-1660* (Cambridge: University Press, 1999)

Clarke Papers, Vol. III (London: Longmans, Green & Co., 1899)

Coffey, J., 'Puritanism and Liberty Revisited: The Case for Toleration in the English Revolution', *The Historical Journal*, Vol. 41, No. 4 (Dec. 1998), pp. 961-98

Coffman, D., *Excise, Taxation and the Origins of Public Debt* (Basingstoke: Palgrave, 2013)

Connolly, S. J., *Divided Kingdom* (Oxford: University Press, 2008)

Coward, B., *Oliver Cromwell* (Harlow: Longman Group, 1991)

Cunningham, J., *Conquest and Land in Ireland: The Transplantation to Connacht, 1649-1680* (Woodbridge: Boydell Press, 2011)

Davies, G., *The Restoration of Charles II* (London: Oxford University Press, 1969)

Davis, J. C., 'Religion and the Struggle for Freedom in the English Revolution', *The Historical Journal*, Vol. 35, No. 3, Sept 1992, pp. 507-530

Diary of Sir Archibald Johnston of Wariston, 1655-1660, Ogilvie, J. D., ed., Vol. III (Scottish History Soc. 3rd ser. Vol. 34, Edinburgh: 1940)

Diary of Thomas Burton, Rutt, J. T., ed., 4 Vols (London: H Colburn, 1828)

Dow, F., *Cromwellian Scotland* (Edinburgh: John Donald, 1999)

Dunlop, R., *Ireland under the Commonwealth* (Manchester: University Press, 1913)

Durston, C., 'Let Ireland be Quiet: opposition in England to the Cromwellian Conquest of Ireland', *History Workshop*, No. 21, 1986, pp. 105-112

Durston, C., *Cromwell's Major-Generals: godly government during the English Revolution* (Manchester: University Press, 2001)

Evelyn, J., *The Diary of John Evelyn* (Oxford: University Press, 1985)

Farnell, J. E., 'The Navigation Act of 1651, the First Dutch War, and the London Merchant Community', *The Economic History Review*, New Series, Vol. 16, No. 3 (1964)

Farr, D., *John Lambert* (Woodbridge: Boydell, 2003)

Firth, C. H., 'Cromwell and the Expulsion of the Long Parliament in 1653', *The English Historical Review*, Vol. 8, No. 31 (Jul., 1893), pp. 526-534

Firth, C. H., *Scotland and the Protectorate* (Edinburgh: University Press, 1899)

Firth, C. H., *The Last Years of the Protectorate*, 2 Vols (London: Longman, Green and Co., 1909)

Firth, C. H., *Oliver Cromwell and the Rule of the Puritans in England* (London: Putnam, 1972)

Firth C. H., Rait, R.S., *Acts and Ordinances of the Interregnum 1642-1660* (England: HMSO, 1911)

Fraser, A., *King Charles II* (London: Weidenfeld and Nicholson, 1979)

Fraser, A., *Cromwell, Our Chief of Men* (London: Phoenix, 2002)

Gardiner, S. R., 'The Transplantation to Connaught', *English Historical Review*, October 1899

Gardiner, S. R., *History of the Commonwealth and Protectorate 1649-1656*, 4 Vols (London: Longman, Green & Co., 1903)

Gardiner, S. R., *Constitutional Documents of the Puritan Revolution* (Oxford: Clarendon Press, 1968)

Gentles, I., 'The Sales of Crown Lands during the English Revolution', *The Economic History Review*, Vol. 26, No. 4 (1973), pp. 614-635

Gentles, I., 'The Impact of the Sales of Confiscated Land on English Society during the Revolution, 1647-1660', *Histoire Sociale/Social History*, Vol. xiii (Nov. 1980)

Bibliography

Gentles, I., *The New Model Army in England, Ireland and Scotland, 1645-1653* (Oxford: Blackwell, 1992)

Gilbert, J. T., ed., *A Contemporary History of Affairs in Ireland 1641-1652* (Dublin: 1879-80)

Habakkuk, 'Public Finance and the Sale of Confiscated Property during the Interregnum', *The Economic History Review*, New Series, Vol. 15, No. 1 (1962), pp. 70-88

Haley, K. H. D., *The First Earl of Shaftesbury* (Oxford: Clarendon Press, 1968)

Herbert, Sir Thomas, *Memoirs of the last years of the reign of King Charles I* (London: G. & W. Nicol, 1813)

Hirst, D., *The Representative of the People?* (Cambridge: University Press, 1975)

HMC Report on the Manuscripts of the Earl of Egmont, Vol I, Part I, ed. Lomas S. C. (London: HMSO, 1905-09)

Houston, R. A., *Literacy in early modern Europe* (Oxford: Routledge, 2013)

Hutchinson, L., *Memoirs of Colonel Hutchinson*, ed. C. Firth (London: Routledge, 1906)

Hutton, R., *Charles II, King of England, Scotland and Ireland* (Oxford: University Press, 1989)

Hutton, R., *The Restoration: a political and religious history of England and Wales 1658-1667* (Oxford: University Press, 1993)

Jones, J. R., *Charles II, Royal Politician* (London: Allen and Unwin, 1987)

Journal of the House of Commons, Vols VII & VII (London: HMSO, 1802)

Judson, M. A., *The Political Thought of Sir Henry Vane the Younger* (Philadelphia: University of Pennsylvania Press, 1969)

Kelsey, S., *Inventing a Republic: The Political Culture of the English Commonwealth 1649-1653* (Stanford: University Press, 1997)

Kenyon, J., Ohlmeyer, J., eds., *The Civil Wars: A Military History of England, Scotland and Ireland 1638-1660* (Oxford: University Press, 1998)

Kirby, E. W., 'The Cromwellian Establishment', *Church History*, Vol. 10, No. 2 (Jun., 1941), pp. 144-158

Kupperman, K. O., *Providence Island 1630-1641* (Cambridge: University Press, 1993)

Lane, J., *The Reign of King Covenant* (London: R. Hale, 1956)

Lenihan, P., 'War and Population 1649-52', *Irish Economic and Social History*, Vol. 24 (1997)

Letters and Memorials of State (London: T. Osborne, 1746)

Letters and Speeches of Oliver Cromwell, ed. Carlyle, T., 3 Vols (London: Methuen, 1904)

'Letter to John Hobart, 12 Feb 1658', *English Historical Review*, VII (1892)

L'Estrange, Sir R., *The Dissenter's Sayings: The Second Part* (1681)

Little, P., *Lord Broghill and the Cromwellian Union with Ireland and Scotland* (Woodbridge: Boydell, 2004)

Little, P., *The Cromwellian Protectorate* (Boydell: Woodbridge, 2007)

Little, P., ed., *Oliver Cromwell, New Perspectives* (Basingstoke: Palgrave Macmillan, 2009)

Little, P., Smith, D. L., *Parliaments and Politics during the Cromwellian Protectorate* (Cambridge: University Press, 2007)

Loomie, A. J., 'Oliver Cromwell's Policy toward the English Catholics: The Appraisal by Diplomats 1654-1658', *Catholic Historical Review*, 90 (2004) pp. 29-44

Ludlow, E., *The Memoirs of Edmund Ludlow*, Firth, C. H. ed., Vol. I (Oxford: Clarendon Press, 1894)

Lynch, K. M., *Roger Boyle, First Earl of Orrery* (Knoxville: University of Tennessee Press, 1965)

Marvell, A., *The Poems of Andrew Marvell*, ed. Smith, N. (Harlow: Pearson/ Longman, 2007)

McCormick, T., *William Petty and the Ambitions of Political Arithmetic* (Oxford: University Press, 2009)

McFarlane, A., *The British in the Americas 1480-1815* (London: Longman, 1994)

Macinnes, A. I., *The British Confederate* (Edinburgh: John Donald, 2011)

Macinnes, A. I., Ohlmeyer, J., *The Stuart Kingdoms in the Seventeenth Century* (Dublin: Four Courts Press, 2002)

Mayer, J., 'Inedited letters', in *Transactions of the Historical Society of Lancashire and Cheshire*, new ser. (1810)

McCormick, T., *William Petty and the Ambitions of Political Arithmetic* (Oxford: University Press, 2009)

Millar, O., 'The Inventories and Valuations of the King's Goods 1649-1651', *The Forty-Third Volume of the Walpole Society 1970-1972* (London: 1972)

Milton, A., *England's Second Reformation* (Cambridge: University Press, 2021)

Montagu, E., Earl of Sandwich, *Journal, 1659-1665* Anderson, R. C., ed. (London: Navy Records, 1929)

Morgan, E. S., *Visible Saints: The History of a Puritan Idea* (New York: University Press, 1963)

Morrill, J., 'Cromwell, Parliament, Ireland and a Commonwealth in Crisis', *Parliamentary History,* June 2011, pp.193-214

Morrill, J., *Revolution and Restoration: England in the 1650s* (London: Collins & Brown, 1992)

Ollard, R. L., *Clarendon and his Friends* (London: Hamish Hamilton, 1987)

Oman, C., *Elizabeth of Bohemia* (London: Hodder and Stoughton Ltd., 1938)

Peacey, J., 'Cromwellian England: A Propaganda State', *History* (London), 2006, Vol.91 (2), pp.176-199

Penn, G., *Memorials of the professionale life and times of Sir William Penn, Knt. Admiral and General of the Fleet: From 1644 to 1670*, Vol. 2 (London: J. Duncan, 1833)

Petty, W., *The Political Anatomy of Ireland* (Dublin: 1691)

Prendergast, F., *The Down Survey of Ireland,* https://arrow.dit.ie

Prendergast, J. P., 'Missing Records. No. I. Records of the Kilkenny Confederate Assembly, A.D. 1642-1650', *Transactions of the Kilkenny Archaeological Society*, Vol. 1, No. 3 (1851)

Prendergast, J. P., *The Cromwellian Settlement of Ireland* (London: Constable, 1996)

Ramsey, R. W., *Henry Ireton* (London: Longmans, Green, 1949)

Reid, C. R., 'The Seventeenth Century Revolution in English Land Law, *Cleveland State Law Revue* (1995) pp. 221-302

Richards, R. D., 'The Exchequer in Cromwellian Times', *Economic History*, suppl. to *Economic Journal*, Vol. II (London: Macmillan & Co.,1933)

Rowe, V. A., *Sir Henry Vane the Younger* (London: The Athlone Press, 1970)

Samuel, E., 'Oliver Cromwell and the Re-admission of the Jews to England', *Cromwelliana*, ser. II (2007) no. 4, pp. 3-7

Scotland and the Protectorate, Firth, C. H., ed. (Edinburgh: Scottish History Society, 1899)

Scott, J., *Algernon Sidney and the English Republic 1623-1677* (Cambridge: University Press, 1988)

Scott, J., 'What Were Commonwealth Principles?' *The Historical Journal* (Sept., 2004)

Sheils, W. J., *Persecution and Toleration* (Oxford: Blackwell, 1984)

Simington, R., *The Transplantation to Connaught 1654-58* (Shannon: Irish University Press, 1970)

Smith, D. L., 'Oliver Cromwell, the First Protectorate Parliament and Religious Reform', *Parliamentary History* 19 (2000), pp. 38-48

Smith, G., *Royalist Agents, Conspirators and Spies: Their Role in the British Civil Wars 1640-1660* (Farnham: Ashgate, 2011)

Spurlock, R. S., *Cromwell and Scotland* (Edinburgh: John Donald, 2007)

Solt, L. F., 'The Fifth Monarchy Men and the Millennium', *Church History*, Vol. 30, No. 3, 1961, pp. 314-324

Spalding, R.; *The Improbable Puritan: a life of Bulstrode Whitelocke, 1605-1675* (London: Faber and Faber, 1975)

Stevenson, D., *Revolution and Counter Revolution in Scotland, 1644-51* (Edinburgh: John Donald, 2011)

Stewart, L. A. M., *Rethinking the Scottish Revolution: Covenanted Scotland, 1637-1651* (Oxford: University Press, 2016)

Survey of London: Volume 14, *The Parish of St Margaret, Westminster* (London: County Council, 1931)

Sydenham, T., *His Life and Original Writings* (Berkeley: University of California Press, 1966)

Tatham, G.B., 'The Sale of Episcopal Lands during the Civil Wars and Commonwealth', *The English Historical Review*, Vol. 23, No. 89 (Jan., 1908), pp. 91-108

Tawney, R. H., *Religion and the Rise of Capitalism* (New Brunswick: Transaction, 2008)

Terry, C. S., *The Cromwellian Union* (Edinburgh: University Press, 1902)

The Letters Speeches and declaration of King Charles II, Bryant, A., ed. (London: Cassell, 1935)

Thirsk, J., 'The Sales of Royalist Land during the Interregnum', *The Economic History Review*, New Series, Vol. 5, No. 2 (1952), pp. 188-207

Thomas, K., & Pennington, D., eds., *Puritans and Revolutionaries* (Oxford: Clarendon Press, 1978)

Thurloe State Papers, Vol. II (London: Fletcher Gyles, 1742)

Tolmie, M., *The Triumph of the Saints: the separate churches of London, 1616-1649* (Cambridge: University Press, 1977)

Underdown, D., *Royalist Conspiracy in England 1649-1660* (New Haven: Yale University Press, 1960)

Underdown, D., 'Party Management in the Recruiter Elections, 1645-1648', *The English Historical Review*, 1968, vol. 83, no. 327

Venning, T., *Cromwellian Foreign Policy* (Basingstoke: Macmillan, 1995)

Waters, I., *Henry Marten and the Long Parliament* (Chepstow: Chepstow Society, 1973)

Weber, M., *The Protestant Ethic and the Spirit of Capitalism* (London: George Allen & Unwin Ltd., 1952)

Wheeler, J. S., 'Navy Finance', *The Historical Journal*, Vol. 39, No. 2 (Jun., 1996), pp. 457-466

Whitelocke, B., *Memorials of the English Affairs* (London: J. Tonson, 1732)

Whitelocke, B., *Memorials of the English Affairs*, 4 Vols (Oxford: University Press, 1853)

Williams, J. B., *A History of English Journalism to the Foundation of the Gazette* (London: Longmans, Green, 1908)

Wolfe, D. M., ed. *Leveller Manifestos of the Puritan Revolution* (New York: Colombia University Press, 1944)

Woolrych, A., *Commonwealth to Protectorate* (Oxford: Clarendon Press, 1982)

Woolrych, A., *Britain in Revolution* (Oxford: University Press, 2002)

Wooton, D., *Republicanism, Liberty and Commercial Society 1649-1776* (Stanford: University Press, 1994)

Worden, B., 'The Bill for a New Representative: The Dissolution of the Long Parliament, April 1653', *The English Historical Review*, 1971, vol. 86, no. 340, pp. 473-49

Worden, B., *The Rump Parliament* (Cambridge: University Press, 1974)

Worden, B., *Literature and Politics in Cromwellian England* (Oxford: University Press, 2007)

Zakai, A., 'Orthodoxy in England and New England: Puritans and the Issue of Religious Toleration, 1640-1650', *Proceedings of the American Philosophical Society*, Vol. 135, no. 3, 1991, pp. 411-429

Index

Also available from Amberley Publishing

THE FALL OF
CHARLES I

JANE HAYTER-HAMES